Collins
Town & Country
BRITAIN

KU-511-072

CONTENTS

Published by Collins
An imprint of HarperCollinsPublishers
77-85 Fulham Palace Road, Hammersmith, London W6 8JB

www.collins.co.uk

Copyright © HarperCollinsPublishers Ltd 2003

Collins® is a registered trademark of HarperCollinsPublishers Limited

Mapping generated from Collins/Bartholomew digital databases

The grid on this map is the National Grid taken from the Ordnance Survey map with the permission of the Controller of Her Majesty's Stationery Office.

| Printed in | PB | ISBN 0 00 716036 4 | Imp. 001 | QC11494 CDDU |
| Great Britain | Spiral | ISBN 0 00 716037 2 | Imp. 001 | QC11495 CDDU |

e-mail: roadcheck@harpercollins.co.uk

Key to route planning maps

SCALE: 1: 440,000 approx.
7 miles to 1inch /
4.4 km to 1cm

0   10   20 m
0   10   20   30 km

M1 under constr.	Motorway
Motorway tunnel	Motorway tunnel
restricted access — Junction number — ②	Junction number
restricted access	Motorway service area
dual A1	Primary route
dual A634 under constr.	'A' road
dual B1246 under constr.	'B' road
Other road	Other road

Gradient	Gradient
Toll	Toll
Railway line / tunnel	Railway line / tunnel
Car ferry	Car ferry
✈ Airport	Airport
Built-up area	Built-up area
○ ○ ○ Settlement	Settlement
18 Distance in miles	Distance in miles

National boundary	National boundary
National / Regional park	National / Regional park
Forest park	Forest park
Woodland	Woodland
Beach	Beach
Canal	Canal
Lake, dam and river	Lake, dam and river
718 △	Height in metres
☆	Place of interest

land below	0	328	657	985	1640	2295	2950	feet
water	sea level 0	100	200	300	500	700	900	metres

Key to approach route maps

SCALE: 1: 160,000 approx.
2.5 miles to 1inch /
1.6 km to 1cm

0   1   2   3   4   5 miles
0 1 2 3 4 5 6 7 8 km

M5	Motorway
full access 30 ⨯ 29 restricted access	Motorway junction
Maidstone Birch Sarn	Motorway service area with full / restricted / off road access
dual A48 single	Primary route
Primary route with passing places	Primary route with passing places
dual A30 single	'A' road
'A' road with passing places	'A' road with passing places
dual B1403 single	'B' road
'B' road with passing places	'B' road with passing places
Minor road	Minor road
Restricted access	Restricted access
Road projected or under construction	Road projected or under construction
⨂ 14	Multi-level junction (occasionally with junction number)
Roundabout	Roundabout
⨂ 10	Road distance in miles

Road tunnel	Road tunnel
Steep hill (arrows point downhill)	Steep hill (arrows point downhill)
⨯ Toll	Level crossing / Toll
Car ferry route	Car ferry route
Railway line / station / tunnel	Railway line / station / tunnel
✈ Airport with scheduled services	Airport with scheduled services
Ⓗ Heliport	Heliport
Ⓟ Park and Ride site*	Park and Ride site*
Built up area	Built up area
□ □ ▫ Town / Village / Other settlement	Town / Village / Other settlement
National boundary	National boundary
National / Regional park	National / Regional park
Forest park boundary	Forest park boundary
Danger Zone Military range	Military range
Woodland	Woodland
•468 ▲941 Spot height / summit height in metres	Spot height / summit height in metres
Beach	Beach
Lake / Dam / River / Waterfall	Lake / Dam / River / Waterfall
Canal / Dry canal / Canal tunnel	Canal / Dry canal / Canal tunnel

A selection of tourist detail is shown on the mapping. It is advisable to check with the local tourist information centre regarding opening times and facilities available.

𝒊 𝒊	Tourist information centre (all year/seasonal)
m	Ancient monument
⚔1738	Battlefield
Castle	Castle
Country Park	Country Park
Ecclesiastical building	Ecclesiastical building
Factory shop village	Factory shop village
Garden	Garden
Golf course	Golf course
Historic house (with or without garden)	Historic house (with or without garden)
Major sports venue	Major sports venue
Motor racing circuit	Motor racing circuit
Museum / Art gallery	Museum / Art gallery
Nature reserve	Nature reserve
Preserved railway	Preserved railway
Theme park	Theme park
Racecourse	Racecourse
Wildlife park or zoo	Wildlife park or zoo
★ Other interesting feature	Other interesting feature
(NT) (NTS)	National Trust / National Trust for Scotla

Key to town plan maps

Motorway	Motorway
dual Primary route	Primary route
dual 'A' road	'A' road
dual 'B' road	'B' road
dual Through route	Through route
dual → Other road / One way street	Other road / One way street

Restricted access / Pedestrian street	Restricted access / Pedestrian street
Path / Footbridge	Path / Footbridge
Ⓟ Ⓟ Car park / Park and Ride site*	Car park / Park and Ride site*
Railway line / Station	Railway line / Station
Ⓤ Ⓜ Underground / Metro / Light rail station	Underground / Metro / Light rail station
𝒊 † Tourist information centre / Ecclesiastical building	Tourist information centre / Ecclesiastical building

Tourist building	Tourist building
Important building	Important building
Higher education building	Higher education building
Hospital	Hospital
Cemetery	Cemetery
Recreational area / Open spa	Recreational area / Open spa

*Park and Ride sites shown in this atlas operate a minimum of five days a week

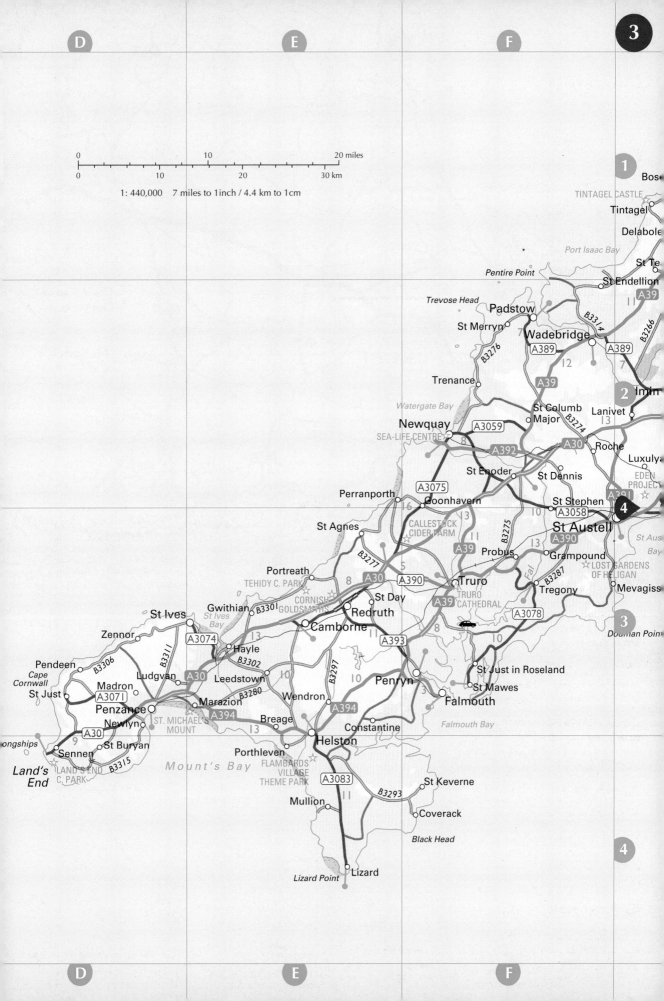

1 : 440,000   7 miles to 1 inch / 4.4 km to 1 cm

0   10   20 miles
0   10   20   30 km

1

Bos

TINTAGEL CASTLE

Tintagel

Delabole

Port Isaac Bay

St Te

Pentire Point

St Endellion

A39

Trevose Head

Padstow

St Merryn

Wadebridge

B3314

B3266

A389

A389

12

7

Trenance

B3276

A39

Watergate Bay

2

Imin

St Columb
Major

Lanivet

B3274

13

Newquay

A3059

A392

A30

Roche

SEA-LIFE CENTRE

8

St Enoder

St Dennis

Luxuly

EDEN
PROJECT
☆

A39

Perranporth

A3075

Goonhaven

St Stephen

A3058

4

St Agnes

CALLESTOCK
CIDER FARM ☆

13

11

B3275

10

St Austell

A390

St Aus
Bay

Portreath

B3277

5

A30

A390

Truro

A39

Probus

13

Grampound

B3287

Tregony

LOST GARDENS
OF HELIGAN ☆

Mevagiss

TEHIDY C. PARK ☆

8

St Day

TRURO
CATHEDRAL

A39

A3078

St Ives

St Ives
Bay

CORNISH
GOLDSMITHS ☆

B3301

Redruth

Camborne

Fal

10

Dodman Poin

3

Zennor

A3074

13

Hayle

A393

8

Pendeen

B3306

B3311

Ludgvan

B3302

10

B3297

10

Penryn

St Just in Roseland

Cape
Cornwall

Madron

Leedstown

Wendron

St Mawes

St Just

A3071

B3280

3

Penzance

Marazion

A394

Falmouth

Newlyn

ST. MICHAEL'S
MOUNT ☆

Breage

Constantine

Falmouth Bay

ongships

A30

9

St Buryan

13

Helston

Sennen

B3315

Porthleven

St Keverne

Land's
End

LAND'S END
C. PARK ☆

Mount's Bay

FLAMBARDS
VILLAGE
THEME PARK ☆

A3083

B3293

Coverack

Mullion

11

Black Head

4

Lizard Point

Lizard

Witheridge
B3137
Tiverton
A396
Bickleigh
13
Bradninch
A3072
Silverton
Copplestone
Crediton
Newton
St Cyres
A377
8
A396
Exeter
EXETER
CATHEDRAL
KILLERTON
HOUSE
ROYAL
ALBERT
MUSEUM
M5
Broadclyst
Pinhoe
29
30
CREALY PARK
A30
31
Exminster
2
Kenton
A3052
Topsham
A373
10
Starcross
A38
Lympstone
B3178
A379
Bovey
Tracey
Chudleigh
Dawlish
B3192
Kingsteignton
A381
A380
Teignmouth
Babbacombe Bay
A383
Newton
Abbot
A379
Kingskerswell
BABBACOMBE MODEL VILLAGE
Ipplepen
A380
COCKINGTON COURT C. PARK
DARTINGTON
CRYSTAL & CIDER
PRESS CENTRE
Marldon
Torquay
A3022
ENGLISH RIVIERA CENTRE
Paignton
totnes
5
A3022
PAIGNTON ZOO
Tor Bay
Berry Head
A381
Brixham
A379
Halwell
A3122
PAIGNTON & DARTMOUTH
STEAM RLY
Dartmouth
WOODLANDS
LEISURE PARK
Kingswear
A379
8
ridge
Stokenham
Start Bay
Start Point
Prawle Point

Culmstock Hemyock
27
Uffculm
Cullompton
28
Feniton
Whimple
Ottery
St Mary
West
Hill
Sidbury
B3180
Sidford
Newton
Poppleford
Sidmouth
Honiton
A373
11
A30
A375
Kilmington
Colyton
Colyford
A3052
Beer
Seaton

Black Down Hills
Combe
St Nicholas
7
16
A30
A358
Chard
Chardstock
A358
South
Chard
Axminster
B3165
Musbury
Charmouth
Uplyme
A3052
Lyme
Regis

14
A303
Ilminster
A356
9
A30
Crewkerne
A356
A358
8
Broadwindsor
B3162
Beaminster
B3165
A3066
Bridport
Bradpole
A35
Bothenhampt
Burton
Bradstock
Abbots
Lyme Bay
ABBOTSB
GARD

D
E
7
F
5

1

2

3

4

0   10   20 miles
0   10   20   30 km
1: 440,000   7 miles to 1inch / 4.4 km to 1cm

D
E
F

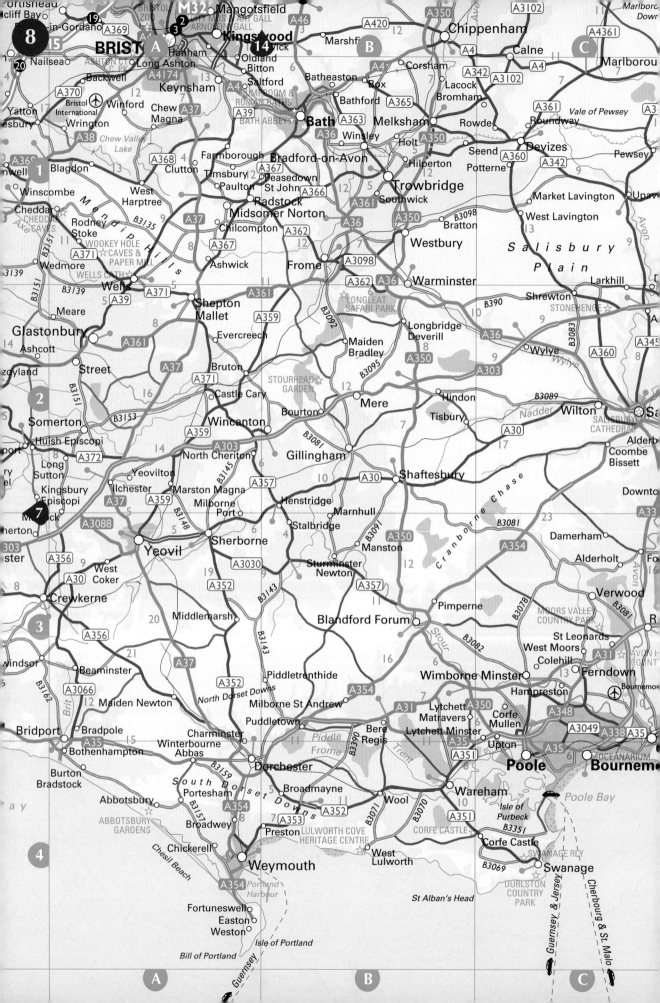

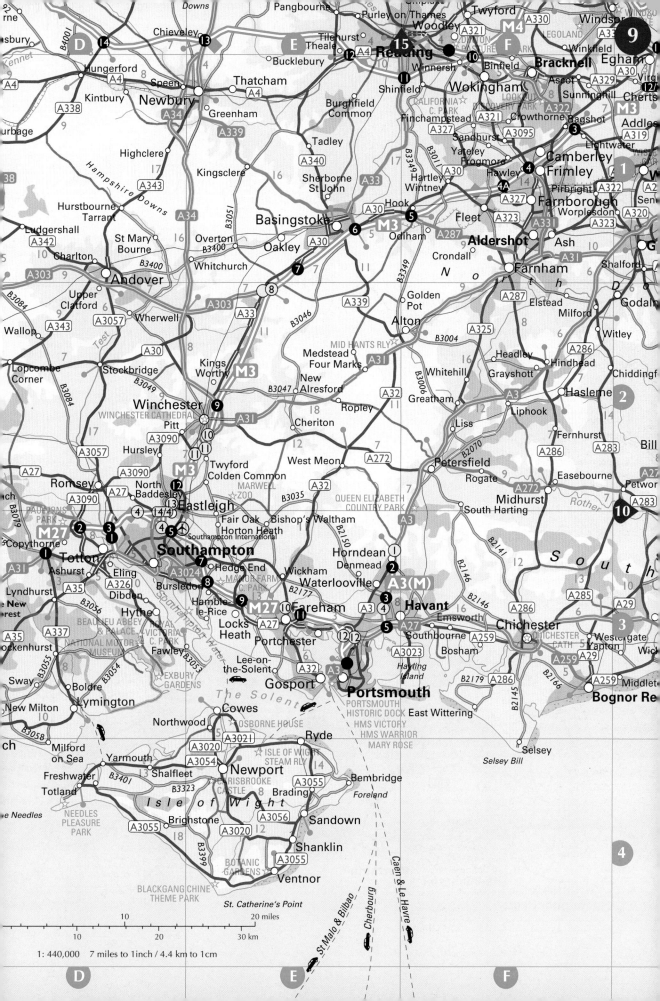

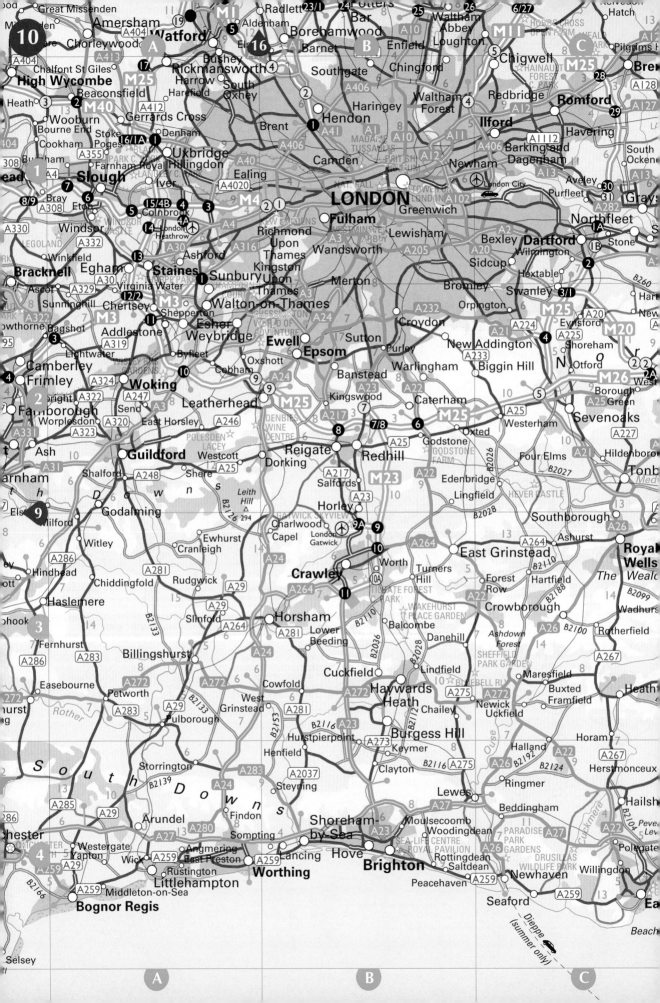

12

18

A   **B**   **C**

Y Llethr **Park**

Map Labels

Inset map (top left):

Bardsey Sd.
Porth Neigwl

Pembrokeshire Coast
National Park

Rosslare
Strumble Head
Dinas Head
Newport Bay
Fishguard Bay

Cardigan
St Dogmaels
A496
Barmouth
Barmouth Bay
A493
Dolgellau
A496
Llanellt
Cadair Idris
893 △ Penygadair

Goodwick
Fishguard
B4313
Newport
B4582
A478
Eglwysw
Llwyngwril
Llangelynin

St David's Head
Scleddau
Letterston
B4329
Crymych
Greenway
Mynydd Preseli
A478
Abergynolwyn
Tywyn
CENTRE FOR ALTERNATIVE TECHNOLOGY
B4405

LLYS-Y-FRAN RESERVOIR C. PARK
Greenway
Maenclochog
TALYLLN RAILWAY
A493
15

St David's
BISHOP'S PALACE
St David's
Solva
A487
Solva
Ramsey Island
SCOLTON MANOR C. PARK
A40
B4313
Taf
A478
Llandissilio
Aberdyfi
Eglwys Fach

St Bride's Bay
Camrose
Clynderwen
Borth
B4353
Taliesin
Nant-y Rese

Skomer Island
Haverfordwest
A40
OAKWOOD LEISURE PARK
A4076
Narberth
Whitla
B4328
Templeton
B4572
18

Broad Haven
B4341
CANASTON CENTRE
Johnston
B4327
Llangwm
A477
A478
FOLLY FARM
Kilgetty
Aberystwyth
A4120
Dev
Skokholm Island
Rosslare
Dale
Milford Haven
Neyland
A477
Saundersf
Llanbadarn Fawr
ABERYSTWYTH ARTS CENTRE
Rheidol
VALE OF RHEIDOL RLY
CEREDIGION MUSEUM

St Ann's Head
Angle
Pembroke Dock
PEMBROKE CASTLE
Pembroke
GREAT WEDLOCK DINOSAUR EXPERIENCE
B4318
Tenby
Penally

Hundleton
A4139
Manorbier
Llanilar
Ystwyth
Ysby
B4340
B4343
Castlemartin
B4319
Freshwater East
Caldey Island
Lledrod
18

Linney Head
St Govan's Head
Llanrhystud
B4576
A485
Pont

0   5 miles

Inset at different scale to main mapping

Llanon
Aberaeron
B4577
Cross Inn
B4577
A485
Tregaron
Teifi

0   10   20 miles
0   10   20   30 km

New Quay
A486
Llanarth
A487
B4342
Temple Bar
Aeron
A482
B4337
B4576

1: 440,000   7 miles to 1inch / 4.4 km to 1cm

Llangranog
Plwmp
Synod Inn
Cambrian
A485
B4343

Aberporth
A487
B4334
Talgarreg
B4337
A482
Lampeter
Bri Rese

Cardigan
St Dogmaels
A484
B4570
B4333
Penrhiw-pal
Ffostrasol
A486
A475
Llanybydder
B4337
A482
Pumsaint
Cothi

Dinas Head
A478
B4582
Teifi
Horeb
A486
Llandysul
A485
Llanfihangel ar-arth
Llansawel
B4302
Llandovery

Newport
Eglwyswrw
Newcastle Emlyn
Llangeler
B4333
Pencader
A484
B4310
Brechfa
Llanwrda
A4069
Llangadog

Fishguard
B4313
Crymych
Mynydd Preseli
Trelech
Cynin
Cothi
B4302
A40
A4069 Bla

Greenway
Maenclochog
A478
Taf
Cynwyl Elfed
B4299
A485
Llanegwad
Llandeilo

Llandissilio
Clynderwen
Meidrim
Carmarthen
A40
Llangunnor
Llanarthney
NATIONAL BOTANIC GARDEN OF WALES
GELLI AUR C. PARK
Llandybie
Brynamm

OAKWOOD LEISURE PARK
CANASTON CENTRE
Templeton
Whitland
Narberth
St Clears
Cwm
Tywi
A48
Llanddarog
A483
Llangendeirne Drefach
Ammanford
A4069 Blac

Red Roses
Llan wror
B4312
A484
B4309
A476
A477

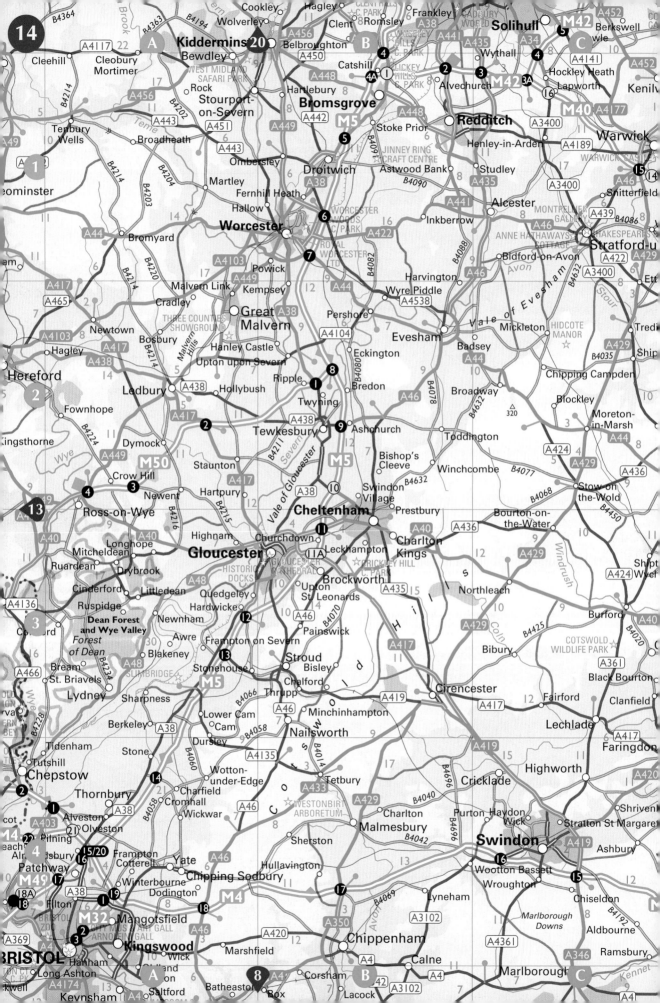

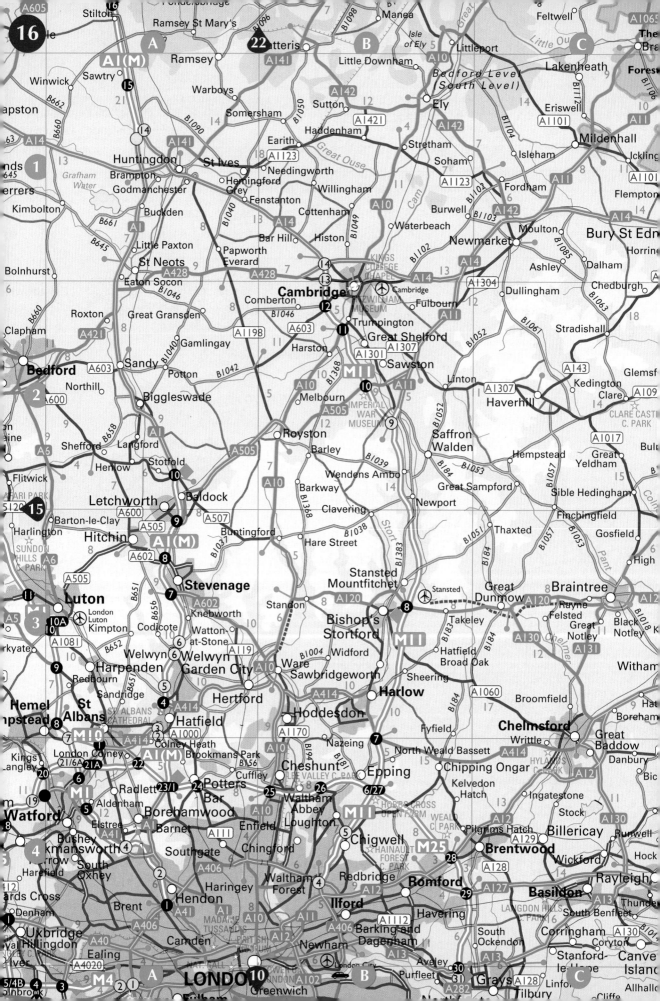

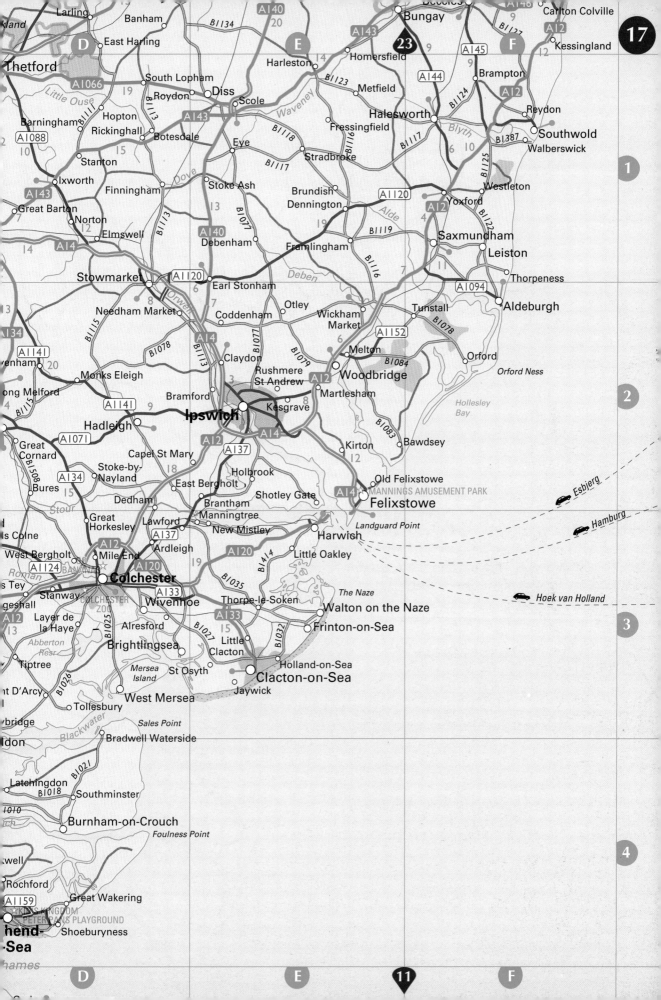

A   B   C

Carmel Head

Dublin & Dún Laoghaire

Holyhead Bay

Holyhead

Holy Island

Llanbadrig

Amlwch

A5025

17

Llyn Alaw

B5111

A5025

Moelfre

Llannerch-y-medd

Benllech

Anglesey

Pentraeth

B5110

17

B5110

B5109

Red Wharf Bay

Valley

Llanynghenedl

8

ANGLESEY HERITAGE GALLERY

B5109

Beaumaris

LLANDUDNO CABLE CAR
NORTH WALES THEATRE
GREAT ORME TRAMWAY

Llandudno

Penrh

Great Ormes Head

Deganwy

4

Conwy

C

Llangoed

BEAUMARIS CASTLE

Conwy Bay

CONWY CASTLE

Llansanff Glan Con

BODNANT GARDENS

A5

A4080

5

B5109

12

A55

Llangefni

A5025

4

Bangor

Penmaenmawr

Llanfairfechan

15

18

B5106

A470

B5113

Llanfaelog

B4422

Llanfairpwllgwyngyll

Menai Bridge

A55

PLAS NEWYDD

PENRHYN CASTLE

Caerhun

11

Aberffraw

20

B4419

A4080

ANGLESEY SEA ZOO

10

Pentir

Bethesda

Dolgarrog

A470

TREFRIW WOOLEN MILLS

Malltraeth Bay

ROYAL WELSH FUSILIERS REG'T MUSEUM

B4366

Llanddeiniolen

12

Carnedd Llywelyn 1064

Trefriw

Llanrwst

CAERNARFON CASTLE

Llanrug

WELSH SLATE MUS.

PADARN C. PARK

14

LLANBERIS LAKE RLY

Llyn Cowlyd

B5113

Menai Castle

Menai Strait

Caernarfon

3

Llanberis

Glyder Fawr 999

A5

Capel Curig

4

Betws-y-

Llanwnda

WELSH HIGHLAND RLY

SNOWDON MOUNTAIN RLY

A4086

SWALLOW FALLS

CONWY VAL RAILWAY M

Llandwrog

1085

Snowdon (Yr Wyddfa)

A498

A470

6

Penygroes

10

A487

16

Llanllyfni

A4085

8

Snowdonia

5

LLECHWEDD SLATE CAVERNS

Conw y

Caernarfon Bay

A499

Beddgelert

6

A4085

FFESTINIOG RAILWAY

Blaenau Ffestiniog

B4407

18

Llanaelhaearn

B4417

Dolbenmaen

A498

Maentwrog

National

18

A4212

Morfa Nefyn

Lleyn Peninsula

Nefyn

B4354

7

Llanystumdwy

Tremadog

Porthmadog

2

Ffestiniog

Arenig Fawr 854

A497

Criccieth

5

PORTMEIRION VILLAGE

Penrhyndeudraeth

9

Llyn C Trawsfynydd

Trawsfynydd

Tudweiliog

B4417

7

Pwllheli

Tremadoc Bay

HARLECH CASTLE

National

Bronaber

15

Llanuwchlly

B4413

Llanbedrog

St Tudwal's Road

Harlech

COED Y BRENIN VISITOR CENTRE

18

Pen n Mawr

A499

Abersoch

754 Y Llethr **Park**

A494

Aberdaron

Llanbedr

11

A496

Bardsey Sound

Porth Neigwl

10

Llanelltyd

Bardsey

A496

Dolgellau

8

A470

Barmouth

A493

Cadair Idris

Mallwy

Barmouth Bay

20

893 Penygadair

13

Llwyngwril

A487

0   10   20 miles

0   10   20   30 km

Llangelynnin

CORRIS CRAFT CENTRE

A47

1: 440,000   7 miles to 1inch / 4.4 km to 1cm

B4405

Abergynolwyn

CENTRE FOR ALTERNATIVE TECHNOLOGY

Dyfi

A489

6

4

Tywyn

TALYLLN RAILWAY

A493

Machynlleth

C a r d i g a n

A493

15

B a y

Aberdyfi

Eglwys Fach

A487

Borth

B4353

Taliesin

Llyn Clywe Reservoir

18

A   **12**   B   C

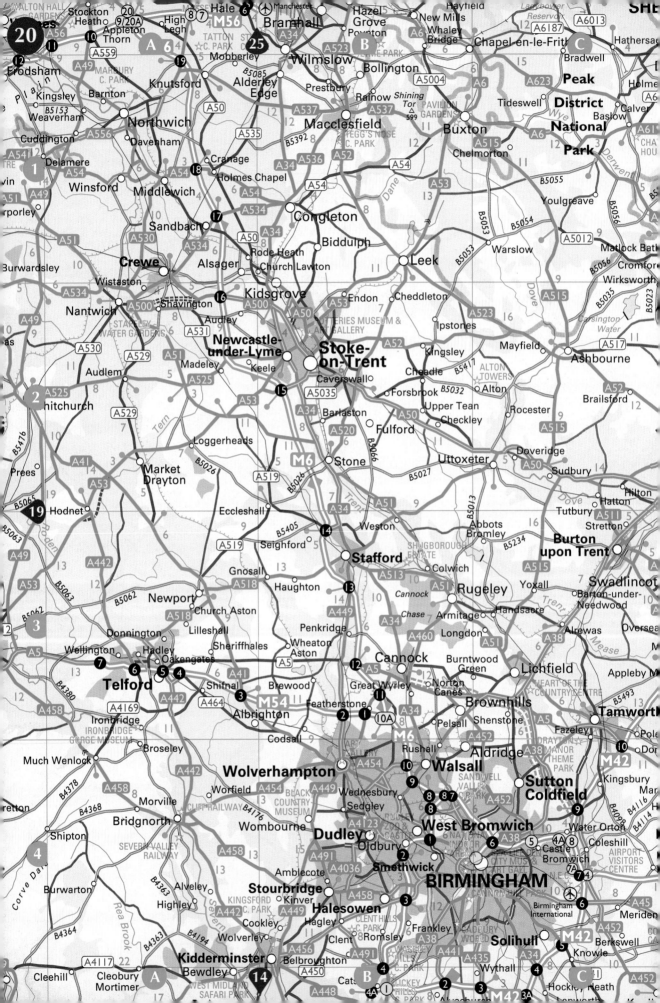

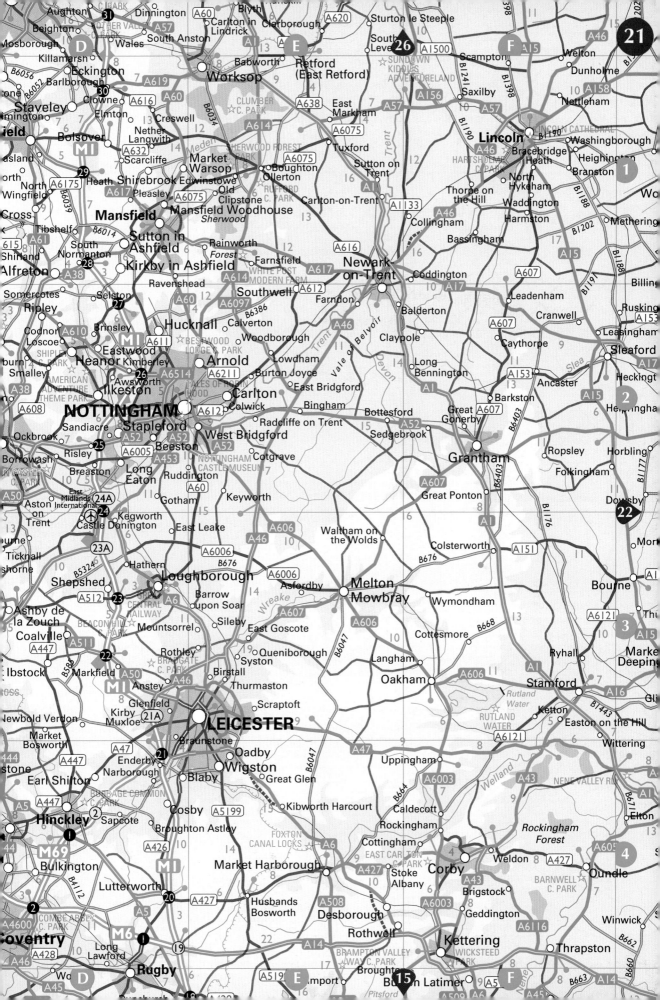

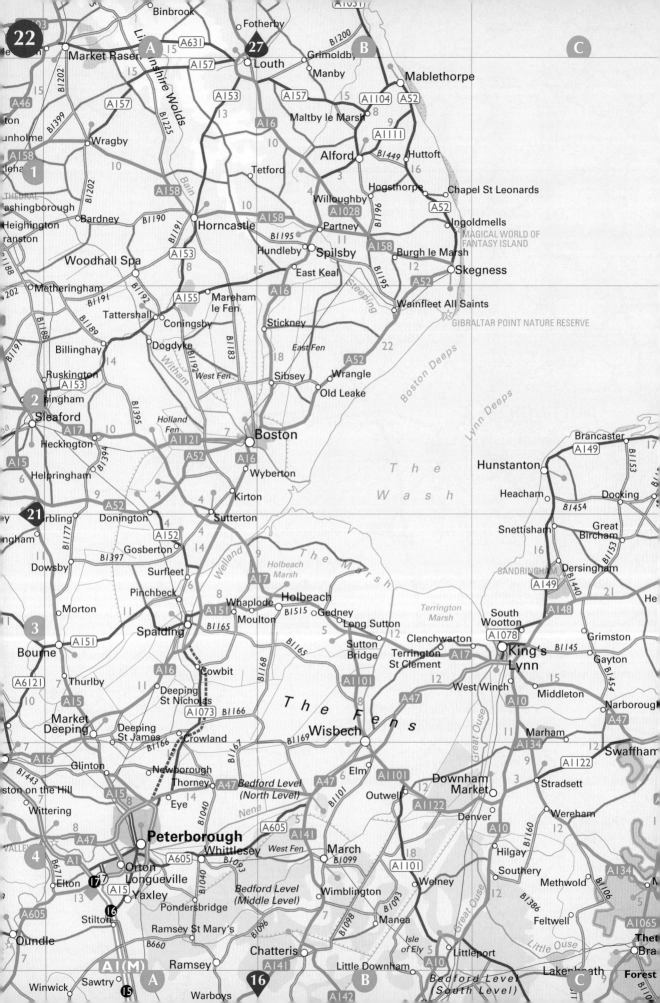

D   E   F

1

0   10   20 miles
0   10   20   30 km

1: 440,000   7 miles to 1inch / 4.4 km to 1cm

2

Blakeney Point

Blakeney   A149   Sheringham   Cromer
Wells-next-the-Sea   19   NORTH NORFOLK RLY
B1105   B1156   A148   8
Letheringsett   Roughton   Mundesley
Holt   Thorpe Market
9   21   B1149   A140   B1145
A148   10   Happisburgh
Briston   B1354   A149
enham   Saxthorpe   BLICKLING HALL   North Walsham   B1159
PENSTHORPE WATERFOWL PARK   B1149   Stalham
Guist   Aylsham   BURE VALLEY RAILWAY   Ant   Low   A149
B1146   A1067   Cawston   B1150   A1151   Street   Hickling
North Elmham   25   B1145   Reepham   Bure   WROXHAM BARNS   Broad   West Somerton
14   B1147   Bawdeswell   A140   11   Horstead   Coltishall   Martham   Hemsby
A145   Swanton Morley   Attlebridge   Horsford   Hoveton   A1062   Filby   A149   Ormesby St Margaret
Wensum   Horning   The   Broad   A1064
East Dereham   A47   Taverham   Spixworth   Rackheath   Broads   Caister-on-Sea
11   Drayton   Norwich   Salhouse   Billockby
A47   16   Sprowston   A1151   Little   Bure   PLEASURE BEACH
A1075   A47 A1074   NORWICH   Plumstead   Acle   A47
B1135   18   Thorpe   Brundall   Great
Norwich   St Andrew   Yarmouth
Hethersett   B1108   Cringleford   A146   SEA-LIFE CENTRE
Kimberley   B1172   Stoke Holy Cross   17   Yare   Bradwell
Hingham   14   Thurton   A143   A12
ney   Wymondham   Mulbarton   B1332   Loddon   Hopton   PLEASUREWOOD HILLS THEME PARK
Watton   B1108   Brooke   Hales   14   B1074   10   Corton
08   B1077   Great Ellingham   B1136   Haddiscoe   Oulton
A1075   13   Hempnall   Woodton   A1117
13   B1111   Attleborough   B1527   B1332   7   Lowestoft
Thet   A11   B1077   Long Stratton   Beccles   A146   Carlton Colville
Larling   13   B1113   A140   Bungay   9   B1127   A12
land   Banham   20   A143   Kessingland
06   B1134   14   A145   12
East Harling   Harleston   Homersfield   9   Bram
Thetford   South Lopham   17   A144   A12
19   Roydon   Diss   B1123   Metfield   24

3

4

D   E   F

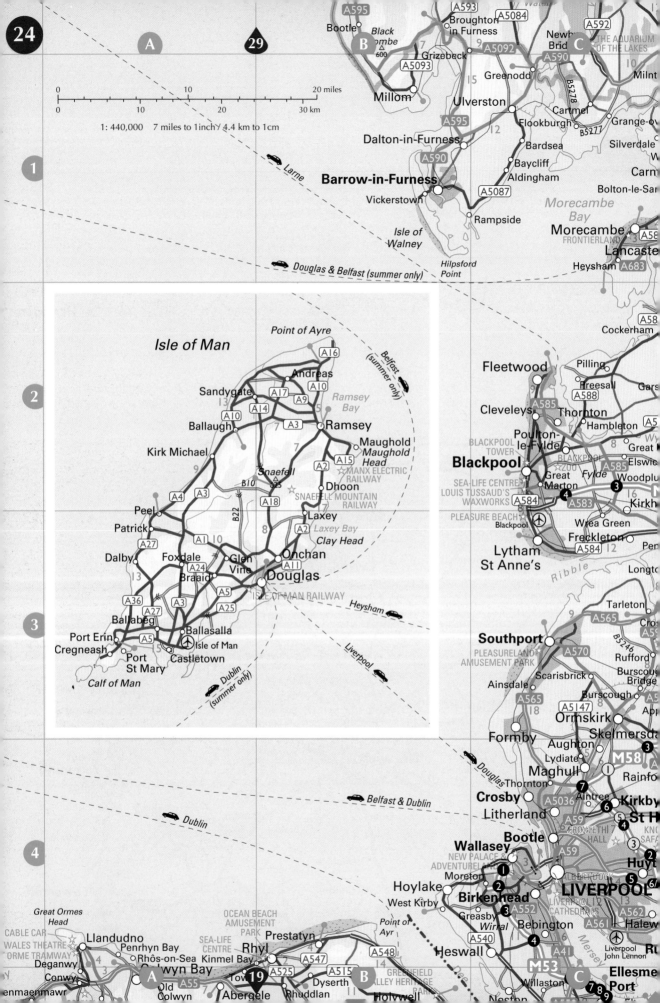

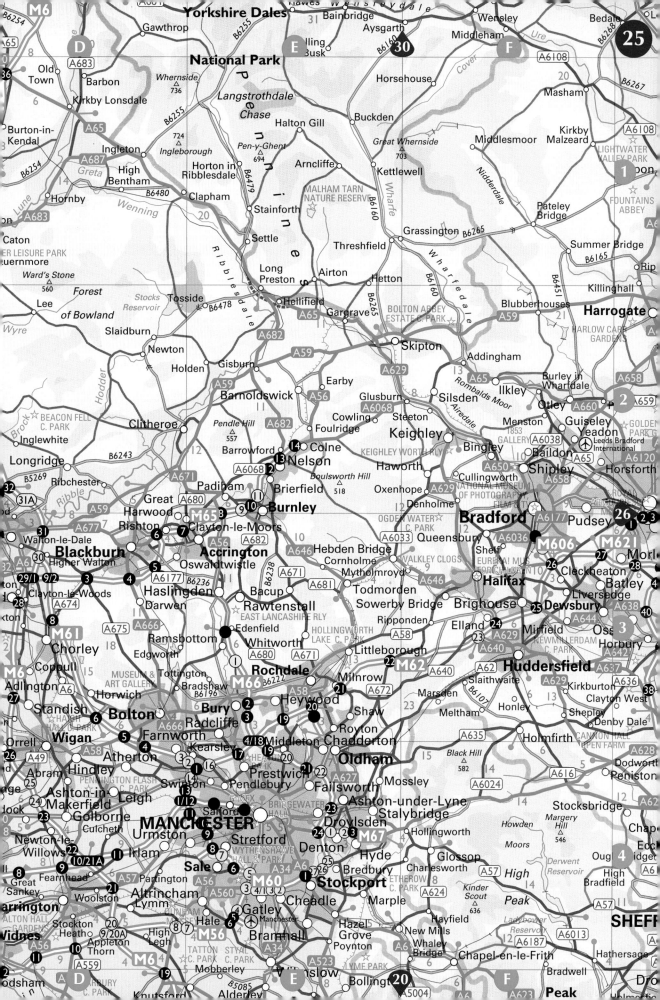

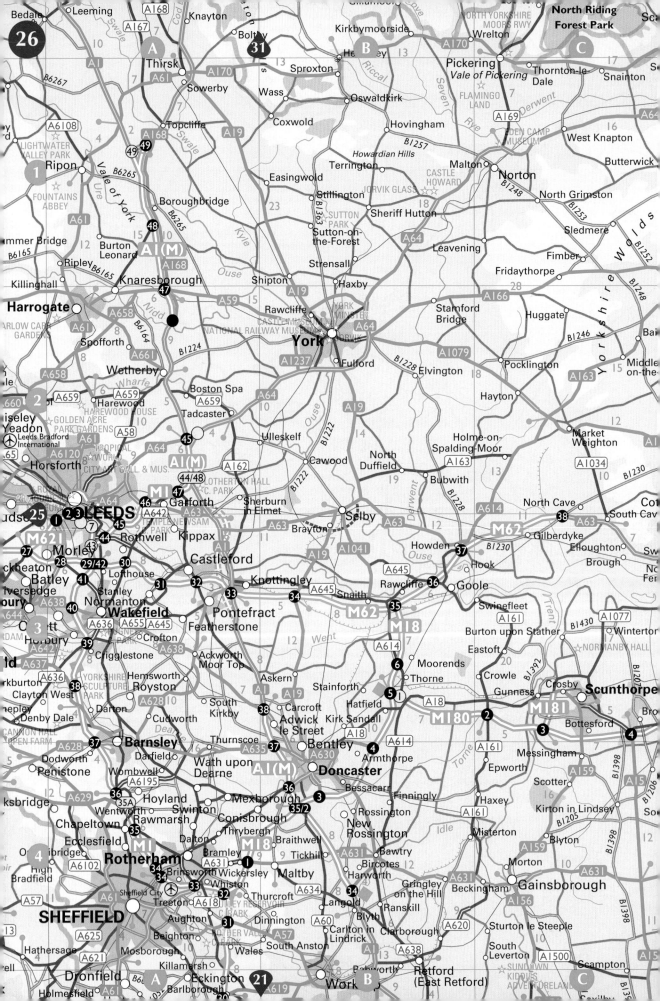

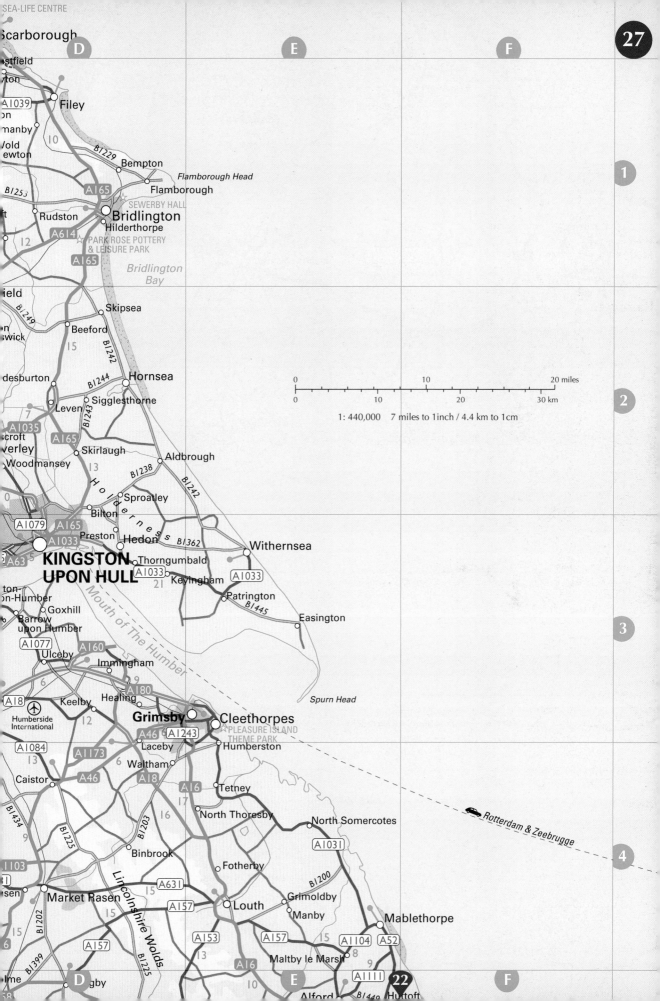

SEA-LIFE CENTRE

Scarborough

astfield

D

E

F

on

A1039

Filey

1

manby

10

Vold
ewton

B1229

Bempton

Flamborough Head

B1255

A165

Flamborough

t

Rudston

SEWERBY HALL

A614

Bridlington

Hilderthorpe

12

PARK ROSE POTTERY
& LEISURE PARK

A165

Bridlington
Bay

ield

Skipsea

B1249

Beeford

2

15

B1242

desburton

B1244

Hornsea

swick

0   10   20 miles

Leven

B1243

Sigglesthorne

0   10   20   30 km

7

A1035

1: 440,000   7 miles to 1inch / 4.4 km to 1cm

scroft
verley

A165

Skirlaugh

Aldbrough

Woodmansey

13

B1238

B1242

Holderness

Sproatley

Bilton

A1079

A165

Preston

Hedon

B1362

2

A1033

Withernsea

KINGSTON
UPON HULL

Thorngumbald

A1033

A63

21

Keyingham

A1033

Patrington

3

ton-
Humber

B1445

Goxhill

Easington

Barrow
upon Humber

A1077

A160

Mouth of The Humber

Ulceby

Immingham

Spurn Head

9

A180

Healing

A18

Keelby

Humberside
International

12

Grimsby

Cleethorpes

PLEASURE ISLAND
THEME PARK

A1084

A1173

A46

A1243

Laceby

Humberston

13

Rotterdam & Zeebrugge

Waltham

A46

A18

Caistor

A16

Tetney

17

16

North Thoresby

B1434

B1203

16

North Somercotes

B1225

Binbrook

A1031

1103

Fotherby

31

B1200

sen

A631

15

Market Rasen

Lincolnshire Wolds

A157

Louth

Grimoldby

15

Manby

Mablethorpe

15

A153

A157

A1104

A52

6

A157

15

8

B1202

B1399

B1225

13

A16

Maltby le Marsh

9

me

D

gby

E

A1111

22

F

10

Alford

B1449

Hurtoft

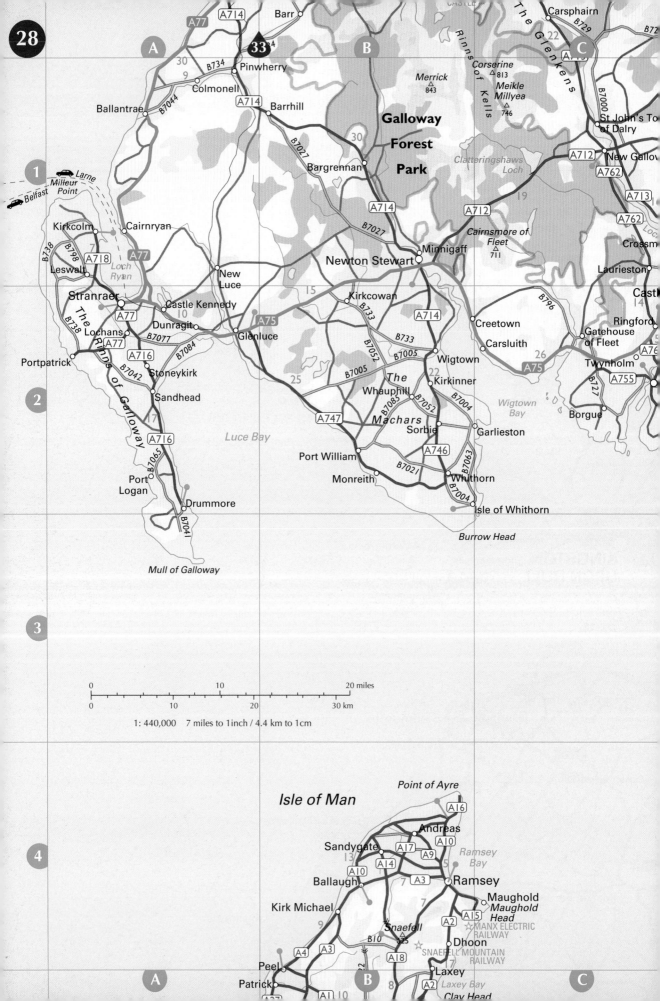

ington
Lynemouth
QUEEN ELIZABETH II
COUNTRY PARK
D
Newbiggin-by-the-Sea
SBECK C. PARK

Blyth
EY PARK
ramlington
Seaton Sluice
Seaton Delaval
Seghill
Whitley Bay
A19
Shiremoor
Tynemouth
North Shields
South Shields
SOUTH SHIELDS MUSEUM & ART GALLERY
Amsterdam
A183
Jarrow
Hebburn
A194
Cleadon
Boldon
A19
A1018

Sunderland
A183
Washington
A182
A690
A1018
Chester-le-Street
Bournmoor
A1231
ughton Spring
Hetton-le-Hole
Seaham
Murton
South Hetton
rham
62
Haswell
Easington Colliery
A182
Easington
Sherburn
Thornley
Peterlee
Horden
IRHAM THEDRAL
Wheatley Hill
Blackhall Colliery
rn
61
A181
Wingate
A1086

Trimdon
A179
Hartlepool
Fishburn
A19
12
Tees Bay
Ferryhill
A1(M)
on
60
6
7
Sedgefield
A177
A689
A689
A178
ewton yeliffe
Billingham
A1085
Redcar
7
8
South Bank
Marske-by-the-Sea
Middlesbrough
ALBERT PARK
Eston
Saltburn-by-the-Sea
Stockton-on-Tees
Thornaby-on-Tees
Skelton
Brotton
12
A66
STEWART PARK
A171
Loftus
Hinderwell
Eaglescliffe
A67
Roseberry Topping
Guisborough
B1366
16
Teesside International
Egglescliffe
A172
320
A174
Sandsend
th-ees
Yarm
Great Ayton
Whitby
A167
Cleveland Hills
ST MARY'S
Hutton Rudby
Stokesley
Danby
Sleights
High Hawsker
B1264
13
Great Broughton
Castleton
Egton
B1416
A19
A172
NORTH YORKSHIRE MOORS RAILWAY
Robin Hood's Bay
North Cowton
Round Hill
454
North York Moors
20
A167
15
B1257
19
Rosedale Abbey
20
Staintondale
Brompton
A169
A171
4
orthallerton
A684
North York Moors
Cloughto
Leeming
A168
National Park
Gillamoor
NORTH YORKSHIRE MOORS RWY
North Riding Forest Park
Burnisto
A167
Knayton
Kirkbymoorside
Lockton
Hackness
Scalby
A165
hirsk
A170
Sproxton
Helmsley
Wrelton
Thorn Dale
Seamer
A61
Boltby
26
ring Vale of Pickering
e
Snainton
Sowerby

0   10   20 miles
0   10   20   30 km
1:440,000   7 miles to 1inch / 4.4 km to 1cm

Stavanger, Haugesund & Bergen
Göteborg & Kristiansand

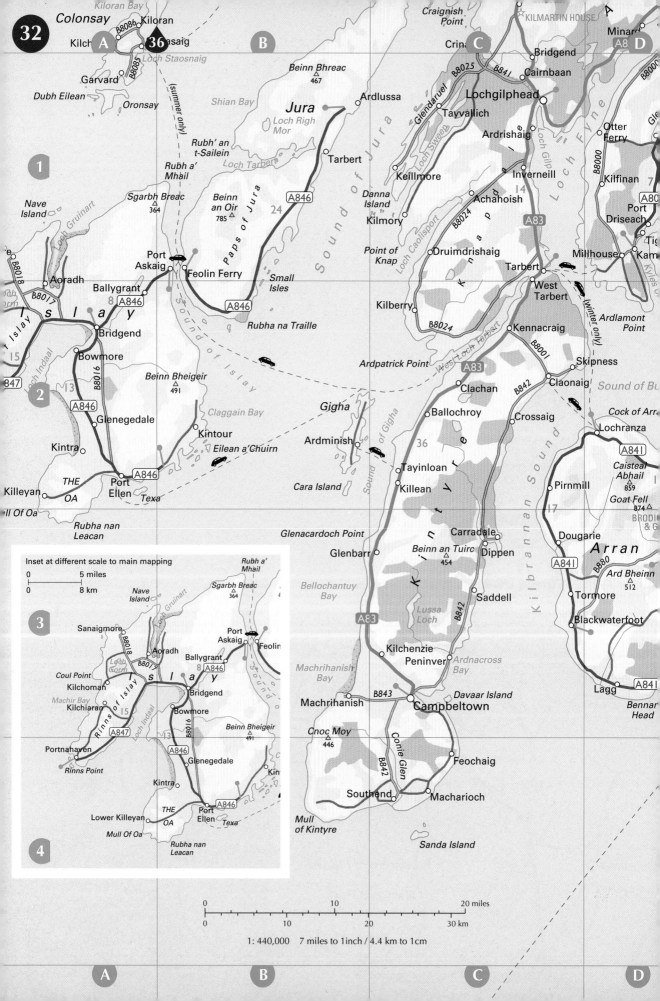

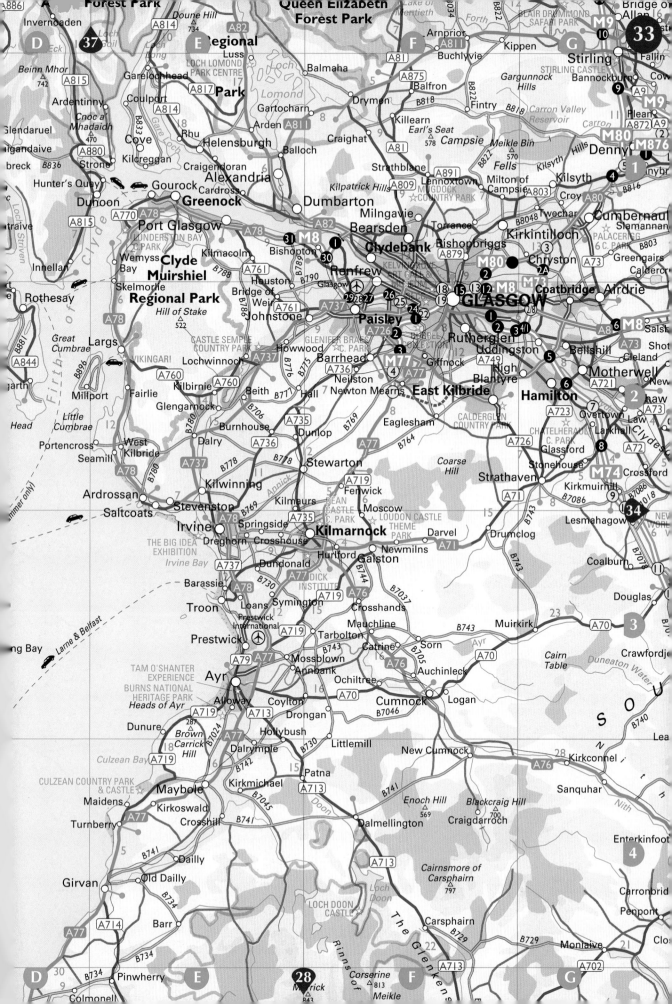

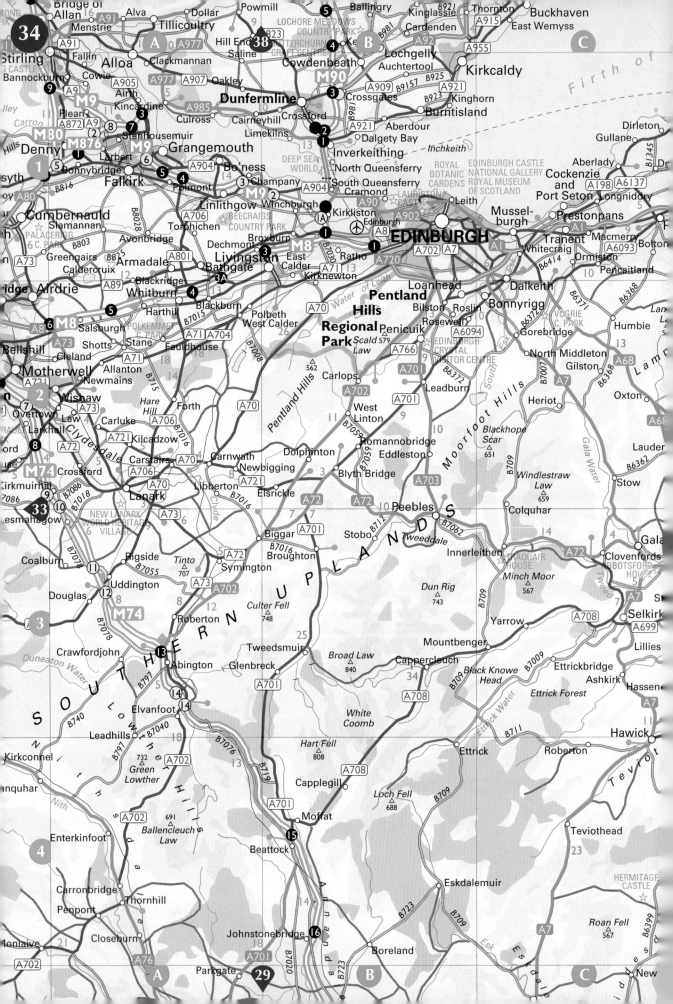

D E 39 F

20 miles

0   10   20 miles
0   10   20   30 km
1: 440,000   7 miles to 1inch / 4.4 km to cm

Bass Rock
Zeebrugge
Berwick
SCOTTISH
SEABIRD CENTRE
A198
JOHN MUIR
COUNTRY PARK
Dunbar

1

B6370 Stenton
Garvald
A1
Cockburnspath
Meikle
Black Law
St Abb's Head
Ecclaw
3
A1107 13
St Abbs
Coldingham
Grantshouse
B6438
9
Cranshaws
A6112
Eyemouth
Hills
Meikle Says
Law
B6355
Auchencrow
Reston
Burnmouth
35
Water
Whiteadder
9
B6438
B6437
Preston
Chirnside
6
A6105
Foulden
Berwick-
upon-Tweed
Dirrington
Great Law
Duns
15
Paxton
B6460
Tweedmouth
2
Water
Blackadder
struther
B6456 Polwarth
B6437
B6461
Norham
B6354
Scremerston
A6105
Ladykirk
Houndslow
8
B6400
Swinton
A6089 Greenlaw
12
A6112
A698
12
Ancroft
Duddo
A1
Gordon
12
Eccles
A697
Coldstream
B6525
Fenwick
Holy Island or
Lindisfarne
A6105
10
B6364
A6089
Stichill
A698
Cornhill-on-Tweed
B6353
Lowick
Burrows Hole
riston
Smailholm
B6350
Crookham
B6353
Ford
B6525
Farne Islands
B6397
Kelso
B6396
Flodden
Cockenheugh
28
B6349
Bamburgh
6356
FLOORS
CASTLE
KELSO ABBEY
B6352
Milfield
211
BAMBURGH CASTLE
B6404
A699
B6352
Kilham
14
Doddington
B1342
Seahouses
10
A698
B6436
Kirknewton
B6348
B1341
North Sunderland
RYBURGH ABBEY
Town
Yetholm
Kirk
Yetholm
Akeld
Chatton
Beadnell
7
9
Nisbet
Eckford
B6351
Wooler
B1340
Beadnell Bay
6400
B6401
Ellingham
3
Bonjedward
Morebattle
Bowmont Water
Cateran
Hill
Christon
Bank
Embleton
JEDBURGH ABBEY
Jedburgh
The Cheviot
815
Craster
698
B6358
Oxnam
Breamish
A697
B6347
Remington
holm
Cheviot
Windy Gyle
619
Eglingham
B6346
B1340
Longhoughton
B6357
A68
Camptown
13
Glanton
Powburn
A1
Hills
Whittingham
Alnwick
Lesbury
14
Chesters
Netherton
B6341
Alnmouth
thdean
A6088
Carter Bar
30
Edlingham
A1068
Shilbottle
Warkworth
A68
13
Thropton
Rothbury
Longframlington
B6345
Coquet Island
Amble
Rochester
B6341
Rothbury
Forest
Felton
Togston
4
National
B6341
18
DRURIDGE BAY
COUNTRY PARK
Kielder
Kielder Forest
Park
Otterburn
Longhorsley
A697
A1068
Istone
Elsdon
B6342
Ulgham
B1337
Ellington
Lynemouth
A189
QUEEN ELIZA
COUNTRY PARK
Kielder Wa
(Reservoir)
Redesdale
Park
D E A696 30 B6343 F
Ashington
A197
A196
Morpeth
Guide
Post
WANSBECK C. PARK
Newbig

3

A · 40 · B · C

I N N E R

H E B R I D E S

Sound of

Rum
(Rhum) · Kinloch · Aird of Sleat

Askival
812 · Point of Sleat

Sound of Rum

Rubha nam
Meirleach

Cleadale

Eilean
nan Each · *Eigg* · An Sgurr
393 · Galmisdale

Sound of Eigg

Sound of A

Muck

Eilean
Shona

Lochboisdale

Castlebay · Ardtoe
Ockle · Achc
Ardtoe

Point of
Ardnamurchan · Achosnich · *A r d n a m u r c h a n*

Eilean Mor

B8007 · Ben Hiant
528 · Glenbeg

Kilchoan · Glenborrodale

Sorisdale

B8072

Clabhach · *Coll* · Ardmore Point

B8071 · Tobermory · Drimnin
M

12 · Arinagour

B8070 · Loch
Eatharna · Caliach
Point · A848 · Killundine
B849

Gunna · Calgary · Dervaig · Loch
Frisa · Fiu

Crossapol
Bay · Calgary Bay · Kilninian

Hough Bay · B8069 · Caolas · Salen · A849

B8068 · Treshnish Isles · Loch Tuath · B8073 · B8035 · 23

Tiree · Scarinish · Gometra · Lagganulva · Knock

Barrapoll · B8065 · Hynish Bay · Ulva

Balephuil · Balemartine · Little
Colonsay · Loch Na Keal · Loch
G · *M u l l*

Staffa · Ben More
966

Balnahard · B8035 · Glen More

Ben Buie
717

IONA ABBEY · Loch Scridain · Pennyghael

Baile Mòr · Fionnphort · A849 · 35 · Carsaig · Loch Buie
Iona · Bunessan

Soa Island · *R o s s   o f   M u l l*

Ardchiavaig · Malcolm's
Point

Garv

0 ——— 10 ——— 20 miles

0 —— 10 —— 20 —— 30 km

1: 440,000   7 miles to 1inch / 4.4 km to 1cm

Kiloran Bay · Rubh' a'Geodha

Colonsay · B8086 · Kiloran

Kilchattan · Scalasaig · Sc

A · 32 · B · C

Garvard · B8085 · Loch Staosnaig · einn Bhreac
467

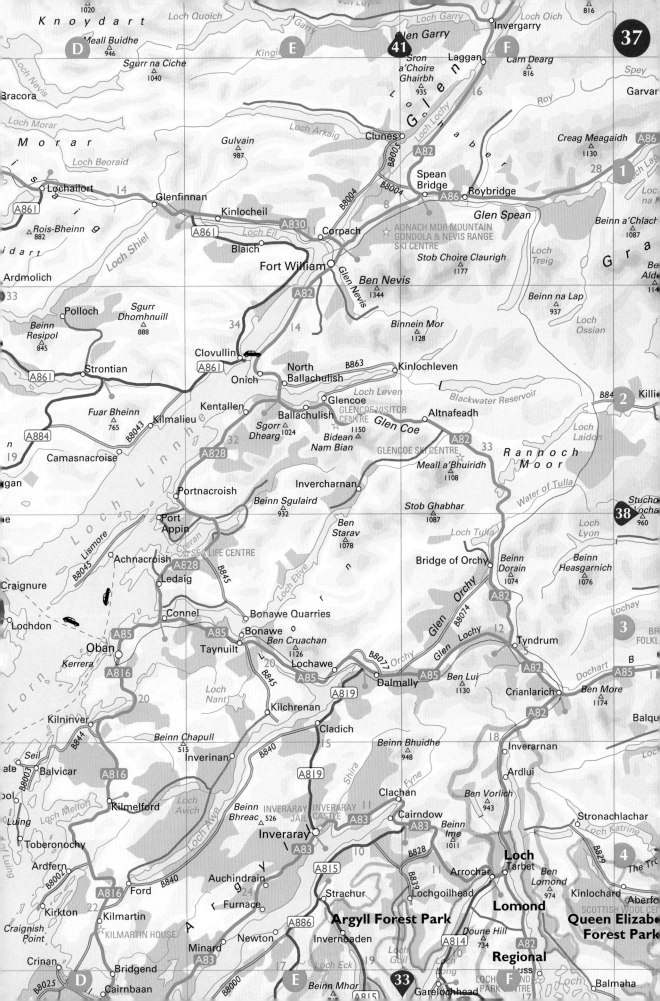

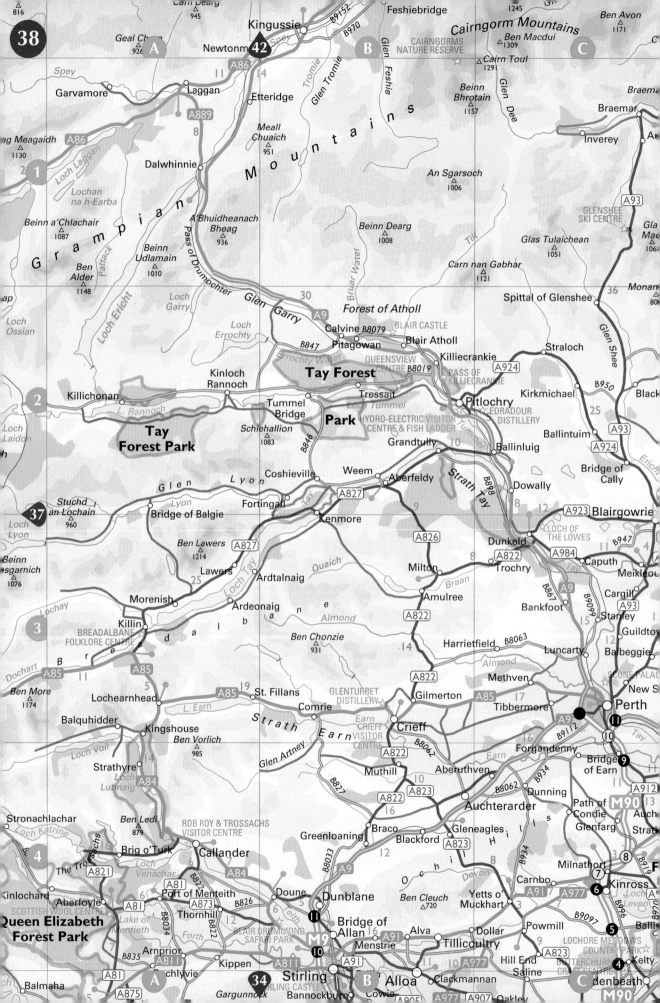

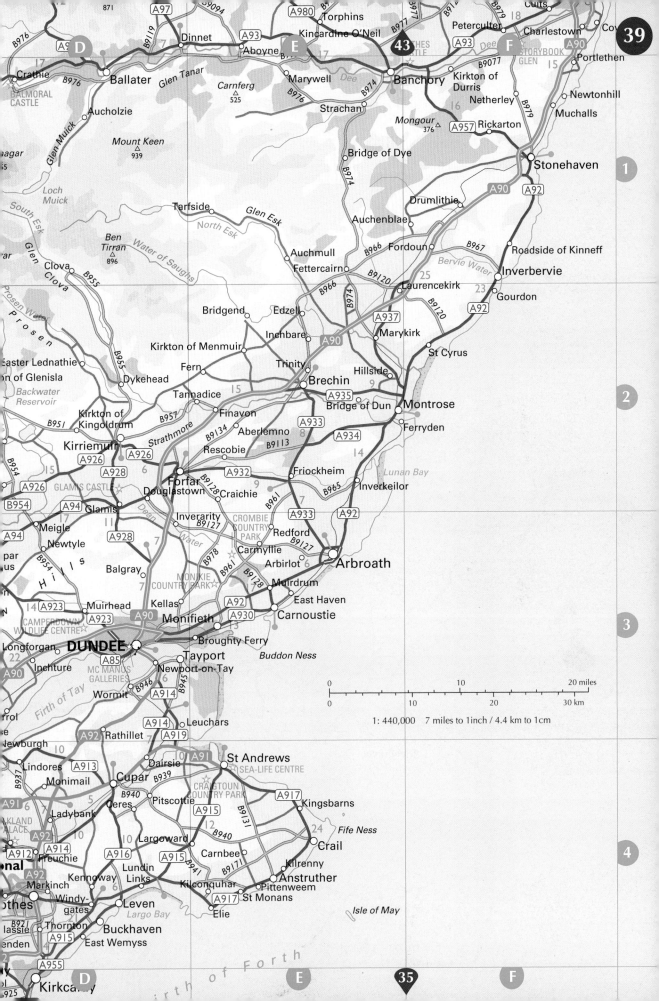

Isles
Culnacraig
D
17
A835
A837
Glen Oy
18
E
44
Invercassley
Oykel Bridge
F
A839
Lairg
8
A836
41
Pit
Isle Martin
Meall Liath Choire
548
Glen Einig
Oykel
Linsidemore
SHIN FALLS
11
A836
Ardmair
Beinn Ghobhlach
635
Ullapool
Strathcarron
12
A836
Bonar Bridge
42
Coast
Badcaul
Little Loch Broom
Leckmelm
Carron
Ardgay
Ardagy
1
B9176
8
A
nning
uinard Bay
12
Inverlael
A835
A832
EASTER
Carn Chuinneag
898
Beinn Tharsuinn
692
Edder
An Teallach
1062
Beinn Dearg
1084
Braeantra
Cn
t-Sa
Loch na Sealga
CORRIESHALLOCH GORGE
ROSS
Beinn nan Eun
742
Boath
Dalnavi
Fionn Loch
Loch Glascarnoch
Loch Morie
Loch Averon
Tomic
ch Maree
Mullach Coire Mhic Fhearchair
1019
Sgurr Mor
1110
Loch Glass
Ben Wyvis
1046
Boath
Alness
A832
Slioch
980
WESTER
20
Aultguish Inn
A835
Black Water
Evanton
Cromarty Firth
2
18
BEINN EIGHE
ATURE RESERVE
ROSS
Loch Fannich
Grudie
16
A832
Garve
Loch Garve
Dingwall
A862
 B817
B9163
ticudde
Liathach
1054
Kinlochewe
A896
A832
9
Achnasheen
Loch Luichart
Strathpeffer
Contin
A834
Conon Bridge
Culbokie
B9169
Black Isle
Fort
16
Sgurr a'Mhuilinn
879
7
Marybank
A835
7
Tore
A9
A832
Sgorr Ruadh
960
18
A890
Craig
Strathconon
Orrin Reservoir
Orrin
A832
6
6
Munloc
7
North Kesso
Balnacra
Sgurr a'Chaorachain
1053
Muir of Ord
A832
A9
42
Achintee
Sgurr a'Choire Ghlais
1083
Loch Monar
Redcastle
Beauly Firth
A862
INV
MU
Attadale
Farrar
Beauly
A831
A833
Dochgarroch
A82
Inv
5
Ling
Glen Cannich
16
12
Lochend
15
B862
B86
3
ch Long
Aonach Buidhe
899
Loch Mullardoch
13
Dores
ch
Ashie
F
AN DONAN CASTLE
Carn Eighe
1183
Cannich
Strathglass
Beauly
LOCH NESS MONSTER EXHIBITION CENTRE
A831
Milton
Drumnadrochit
URQUHART CASTLE
A82
13
Loch Duntelchaig
B852
B862
B851
ie
Glen Affric
Loch Affric
Meal Fuar-mhonaidh
696
13
Errogie
Carn Odhar
802
dge
Sgurr Fhuaran
1068
A'Chralaig
1120
Invermoriston
16
Foyers
Loch Mhor
Fin
Glen Shiel
A87
22
Dundreggan
A887
Glen Moriston
Moriston
M
ò
r
3
Feehlin
Aonach air Chrith
1021
Meall Dubh
788
Glen Moriston
Fort Augustus
B862
Carn Dearg
945
Kinloch Hourn
Loch Cluanie
A87
14
A82
FORT AUGUSTUS ABBEY VISITOR CENTRE
Carn a'Chuilinn
816
Loch Quoich
Loch Loyne
Loch Garry
Invergarry
Garry
Geal Charn
926
Newtonm
Kingie
Glen Garry
Loch Oich
Spey
A86
Ciche
D
Sron a'Choire Ghairbh
935
E
Laggan
Carn Dearg
816
37
Garvamore
Laggan
11

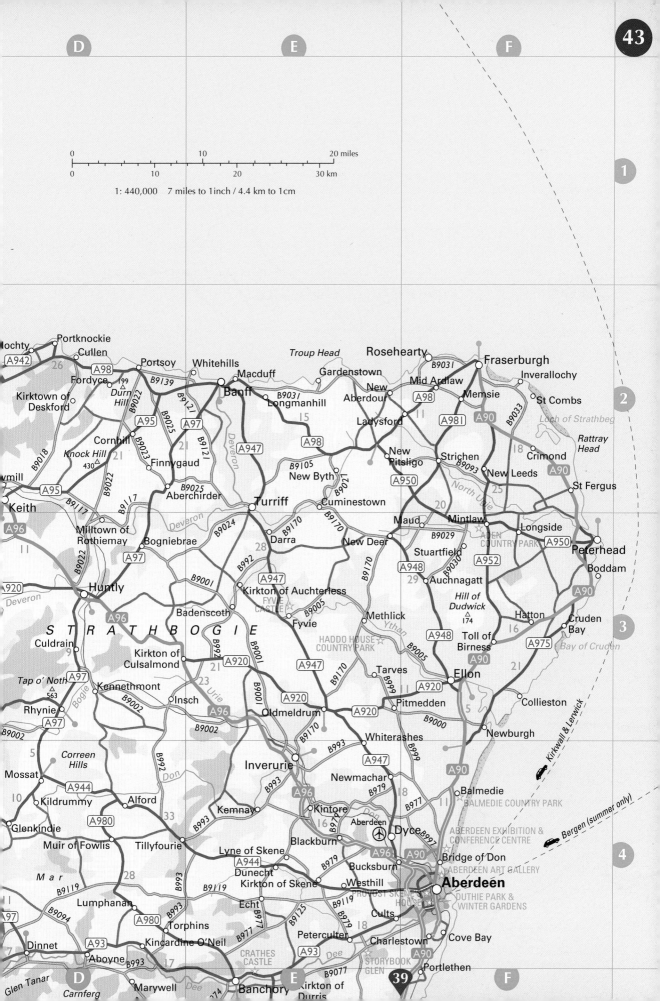

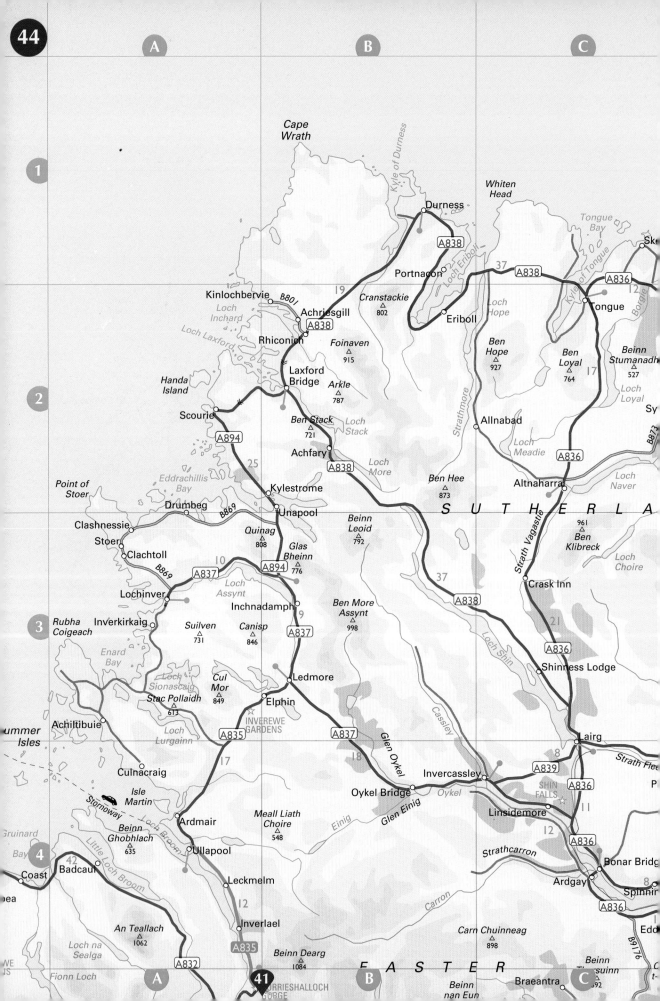

A   B   C

1

Cape
Wrath

Whiten
Head

Durness

Tongue
Bay

Sk

A838

Portnacon   37   A838

A836

12

Kinlochbervie   B801   Cranstackie
                                  802   Eriboll   Tongue

Loch   Achriesgill
Inchard   Loch
                             Hope

Ben   Beinn
Loch Laxford   Rhiconich   Hope   Loy al   Stumanadh
                            Foinaven   927   764   527
                                  915
               Laxford
               Bridge   17
Handa   Arkle
Island   787   Loch
                                         Strathmore   Loyal
2
Scourie   Sy
           A894   Ben Stack   Loch   Allnabad
                     721   Stack   B873
                                                          Loch
                     Achfary   Meadie
        Eddrachillis   A838   Ben Hee   Altnaharra   A836   Loch
        Bay   Loch   873   Naver
                     Kylestrome   More
Point of   Ben
Stoer   Drumbeg   B869   Unapool   SUTHERLA   961   Klibreck
                                         Beinn   Ben
Clashnessie   Leoid   Strath Vagastie   Loch
Stoer   Quinag   792   Choire
        Clachtoll   808
                     Glas
           A837   Bheinn   Crask Inn
        B869   A894   776
Lochinver   Loch
                 Assynt   21   A836
        Inchnadamph   Ben More
3   Rubha   9   Assynt   Shinness Lodge
     Coigeach   Suilven   Canisp   A837   998
                 731   846   Loch
     Enard   Shin
     Bay   Cul   Cassley
           Loch   Mor   Ledmore   Lairg
           Sionascaig   849   8
           Stac Pollaidh   Elphin   A839   Strath Fle
Achiltibuie   613   Glen Oykel   Invercassley   A836
           Loch   INVEREWE   SHIN   11
ummer   Lurgainn GARDENS   Oykel   FALLS
Isles   A835   A837   18   Linsidemore
                                         Oykel Bridge   Glen Einig   12
           Isle   A836
           Martin   Einig
     Stornoway   Ardmair   Meall Liath   Bonar Bridg
           Beinn   Choire   Ardgay
4   42   Ghobhlach   548   Strathcarron   8
Coast Badcaul   635   Spinnir
                     Ullapool
                     Leckmelm   Carron   A836
           12   Edd
           Inverlael   B9176
                     A835   An Teallach   Carn Chuinneag   Beinn
Loch na   1062   Beinn Dearg   898   suinn
Sealga   A832   1084   EASTER   92
Fionn Loch   A   41   B   Beinn   Braeantra   C
              CORRIESHALLOCH   nan Eun
              GORGE

South *F*...

Longhope

South
Wa...

A961

Cleat

Burwick

Brough Ness

Pentland Firth

Swona

Pentla...
Skerrie...

(Summer only)

Island of
Stroma

Dunnet Head

*Strathy
Point*

Strathy

Melvich

Dounreay

Buldoo

Reay

A836

Scrabster

*Thurso
Bay*

Thurso

*Dunnet
Bay*

A836

Brough

A836

Castletown

Mey

Barrock

Dunnet

20

*Loch
Heilen*

Freswick

John o'
Groats

Duncansby
Head

1

A9

B876

Keiss

17

A99

ill

A836

15

Strathy
Point

Strath Halladale

*Loch
Calder*

B870

B874

Halkirk

Roadside

B874

*Loch
Watten*

B870

Sinclair's
Bay

Noss
Head

A882

Olgrinmore

21

Spittal

Watten

Reiss

Westerdale

B870

Mybster

23

Bilbster

Wick

Forsinard

A897

21

Halladale

C A I T H N E S S

Thurso

*Loch
More*

Achavanich

A9

Badlipster

Thrumster

Ulbster

17

B871

Lybster

A99

Kinbrace

Helmsdale

Strath of Kildonan

Morven
△
706

Scaraben
△
626

Latheron

Latheronwheel

Dunbeath

20

Newport

Borgue

Kildonan Lodge

17

A897

Berriedale

A9

Helmsdale

3

Lothmore

Ben Horn
△
521

17

A9

*Loch
Brora*

ogart

Brora

839

A9

4

Golspie

Loch Fleet

7

0   10   20 miles

0   10   20   30 km

...nore

Dornoch

Dornoch Firth

Tarbat Ness

Portmahomack

1 : 440,000   7 miles to 1 inch / 4.4 km to 1cm

Tain

B9166

B9165

Tarrel

of Fearn

A **B** **C**

1

Shillay

Pabbay

Sound of Pabbay

Taobh Tuath

A859

47

HARRIS
(Ceann a Deas
na Hearadh)

An t-Òb

Roghadal

Renish Point

Boreray

Eilean Bhearnaraigh

Sound of Harris

Port nan Long

Griminis Point

Vallay

Solas

25

Baile Mhartainn

B893

NORTH UIST
(Uibhist a' Tuath)

A865

8

Ceann a'Bháigh

Lochmaddy
(Loch na Madadh)

Lochmaddy

Little Minch

Vaternish Point

A865

A867

Saighdinis

Loch Euphoirt

Ben C

28

2

Heisker or
Monach Islands

Baleshare

Sound of Monach

Dunvegan Head

Boreraig

Mileovaig

Loch Dunvegan

Baile a'Mhanaich

Uachdar

Ronay
(Ronaigh)

BENBECULA
(Beinn na Faoghla)

B892

4

Creag Ghoraidh

B891

B884

Ardivachar Point

Wiay

Loch Bee

Bagh nam Faoilean

Healabhal
Bheag
△
488

A865

B890

Stadhlaigearraidh

Loch Sgioport

SOUTH UIST
(Uibhist a' Deas)

Rubha Ardvule

Beinn Mhor
△
620

21

Loch Eynor

3

A865

Dalabrog

B888

Lochboisdale (Loch Baghasdail)

Loch Baghasdail

Sea of the Hebrides

Cille Bhrighde

Ludag

Scurrival Point

Sound of Barra

Eriskay
(Eiriosgaigh)

Canna

Greian Head

Fuday

BARRA
(Eilean Barraigh)

Oban

Borgh

A888

Earsairidh

Castlebay
(Bagh a' Chaisteil)

4

Vatersay
(Bhatarsaigh)

Sanndraigh

Oban

Pabbay
(Pabaigh)

Mingulay
(Miughalaigh)

A **B** 36 **C**

Bearnaraigh

Isle of Lewis / Isle of Harris Map

ISLE OF LEWIS (Eilean Leodhais)

Rubha Robhanais
Eoropaidh
Tabost
Port Nis
Sgiogarstaigh
Dail Bho Thuath

A857 15

Barabhas
Muirneag 248
Tolastadh Úr
Tolsta Head

Arnol
Siabost
Bragar

A858

Carlabhagh
20

Beinn Mholach 292
Griais

West Loch Roag
East Loch Roag

Tolastadh a'Chaolais
A857
Tunga
B895

Great Bernera
Breascleit
Calanais
Stornoway (Steornabhagh)
Newmarket
Loch a' Tuath

Miabhig
Crulabhig
B8059
B8011
Gearraidh na h-Aibhne
A858
13
A866
An Rubha

Rubha an t-Siumpain
Port nan Giúran
Siulaisiadar

Timsgearraidh
Loch Suainaval
Achadh Mór
A859
12
B897

Breanais
Mealisval 574
Einacleit
B8011
Crosbost

ealasta Island

NORTH HARRIS (Ceann a Tuath na Hearadh)

Baile Ailein
B8060
Cearsiadar
Loch Erisort

arp
Loch Langavat
21
Airidh a'Bhruaich
A859
Grabhair
Ullapool

Loch Resort
B8060
Leumrabhagh
Kebock Head

Huisinis
Tirga Mor 679
Clishham 799
A859
Beinn Mhór 572
Loch Shell

Abhainnsuidhe
B887
A859
Loch Claidh

Tarànsay (Taransaigh)
Aird Asaig
Tarbert (An Tairbeart)
Loch Bhrollum

Head
Sound of Taransay
A859
Caolas Scalpaigh
Shiant Islands

25
East Loch Tarbert
Scalpay (Eilean Scalpaigh)

SOUTH HARRIS (Ceann a Deas na Hearadh)
A859
Rubha

Taobh Tuath
A859
Loch Langavat
Me

An t-Ób
Roghadal
Renish Point

Sound of Harris

Rubha Hunish
Kilmaluag
Staffin Bay

gh
chmaddy och na Madadh)
Little Minch
Vaternish Point
A855
19
Staffin
Redp

Balgown

Loch Euphoirt
Ben Geary 284
Idrigil
Uig
A87
Culnaknock
Fearnm

Loch Snizort
Trotternish
Rona

Scale
0 .... 10 .... 20 miles
0 ...... 10 ...... 20 ...... 30 km

1: 440,000   7 miles to 1inch / 4.4 km to 1cm

A   B   C

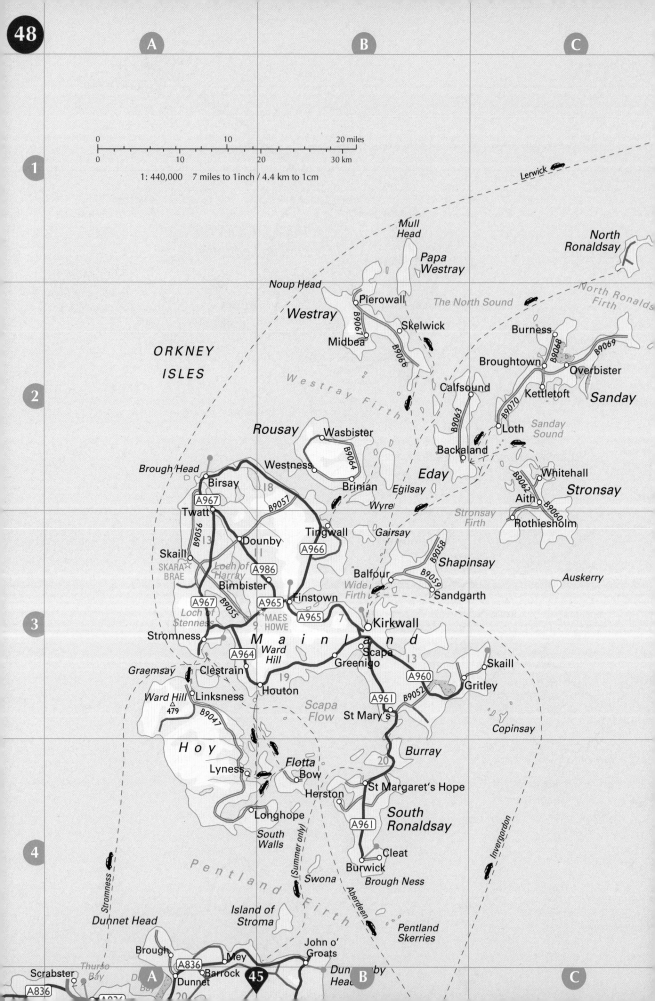

0   10   20 miles
0   10   20   30 km

1: 440,000   7 miles to 1inch / 4.4 km to 1cm

Lerwick

1

Mull
Head

Papa
Westray

North
Ronaldsay

Noup Head

The North Sound

North Ronaldsay
Firth

Westray

Pierowall

Skelwick

Burness

B9067

Midbea

B9066

Broughtown

B9068

Overbister

ORKNEY
ISLES

Westray Firth

Calfsound

Kettletoft

B9069

Sanday

2

B9063

Loth

B9070

Sanday
Sound

Rousay

Wasbister

Backaland

Eday

Whitehall

Westness

B9064

Stronsay

Brough Head

Birsay

Brinian

Egilsay

Aith

B9062

B9060

A967

18

B9057

Wyre

Rothiesholm

Twatt

B9056

Tingwall

Gairsay

Stronsay
Firth

Dounby

11

A986

A966

B9058

Shapinsay

Skaill

B913

SKARA
BRAE

Loch of
Harray

Bimbister

A965

Balfour

B9059

Auskerry

A967

B9055

Finstown

Wide
Firth

Sandgarth

3

Loch of
Stenness

A965

MAES
HOWE

9

7

Kirkwall

M a i n l a n d

Stromness

A964

Ward
Hill

Scapa

13

Skaill

Clestrain

Greenigo

A960

Gritley

Graemsay

19

Houton

B9052

Ward Hill
△
479

Linksness

Scapa
Flow

A961

St Mary's

Copinsay

B9047

Hoy

Flotta

Burray

4

Lyness

Bow

20

Herston

St Margaret's Hope

Longhope

South
Walls

South
Ronaldsay

A961

Swona

Cleat

Burwick

Brough Ness

Stromness

(Summer only)

Pentland
Skerries

Invergordon

Aberdeen

Pentland   Firth

Dunnet Head

Island of
Stroma

John o'
Groats

Scrabster

Brough

A836

Mey

Barrock

45

Dunby
Head

Thurso
Bay

A836

Dunnet

A
B
C

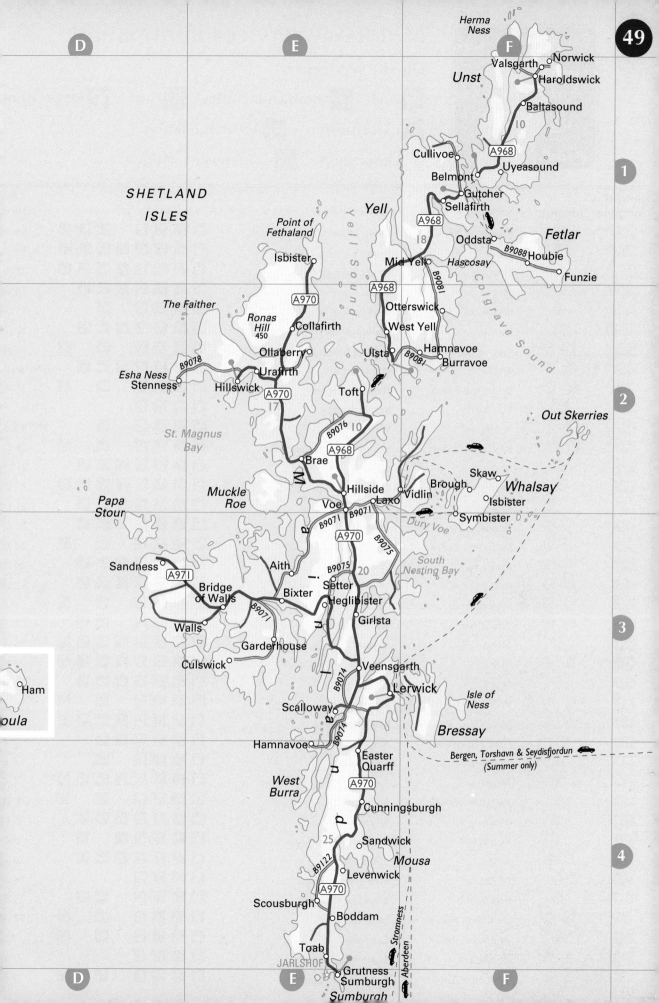

SHETLAND
ISLES

Unst

Herma
Ness

Valsgarth   Norwick
Haroldswick
Baltasound
10
A968
Uyeasound
Cullivoe
Belmont
Gutcher
Sellafirth
A968
Oddsta
B9088   Houbie
Fetlar
Funzie

Yell

Point of
Fethaland

Isbister

A970

Mid Yell
Hascosay
B9081
Otterswick
West Yell
Hamnavoe
Burravoe
B9081
Ulsta

Colgrave Sound

Out Skerries

The Faither

Ronas
Hill
450
Collafirth
Ollaberry
Urafirth
B9078
Esha Ness
Stenness
Hillswick
A970
17

18

Yell Sound

Toft

A970

B9076   10

A968

St. Magnus
Bay

Brae

M

Muckle
Roe

Papa
Stour

a

Hillside
Voe
Laxo
B9071   B9071

Vidlin
Brough   Skaw
Whalsay
Isbister
Symbister

Dury Voe

South
Nesting Bay

A970

B9075

20

Sandness
A971

Aith

B9075

Bridge
of Walls
Bixter
B9071

Setter
Heglibister

Girlsta

Walls

n

i

Garderhouse
Culswick

B9074

Veensgarth

Lerwick

Isle of
Ness

Scalloway

a

Bressay

Hamnavoe
B9074

Easter
Quarff

Bergen, Torshavn & Seydisfjordun
(Summer only)

West
Burra

r

u

A970

Cunningsburgh

p

25

Sandwick

Mousa

B9122

Levenwick

Scousburgh
A970

Boddam

Stromness

Toab
JARLSHOF
Grutness
Sumburgh
Sumburgh

Aberdeen

Ham

oula

D   E   F

1

2

3

4

50

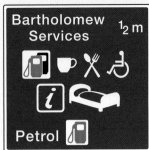

Motorway services information

On-site services:

- ⛽ Fuel
- ♿ Disabled facilities
- 🍴 Food
- £ Service shop
- *i* Information
- 🛏 Accommodation
- ₤ Other shops
- 👥 Conference facilities

Motorway number	Junction	Service provider	Service name	Fuel	Disabled	Food	Service shop	Information	Accommodation	Other shops	Conference	Map reference
A1(M)	1	Welcome Break	South Mimms	●	●	●	●		●	●	●	16 A
A1(M)	10	Extra	Baldock	●	●	●	●	●	●	●	●	16 A
A1(M)	17	Extra	Peterborough	●	●	●	●	●	●	●	●	22 A
A1(M)	34	Moto	Blyth	●	●	●	●	●	●	●		26 B
A1(M)	61	RoadChef	Durham	●	●	●	●		●			31 D
A1(M)	64	Moto	Washington	●	●	●	●	●	●	●		31 D
M1	2–4	Welcome Break	London Gateway	●	●	●	●		●		●	16 A
M1	11–12	Moto	Toddington	●	●	●	●	●	●	●		15 F
M1	14–15	Welcome Break	Newport Pagnell	●	●	●	●		●		●	15 F
M1	15A	RoadChef	Rothersthorpe	●	●	●	●					15 E
M1	16–17	RoadChef	Watford Gap	●	●	●	●		●			15 E
M1	21–21A	Welcome Break	Leicester Forest East	●	●	●	●		●		●	21 D
M1	22	Moto	Leicester	●	●	●	●	●	●	●		21 D
M1	23A	Moto	Donington Park	●	●	●	●	●	●	●	●	21 D
M1	25–26	Moto	Trowell	●	●	●	●	●	●	●		21 D
M1	28–29	RoadChef	Tibshelf	●	●	●	●		●	●		21 D
M1	30–31	Welcome Break	Woodall	●	●	●	●		●		●	26 A
M1	38–39	Moto	Woolley Edge	●	●	●	●	●	●	●		26 A
M2	4–5	Moto	Medway	●	●	●	●	●	●	●		11 D
M3	4A–5	Welcome Break	Fleet	●	●	●	●		●		●	9 F
M3	8–9	RoadChef	Winchester	●	●	●	●		●	●		9 E
M4	3	Moto	Heston	●	●	●	●	●	●	●	●	10 A
M4	11–12	Moto	Reading	●	●	●	●	●	●	●		9 E
M4	13	Moto	Chieveley	●	●	●	●	●	●	●		15 D
M4	14–15	Welcome Break	Membury	●	●	●	●		●		●	14 C
M4	17–18	Moto	Leigh Delamere	●	●	●	●	●	●	●	●	14 B
M4	23A	First Motorway	Magor	●	●	●	●	●	●			7 F
M4	30	Moto	Cardiff Gate	●	●	●	●		●			7 E
M4	33	Moto	Cardiff	●	●	●	●	●	●	●	●	7 E
M4	36	Welcome Break	Sarn Park	●	●	●	●		●		●	7 D
M4	47	Moto	Swansea	●	●	●	●	●	●	●		6 C
M4	49	RoadChef	Pont Abraham	●	●	●	●	●		●		6 C
M5	3–4	Moto	Frankley	●	●	●	●	●	●	●		20 B
M5	8	RoadChef	Strensham (South)	●		●	●					14 B
M5	8	RoadChef	Strensham (North)	●	●	●	●		●	●		14 B
M5	13–14	Welcome Break	Michael Wood	●	●	●	●		●		●	14 A
M5	19	Welcome Break	Gordano	●	●	●	●		●		●	7 F
M5	21–22	RoadChef	Sedgemoor (South)	●		●	●					7 F
M5	21–22	Welcome Break	Sedgemoor (North)	●	●	●	●		●		●	7 F

Motorway number	Junction	Service provider	Service name	On-site services	
M5	24	Moto	Bridgwater		7 F4
M5	25–26	RoadChef	Taunton Deane		7 E4
M5	28	Margram	Cullompton		5 E1
M5	29–30	Moto	Exeter		5 D1
M6	3–4	Welcome Break	Corley		20 C4
M6	10–11	Moto	Hilton Park		20 B3
M6	14–15	RoadChef	Stafford (South)		20 B2
M6	14–15	Moto	Stafford (North)		20 B2
M6	15–16	Welcome Break	Keele		20 A2
M6	16–17	RoadChef	Sandbach		20 A1
M6	18–19	Moto	Knutsford		20 A1
M6	27–28	Welcome Break	Charnock Richard		25 D3
M6	32–33	Moto	Lancaster		25 D2
M6	35A–36	Moto	Burton-in-Kendal (North)		25 D1
M6	36–37	RoadChef	Killington Lake (South)		30 A4
M6	38–39	Westmorland	Tebay		30 A4
M6	41–42	Moto	Southwaite		29 F2
M8	4–5	RoadChef	Harthill		34 A2
M9	9	Moto	Stirling		34 A1
M11	8	Welcome Break	Birchanger Green		16 B3
M18	5	Moto	Doncaster North		26 B3
M20	8	RoadChef	Maidstone		11 D2
M23	11	Moto	Pease Pottage		10 B3
M25	5–6	RoadChef	Clacket Lane		10 C2
M25	23	Welcome Break	South Mimms		16 A4
M25	30	Moto	Thurrock		10 C1
M27	3–4	RoadChef	Rownhams		9 D3
M40	8	Welcome Break	Oxford		15 E3
M40	10	Moto	Cherwell Valley		15 D2
M40	12–13	Welcome Break	Warwick		15 D1
M42	2	Welcome Break	Hopwood Park		14 B1
M42	10	Moto	Tamworth		20 C3
M48	1	Moto	Severn View		14 A4
M50	4	Welcome Break	Ross Spur		14 A2
M56	14	RoadChef	Chester		19 F1
M61	6–7	First Motorway	Bolton West		25 D3
M62	7–9	Welcome Break	Burtonwood		25 D4
M62	18–19	Moto	Birch		25 E3
M62	25–26	Welcome Break	Hartshead Moor		25 F3
M62	33	Moto	Ferrybridge		26 A3
M65	4	Supermart	Blackburn Interchange		19 F1
M74	4–5	RoadChef	Bothwell (South)		33 F2
M74	5–6	RoadChef	Hamilton (North)		33 F2
M74	11–12	Cairn Lodge	Happendon		34 A3
M74	12–13	Welcome Break	Abington		34 A3
M74(M)	16	RoadChef	Annandale Water		34 B4
M74(M)	22	Welcome Break	Gretna Green		29 F1
M90	6	Moto	Kinross		38 C4

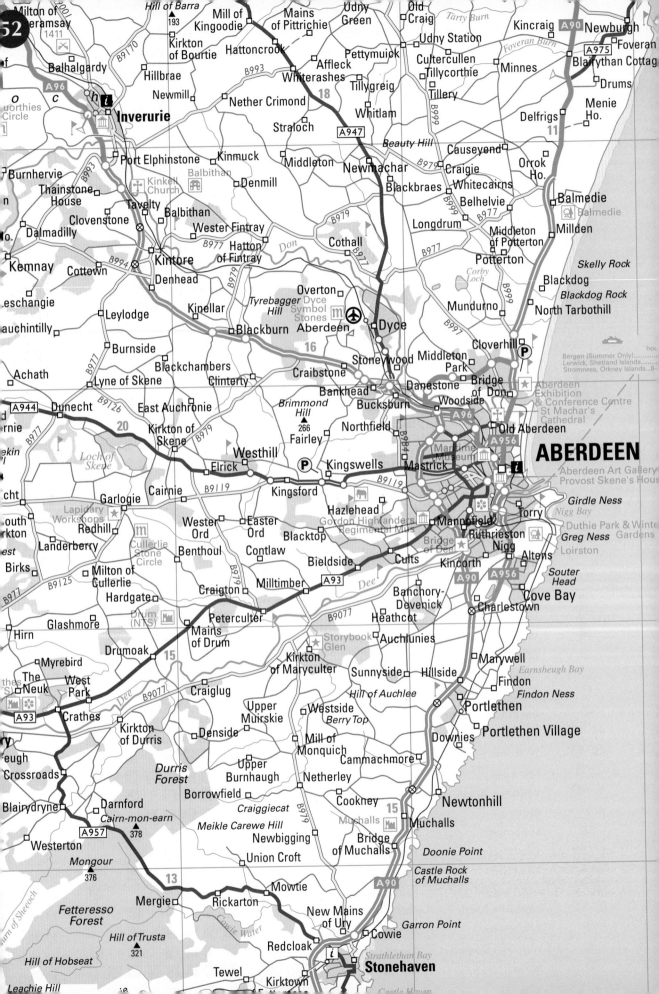

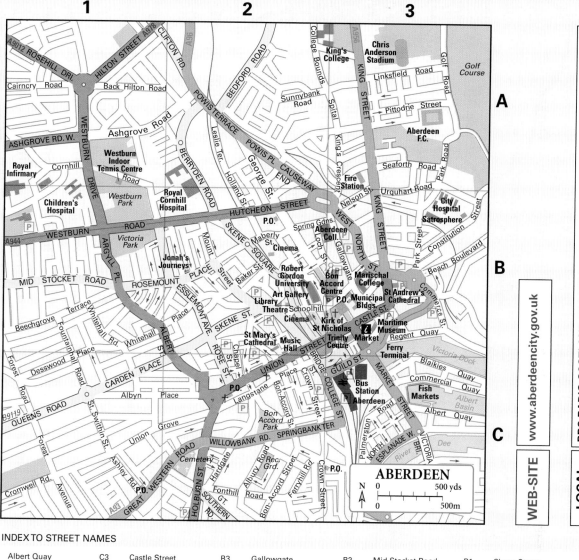

Area Code 01224

ABERDEEN

www.aberdeencity.gov.uk

WEB-SITE

BBC RADIO SCOTLAND 93.9 FM & 810 AM
NORTHSOUND 1 96.9 FM, NORTHSOUND 2 1035 AM

LOCAL RADIO

ABERDEEN

N

0 — 500 yds

0 — 500m

INDEX TO STREET NAMES

TOURIST INFORMATION ☎ 01224 288828
23 UNION STREET,
ABERDEEN, AB10 1YL

HOSPITAL A & E ☎ 01224 681818
ABERDEEN ROYAL INFIRMARY, FORESTERHILL,
ABERDEEN, AB25 2ZN

COUNCIL OFFICE ☎ 01224 522000
TOWN HOUSE, BROAD STREET,
ABERDEEN, AB10 1FY

Aberdeen Population: 189,707. City, cathedral and university city and commercial centre on E coast 57m/92km NE of Dundee. Known as 'The Granite City', local stone having been used in many of its buildings. By 13c, Aberdeen had become an important centre for trade and fishing and remains a major port and commercial base. In 19c shipbuilding brought great prosperity to the city. These industries had receded by mid 20c but the city's prospects were transformed when North Sea oil was discovered in 1970, turning it into a city of great wealth. St. Machar's Cathedral at Old Aberdeen. Many museums and art galleries. Extensive flower gardens. Airport at Dyce, 6m/9km NW of Aberdeen.

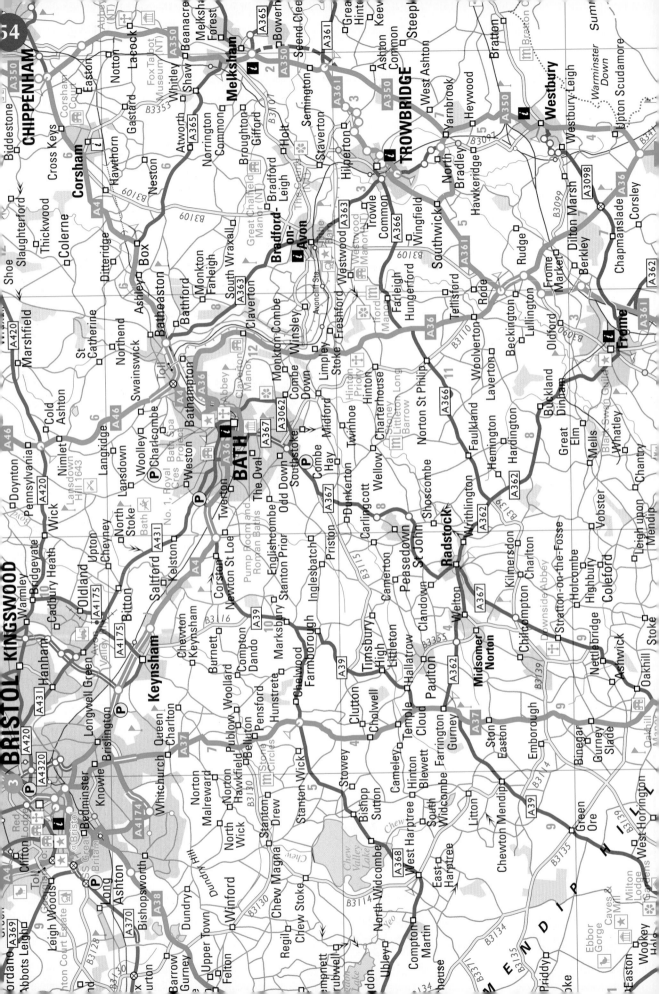

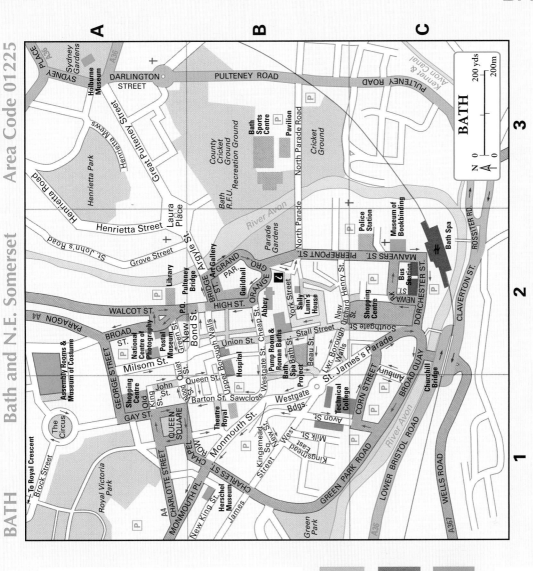

BATH   Bath and N.E. Somerset   Area Code 01225

TOURIST INFORMATION ☎ 01225 477101
AVVEY CAMBERS, ABBEY CHURCHYARD,
BATH, BA1 1LY

HOSPITAL A & E ☎ 01225 428331
ROYAL UNITED HOSPITAL, COMBE PARK,
BATH, BA1 3NG

COUNCIL OFFICE ☎ 01225 477000
THE GUILDHALL, HIGH STREET,
BATH, BA1 5AW

Bath *B. & N.E.Som.* Population: 85,202. City, spa on River Avon, 11m/18km SE of Bristol. Abbey church rebuilt 1501. Natural hot springs unique in Britain drew Romans to Bath, which they named 'Aquae Sulis'. Roman baths and 18c Pump Room are open to visitors. In 18c, it was most fashionable resort in country. Many Georgian buildings and elegant crescents remain, including The Circus and Royal Crescent. Museum of Costume in restored Assembly Rooms. Holds annual summer music festival. American Museum housed in Claverton Manor and University 3m/4km SE.

WEB-SITE www.bathnes.gov.uk

LOCAL RADIO BBC RADIO BRISTOL 1548 AM & 104.6 FM
CLASSIC GOLD 1260 AM, 103 GWR FM 103 FM

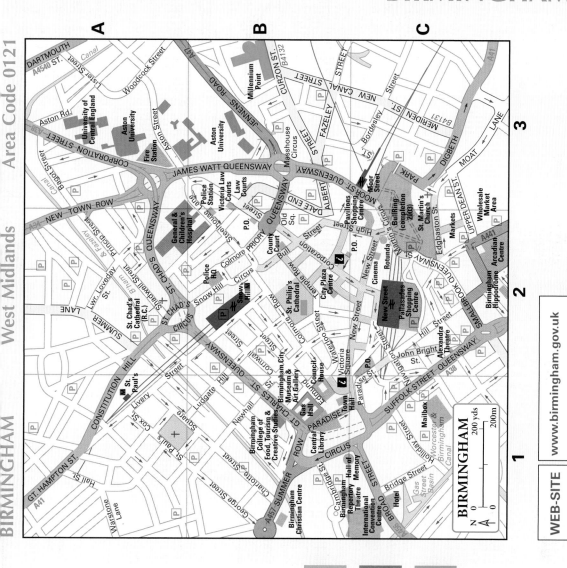

LOCAL RADIO

BBC RADIO WM 95.6 FM
RADIO XL 1296 AM, BRMB 96.4 FM, HEART FM 100.7 FM, GALAXY 102.2 FM

WEB-SITE

www.birmingham.gov.uk

INDEX TO STREET NAMES

Albert Street	B3	Great Charles Street	B1	Paradise Circus	B1
Aston Road	A3	Queensway		Paradise Street	C1
Aston Street	A3	Great Hampton Street	A1	Park Street	C3
Bagot Street	A3	Hall Street	A1	Princ Street	A2
Bordesley Street	C3	High Street	C2	Priory Queensway	B2
Bridge Street	C1	Hill Street	C2	Queensway	B2
Broad Street	C1	Holliday Street	C1	St. Chad's Circus	A2
Bull Street	B2	James Watt	A3	St. Chad's Queensway	A2
Cambridge Street	B1	Queensway		St. Martin's Circus	C2
Charlotte Street	B1	Jennens Road	B3	St. Paul's Square	A1
Colmore Circus	B2	John Bright Street	C2	Shadwell Street	A2
Colmore Row	B2	Lister Street	A3	Smallbrook	C2
Constitution Hill	A1	Livery Street	A2	Queensway	
Cornwall Street	B2	Lower Loveday Street	A2	Snow Hill	B2
Corporation	B2/A3	Ludgate Hill	B1	Steelhouse Lane	B2
Street		Masshouse Circus	B3	Suffolk Street	C1
Cox Street	A1	Meriden Street	C3	Queensway	
Curzon Street	B3	Moat Lane	C3	Summer Lane	A2
Dale End	B2	Moor Street	B2	Summer Row	B1
Dartmouth Street	A3	Queensway		Temple Row	B2
Digbeth	C3	Navigation Street	C1	Upper Dean Street	C2
Edgbaston Street	C2	New Canal Street	C3	Victoria Square	B2
Edmund Street	B1	New Street	C2	Warstone Lane	A1
Fazeley Street	B3	New Town Row	A3	Waterloo Lane	B2
George Street	B1	Newhall Street	B1	Woodcock Street	A3

TOURIST INFORMATION ☎ 0121 643 2514
2 CITY ARCADE, BIRMINGHAM,
WEST MIDLANDS, B2 4TX

HOSPITAL A & E ☎ 0121 554 3801
CITY HOSPITAL, DUDLEY ROAD,
BIRMINGHAM, B18 7QH

COUNCIL OFFICE ☎ 0121 303 9944
COUNCIL HOUSE, VICTORIA SQUARE,
BIRMINGHAM, B1 1BB

Birmingham *W.Mid.* City, England's second city and manufacturing, commercial and communications centre, 100m/160km NW of London. Birmingham was home to many pioneers of industrial revolution. Current economic trend is towards post-industrial activities, concentrating on convention and exhibition trades and tourism. To S of city is planned village of Bournville, established by Quaker chocolate magnates George and Richard Cadbury in 1879, influenced by utopian ideas of William Morris. Universities. City has many galleries and museums, particularly around 19c Victoria and Chamberlain Squares. Anglican and Catholic cathedrals. Birmingham International Airport 7m/11km E of city centre.

Area Code 01253

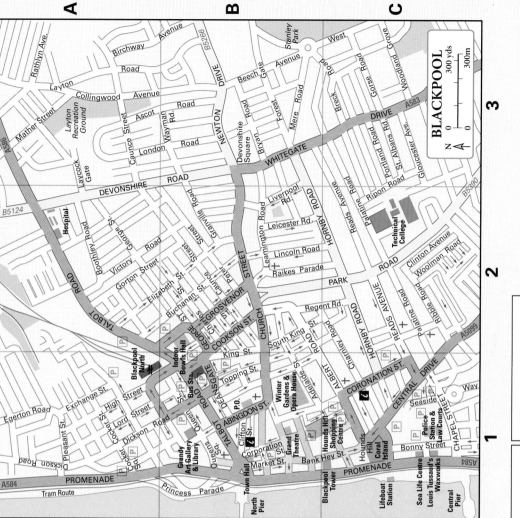

TOURIST INFORMATION ☎ 01253 478222
1 CLIFTON STREET,
BLACKPOOL, FY1 1LY

HOSPITAL A & E ☎ 01253 300000
VICTORIA HOSPITAL, WHINNEY HEYS ROAD,
BLACKPOOL, FY3 8NR

COUNCIL OFFICE ☎ 01253 477477
TOWN HALL, TALBOT SQUARE,
BLACKPOOL, FY1 1NA

Blackpool *B'pool* Population: 146,262. Town, large coastal resort and conference centre on Irish Sea, 15m/24km W of Preston. 19c fashionable resort, still very popular today. 7m/11km long 'Golden Mile' of tram route, beach, piers and amusement arcades. Blackpool Pleasure Beach funfair park, 518ft/158m high Tower entertainment complex, annual autumn illuminations along 5m/8km of Promenade, Zoo, Sea Life Centre, The Sandcastle indoor pool complex and Winter Gardens. Airport 3m/5km S.

WEB-SITE www.blackpool.gov.uk

LOCAL RADIO
BBC RADIO LANCASHIRE 104.5 FM
MAGIC 999 AM, RADIO WAVE 96.5 FM, ROCK FM 97.4 FM

BOURNEMOUTH

Area Code 01202

Map legend:

BOURNEMOUTH

N 0   400 yds
0   400m

Undercliff Drive closed to vehicular traffic in summer season.

INDEX TO STREET NAMES

TOURIST INFORMATION ☎ 0906 802 0234
WESTOVER ROAD,
BOURNEMOUTH, BH1 2BU

HOSPITAL A & E ☎ 01202 303626
ROYAL BOURNEMOUTH HOSPITAL,
CASTLE LANE EAST, BOURNEMOUTH, BH7 7DW

COUNCIL OFFICE ☎ 01202 451451
TOWN HALL, BOURNE AVENUE,
BOURNEMOUTH, BH2 6DY

Bournemouth *Bourne.* Population: 155,488. Town, large seaside resort with mild climate, 24m/39km SW of Southampton. Town developed from a few cottages in 1810 to present conurbation. Sandy beach and pier. Extensive parks and gardens including Compton Acres, a display of international garden styles. Russell-Cotes Art Gallery and Museum houses Victorian and oriental collection. University. Conference, business and shopping centre. Bournemouth International Airport, 5m/8km NE of town centre.

WEB-SITE www.bournemouth.gov.uk

LOCAL RADIO BBC RADIO SOLENT FOR DORSET 103.8 FM
CLASSIC GOLD 828 AM, 2CR FM 102.3 FM, FIRE 107.6 FM

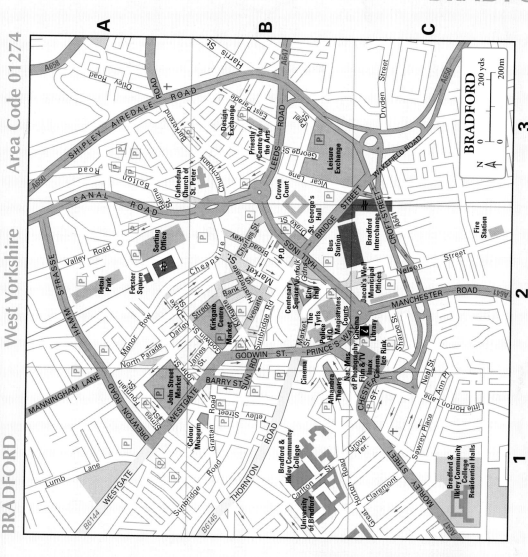

TOURIST INFORMATION ☎ 01274 753678
CENTRAL LIBRARY, PRINCES WAY,
BRADFORD, W. YORKS, BD1 1NN

HOSPITAL A & E ☎ 01274 542200
BRADFORD ROYAL INFIRMARY, DUCKWORTH LANE,
BRADFORD, BD9 6RJ

COUNCIL OFFICE ☎ 01274 752111
CITY HALL, CHANNING WAY,
BRADFORD, BD1 1HY

WEB-SITE www.bradford.gov.uk

LOCAL RADIO
BBC RADIO LEEDS 102.7 FM
WEST YORKS CLASSIC GOLD 1278 AM, THE PULSE 97.5 FM, SUNRISE RADIO 103.2 FM

Bradford W. Yorks. Population: 289,376. City, industrial city, 8m/13km W of Leeds. Cathedral is former parish church. Previously known as wool capital of the world. Bradford is now less dependent upon the textile industry. Colour Museum documents history of dyeing and textile printing. University. Home to National Museum of Photography, Film and Television with IMAX cinema screen. Titus Salt built Saltaire 3m/5km N, which is now considered a model industrial village. Salt's Mill, originally for textiles, now houses David Hockney art in the 1853 gallery. Leeds Bradford International Airport at Yeadon, 6m/10km NE.

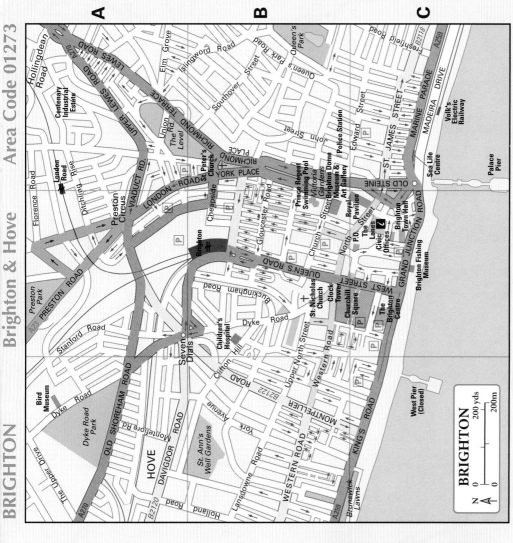

BRIGHTON

N

0   200 yds
0   200m

TOURIST INFORMATION ☎ 0906 711 2255
10 BARTHOLOMEW SQUARE,
BRIGHTON, BN1 1JS

HOSPITAL A & E ☎ 01273 696955
ROYAL SUSSEX COUNTY HOSPITAL, EASTERN ROAD,
BRIGHTON, BN2 5BE

COUNCIL OFFICE ☎ 01273 290000
TOWN HALL, BARTHOLOMEWS,
BRIGHTON, BN1 1JA

Brighton *B. & H.* Population: 124,851. Town, seaside resort, sailing and conference centre, 48m/77km S of London. Previously a fishing village known as Brighthelmstone, centred on current Lanes area. Brighton became fashionable as a sea-bathing resort in the 18c. Patronized by the Prince Regent in 1780s who built the Royal Pavilion in Oriental style as a summer palace. Regency squares at Kemp Town. Amusement arcades on 1899 Palace Pier. Annual festivals. Language schools. Universities.

WEB-SITE   www.brighton-hove.gov.uk

LOCAL RADIO   BBC SOUTHERN COUNTIES RADIO 95.3 FM
CAPITAL GOLD 1323 AM, SOUTHERN FM 103.5

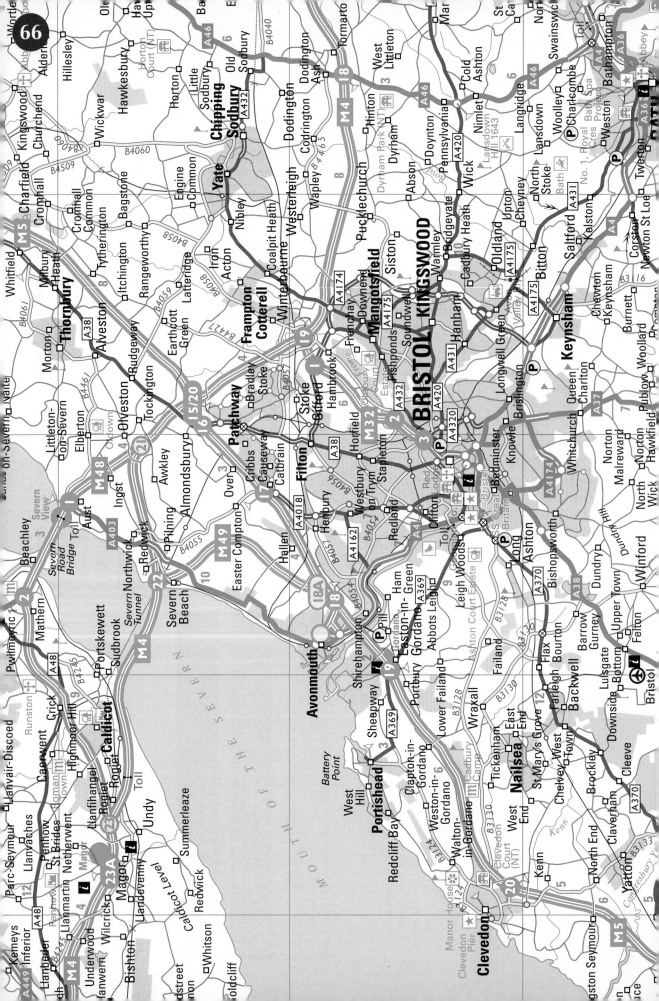

Area Code 0117

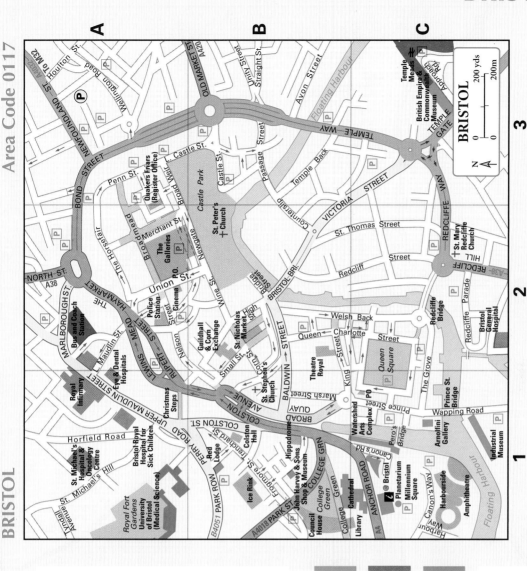

BRISTOL

N

0   200 yds
0   200m

TOURIST INFORMATION ☎ 0117 926 0767
THE ANNEXE, WILDSCREEN WALK, HARBOURSIDE,
BRISTOL, BS1 5UD

HOSPITAL A & E ☎ 0117 923 0000
BRISTOL ROYAL INFIRMARY,
MARLBOROUGH STREET, BRISTOL, BS2 8HW

COUNCIL OFFICE ☎ 0117 922 2000
THE COUNCIL HOUSE, COLLEGE GREEN,
BRISTOL, BS1 5TR

Bristol Population: 407,992. City, 106m/171km W of London. Port on River Avon dates from medieval times. Bristol grew from transatlantic trade in rum, tobacco and slaves. In Georgian times, Bristol's population was second only to London and many Georgian buildings still stand, including the Theatre Royal, the oldest working theatre in the country. Bristol is now a commercial and industrial centre. Cathedral dates from 12c and was originally an abbey. 15c Temple Church tower and walls (English Heritage). Restored iron ship SS Great Britain and Industrial Museum in city docks area. Universities. 245ft/75m high Clifton Suspension Bridge completed in 1864 across the Avon Gorge NW of the city. Bristol International Airport at Lulsgate 7m/11km SW.

WEB-SITE www.bristol-city.gov.uk

LOCAL RADIO BBC RADIO BRISTOL 94.9 FM
BRUNEL CLASSIC GOLD 1260 AM, GWR FM 96.3 FM, GALAXY 101 & 97.2FM, STAR 107.3 FM

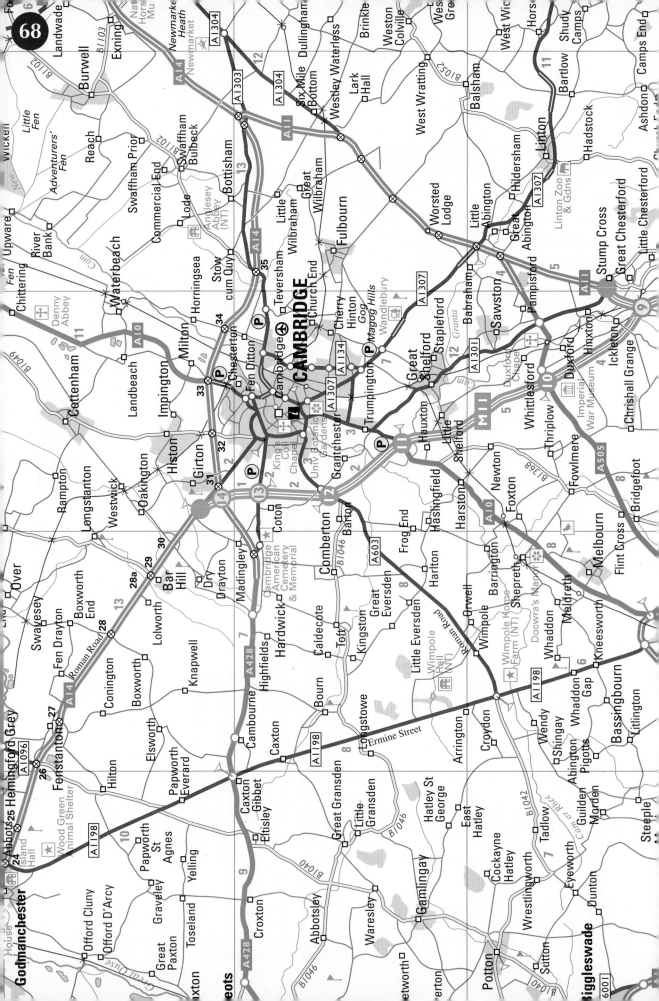

CAMBRIDGE Cambridgeshire Area Code 01223

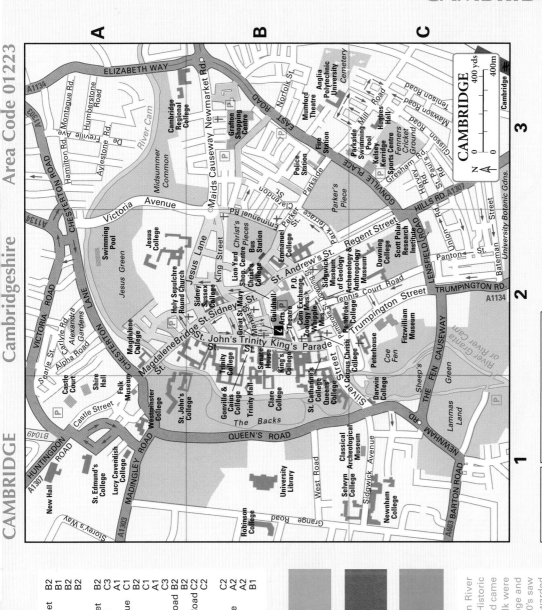

TOURIST INFORMATION ☎ 01223 322640
WHEELER STREET, CAMBRIDGE,
CAMBRIDGESHIRE, CB2 3QB

HOSPITAL A & E ☎ 01223 245151
ADDENBROOKE'S HOSPITAL, HILLS ROAD,
CAMBRIDGE, CB2 2QQ

COUNCIL OFFICE ☎ 01223 457000
THE GUILDHALL, MARKET SQUARE,
CAMBRIDGE, CB2 3QJ

WEB-SITE www.cambridge.gov.uk

LOCAL RADIO BBC RADIO CAMBRIDGESHIRE 96 FM
Q 103 FM, STAR 107.9 FM

Cambridge Cambs. Population: 95,682. City, university city on River Cam 49m/79km N of London. First college founded here in 1271. Historic tensions existed between students and townspeople since 14c, and came to a head during Peasants' Revolt of 1381 in which five townsfolk were hanged. Oliver Cromwell was a graduate of Sidney Sussex College and local MP at a time when the University was chiefly Royalist. 1870's saw foundation of first women's colleges, but women were not awarded degrees until after 1947. University's notable graduates include prime ministers, foreign heads of state, literary giants, philosophers and spies. Cambridge Footlights regularly provide a platform for future stars of stage, screen and television. Cambridge boasts many fine museums, art galleries and buildings of interest, including King's College Chapel and Fitzwilliam Museum. Airport at Teversham 3m/4km E.

MARGATE

HERNE BAY

WHITSTABLE

CANTERBURY

Sandwich

Faversham

ISLE OF THANET — Manston, Minster, Monkton, Acol, Birchington, Westgate on Sea, Cliffs End, Clifs End

St Nicholas at Wade, Sarre, West Stourmouth, East Stourmouth, Boyden Gate, Grove, Preston, Stodmarsh, Hersden, Upstreet, Westbere, Sturry

Richborough Castle, Roman Amphitheatre, Stonar Cut, Great Stonar, Ham, Worth, Woodnesborough, Eastry, Marshborough, Staple, Wingham, Ash, Ware, Cop Street, Elmstone, Hoaden, Wickhambreaux, Ickham, Bramling, Littlebourne, Bekesbourne, Patrixbourne, Howletts Animal Park, Bridge

Knowlton, Goodnestone, Chillenden, Nonington, Easole Street, Adisham, Aylesham, Barham, Kingston, Bishopsbourne, Lower Hardres, Nackington, Street End, Bossingham, Stelling Minnis, Sixmile Cottages, Petham, Upper Hardres Court, Waltham, Sole Street, Bodsham Green, Hassell Street, Stelling

Betteshanger, Sholden, Northbourne, Great Mongeham, East Studdal, Ashley, West Langdon, East Langdon, Ripple, Sutton, Whitfield, Coldred, Shepherdswell (Sibertswold), Eythorne, Elvington, Tilmanstone, Barfrestone, Woollage Green, Lydden, Wootton, Denton, Selstead, Wingmore, Breach, Bladbean, Derringstone, Elham, Lyminge Forest

Westgate, Reculver, Hillborough, Broomfield, Highstead, Hunters Forstal, Beltinge, Herne, Herne Common, Maypole, Hoath, Chislet, Calcott, Hales Place, St Augustine's Abbey, Fordwich, Broadoak, Blean, Tyler Hill, Pean Hill, Clapham Hill, Chestfield, Swalecliffe, Seasalter, Yorkletts, Honey Hill, Rough Common, Harbledown, Thanington, Chartham, Chartham Hatch, Old Wives Lees, Shalmsford Street, Chartham, Street End, Bishopsbourne

Dargate, Hernhill, Goodnestone, Boughton Street, Dunkirk, Overland, Selling, Shottenden, Chilham, Chilham Castle, Molash, Godmersham, Bilting, Crundale, Wye, Brook, Kennington, Eastwell Park, Boughton Lees, Boughton Aluph, Challock

Preston, North Street, Sheldwich, Badlesmere, Leaveland, Throwley, Eastling, Frith, Whitehill, Ospringe, Maison Dieu, Brogdale Horticultural Trust, Oare, Uplees, Luddenham Court, Teynham Sta., Lynsted, Conver, Graveney

ISLE OF SHEPPEY — Eastchurch, Leysdown-on-Sea, Warden, Eastchurch Marshes, Isle of Harty, Shell Ness

Stalisfield Green, Westwell, Westwell Leacon, Charing, Ram Lane, Hothfield, Westwell, Lenham

A256, A253, A28, A299, A291, A290, A2, A2050, A257, A258, A256, A2, A260, A251, A252, A20, A2205, A2090, M2, B2046, B2068, B2205, B2231, B2233, B2050

Area Code 01227

Kent

CANTERBURY

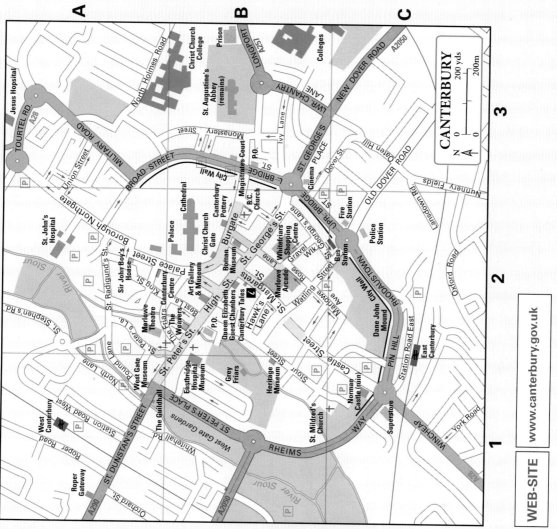

TOURIST INFORMATION ☎ 01227 766567
34 ST. MARGARET'S STREET,
CANTERBURY, KENT, CT1 2TG

HOSPITAL A & E ☎ 01227 766877
KENT & CANTERBURY HOSPITAL, ETHELBERT ROAD,
CANTERBURY, CT1 3NG

COUNCIL OFFICE ☎ 01227 862000
COUNCIL OFFICES, MILITARY ROAD,
CANTERBURY, CT1 1YW

WEB-SITE www.canterbury.gov.uk

LOCAL RADIO BBC RADIO KENT 97.6 FM
INVICTA FM 103.1 FM, 106 CTFM 106 FM

Canterbury *Kent* Population: 36,464. City, premier cathedral city and seat of Primate of Church of England on Great Stour River, 54m/88km E of London. Site of Roman settlement Durovernum. After Romans left, Saxons renamed town Cantwarabyrig. First cathedral in England built on site of current Christ Church Cathedral in AD 602. Thomas à Becket assassinated in Canterbury in 1170, turning Cathedral into great Christian shrine and destination of many pilgrimages, such as those detailed in Geoffrey Chaucer's Canterbury Tales. Becket's tomb destroyed on orders of Henry VIII. Cathedral was backdrop for premiere of T.S. Eliot's play 'Murder in the Cathedral' in 1935. City suffered extensive damage during World War II. Many museums and galleries explaining city's rich heritage. Roman and medieval remains, including city walls. Modern shopping centre; industrial development on outskirts. University of Kent on hill to N.

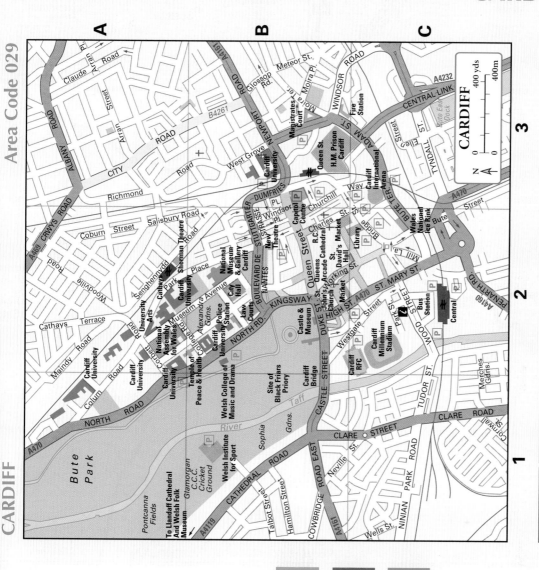

TOURIST INFORMATION ☎ 029 2022 7281
CARDIFF VISITOR CENTRE, 16 WOOD STREET,
CARDIFF, CF10 1ES

HOSPITAL A & E ☎ 029 2074 7747
CARDIFF UNIVERSITY OF WALES HOSPITAL, HEATH PARK,
CARDIFF, CF14 4XW

COUNCIL OFFICE ☎ 029 2087 2087
THE HELP CENTRE, MARLAND HOUSE, CENTRAL SQUARE,
CARDIFF, CF10 1EP

Cardiff (Caerdydd). Population: 272,129. City, capital of Wales since 1955. Romans founded military fort and small settlement on site of present day Cardiff. Uninhabited between departure of Romans and Norman conquest centuries later. Fishing village until development of coal mining in 19c. Population rose from 1000 in 1801 to 170,000 a century later, with city becoming one of busiest ports in the world. Dock trade collapsed in 1930's. Since establishment as Welsh capital, many governmental, administrative and media organisations have moved to city. Major refurbishment and development programme still under way. Cardiff Bay area now major tourist centre and includes Techniquest, a science discovery centre, and has been selected as the location of the new Welsh Assembly building. Millennium Stadium Cardiff Arms Park is the home of the Welsh Rugby Union and also hosts other sporting and entertainment events. Many museums including National Museum of Wales. Universities.

WEB-SITE www.cardiff.gov.uk

LOCAL RADIO BBC RADIO WALES 96.8 FM
CAPITAL GOLD 1305 & 1359 AM, RED DRAGON FM 103.2 FM

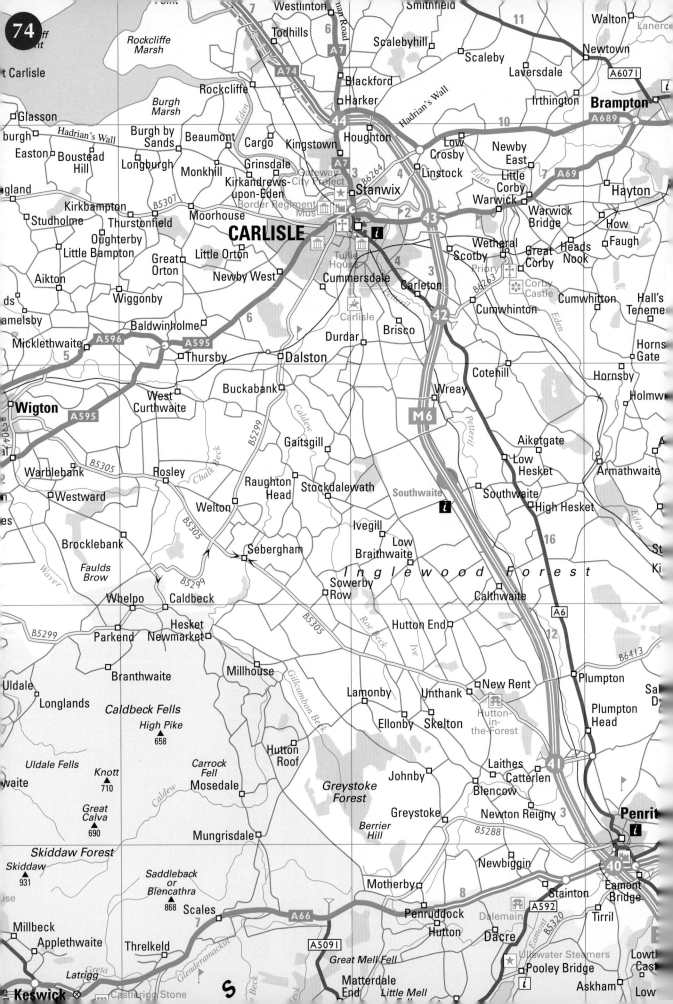

Area Code 01228

Cumbria

CARLISLE

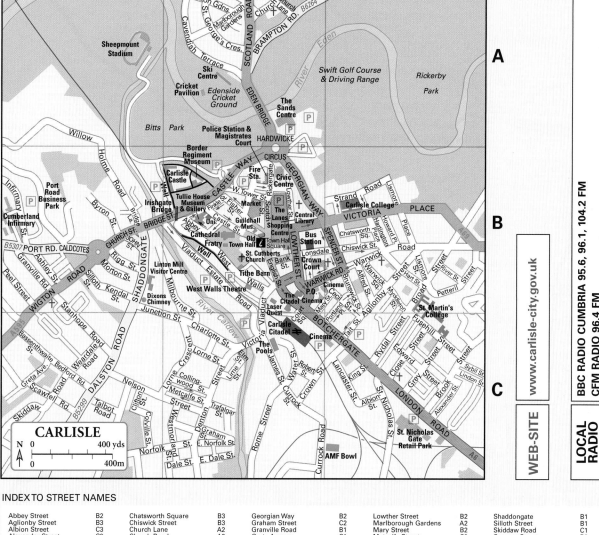

INDEX TO STREET NAMES

TOURIST INFORMATION ☎ 01228 625600
OLD TOWN HALL, GREEN MARKET,
CARLISLE, CA3 8JH

HOSPITAL A & E ☎ 01228 523444
CUMBERLAND INFIRMARY, NEWTOWN ROAD,
CARLISLE, CA2 7HY

COUNCIL OFFICE ☎ 01228 817000
CARLISLE CITY COUNCIL, THE CIVIC CENTRE,
CARLISLE, CA3 8QG

Carlisle *Cumb.* Population: 72,439. Cathedral city at confluence of River Eden and River Caldew, 54m/87km W of Newcastle upon Tyne. Once a Roman military base and later fought over by Scots and English, line of Hadrian's wall runs through the northern suburbs. Castle above the River Eden, completed in 12c, houses a military museum. Cathedral partially destroyed by fire in 17c has two surviving bays of 12c and a magnificent East window. Tullie House Museum imaginatively tells of the city's turbulent past. University of Northumbria. Racecourse 2m/4km S. Airport 6m/9km NE.

Three Counties Showground

Malvern lls

Welland

A4104

Hollybush

A438

Camer's Green

Birts Street

Pendock

Castlemorton

Little Welland

Longdon

Sledge Green

Eldersfield

Corse

Staunton

Corse Lawn

A4208

A417

Ashleworth

Nup End White End

Ashleworth Tithe Barn (NT)

Hartpury

Highleadon

Sandhurst

Nature in Art

Maisemore

Twigworth

Longford

Lassington

Highnam

A48

A40

Nat Waterways Mus

Blackfriars

Cath

GLOUCESTER

Hempsted

A430

A38

Barnwood

Hucclecote

Matson

Robinswood Hill

Tuffley

Quedgeley

Whaddon

Hardwicke

A38

M5

Brookthorpe

A4173

Rococo Gardens

Brimscombe

Moreton Valence

Haresfield

Harescombe

Edge

Pitchcombe

Stroud Green

Whiteshill

Randwick

STROUD

Stonehouse

A419

Eastington

Leonard Stanley

King's Stanley

Frocester

Coaley

Woodchester

Thrupp

A46

Rodborough

Bussage

Chalford

Hyde

Amberley

Hanley Castle

Baughton

Holly Green

Eckington

Upton upon Severn

Naunton

Stratford

Uckinghall

Ripple

Twyning Green

Twyning

Shuthonger

Bredon's Hardwick

The Mythe

Bushley

Forthampton

Tewkesbury

Tewkesbury 1471

Deerhurst

Tirley

Apperley

Odda's Chapel

Tredington

Hasfield

Lower Apperley

Coombe Hill

The Leigh

Boddington

Norton

Down Hatherley

Staverton

Staverton Bridge

Gloucestershire

Innsworth

Churchdown

Twyning

M50

A38

Strensham

A38

Walton Cardiff

Ashchurch

Fiddington

Hardwicke

Stoke Orchard

Golden Valley

Up Hatherley

Leckhampton

Badgeworth

Shurdington

Crickley Hill

Bentham

Brockworth

Upton St Leonards

Roman Villa

Little Witcombe

Great Witcombe

Cranham

The Camp

Painswick

Slad

Miserden

Misarden Park Gardens

Sudgrove

Edgeworth

Bisley

Eastcombe

Bournes Green

Oakridge Lynch

Sapperton

Frampton Mansell

Bricklehampton (ruins)

A46

Great Comberton

Elmley Castle

Netherton

Bredon Hill 293

Hinton on the Green

Bredon's Norton

Kemerton

Overbury

Conderton

Ashton under Hill

Sedgeberrow

Dumbleton

Great Washbourne

Alderton

Toddington

New Town

Bredon

Elaine Rippon Hand Painted Silk

Tithe Barn (NT)

Northway

Aston Cross

Pamington

Teddington

Alstone

A4077

B4079

Beckford

Oxenton

Dixon

Greet

Gretton

Gotherington

223

Langley Hill

BISHOP'S CLEEVE

Winchcombe

Cleeve Hill

Sudel

Roman Villa

Belas Knap Long Barrow

Woodmancote

Elmstone Hardwicke

Uckington

Swindon Village

Southam

Cheltenham

Prestbury

Charlton Abb

CHELTENHAM

Sevenhampton

Broc

Whittington

Syreford

Charlton Kings

Dowdeswell

Andoversfo

A40

A435

Kilkenny

Foxcote

Pilley

295

Ullenwood

Coberley

Upper Coberley

Withington Woods

Chedw Roman

Birdlip

297

Seven Springs

Cowley

A417

Roman Road

Elkstone

Colesbourne

Chedw

Whiteway

Syde

Winstone

Woodmancote

Calmsden

Duntisbourne Abbots

Duntisbourne Leer

North Cerney

Bagendon

Ermin Way

Duntisbourne Rouse

Daglingworth

Baunton

Rendcomb

A435

A429

Stratton

Corinium

Cirencester

A419

Area Code 01242

Gloucestershire

CHELTENHAM

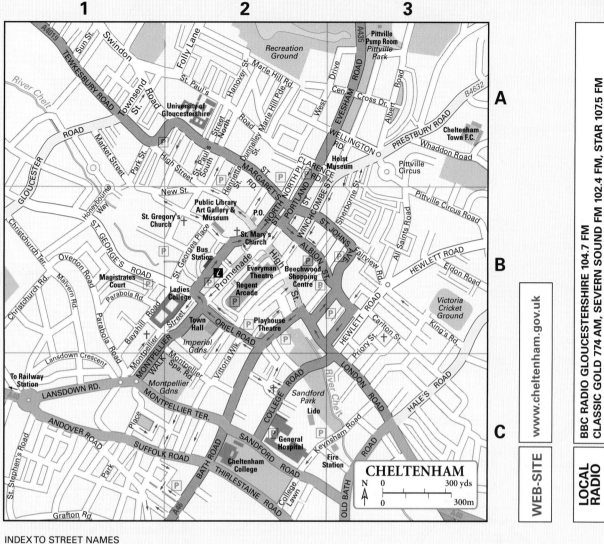

CHELTENHAM
N 0 — 300 yds
0 — 300m

WEB-SITE www.cheltenham.gov.uk

LOCAL RADIO BBC RADIO GLOUCESTERSHIRE 104.7 FM CLASSIC GOLD 774 AM, SEVERN SOUND FM 102.4 FM, STAR 107.5 FM

INDEX TO STREET NAMES

TOURIST INFORMATION ☎ 01242 522878
77 THE PROMENADE, CHELTENHAM,
GLOUCESTERSHIRE, GL50 1PP

HOSPITAL A & E ☎ 01242 222222
CHELTENHAM GENERAL HOSPITAL,
SANDFORD ROAD, CHELTENHAM, GL53 7AN

COUNCIL OFFICE ☎ 01242 262626
MUNICIPAL OFFICES, THE PROMENADE,
CHELTENHAM, GL50 1PP

Cheltenham *Glos.* Population: 91,301. Town, largest town in The Cotswolds, 8m/12km NE of Gloucester. Shopping and tourist centre, with some light industry. Mainly residential, with many Regency and Victorian buildings and public gardens. Formerly a spa town, Pittville Pump Room built between 1825 and 1830 overlooks Pittville Park and is now used for concerts. Art Gallery and Museum. Ladies' College founded 1853. Racecourse to the N hosts Cheltenham Gold Cup race meeting, Cheltenham International Music Festival and Festival of Literature, among other events. Birthplace of composer Gustav Holst. University of Gloucestershire.

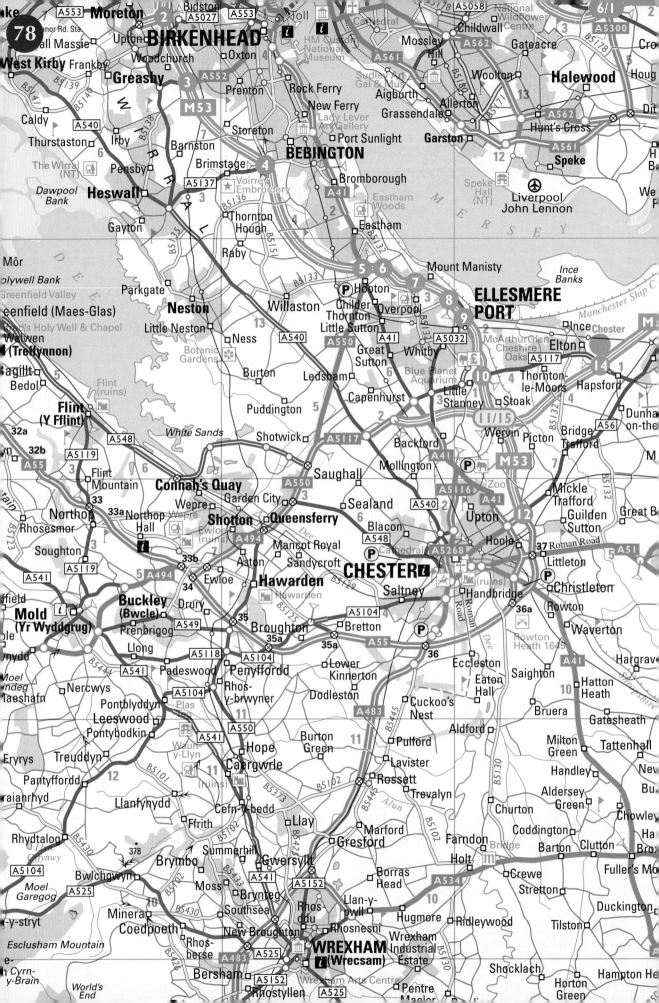

Area Code 01244

Cheshire

CHESTER

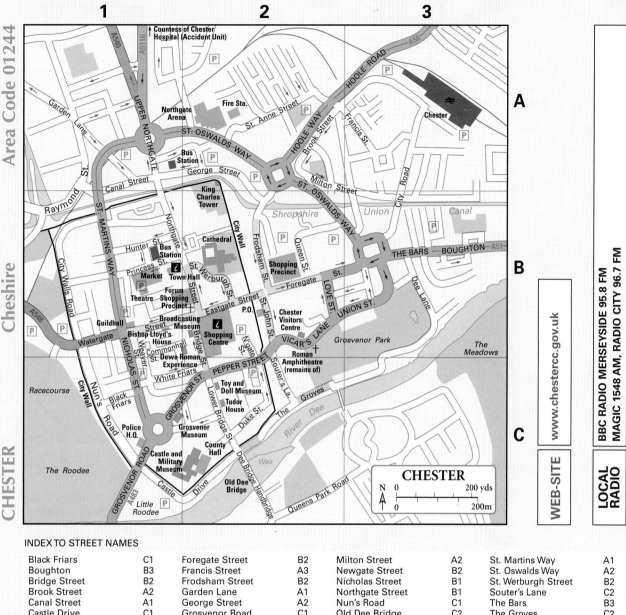

www.chestercc.gov.uk

WEB-SITE

BBC RADIO MERSEYSIDE 95.8 FM
MAGIC 1548 AM, RADIO CITY 96.7 FM

LOCAL RADIO

INDEX TO STREET NAMES

TOURIST INFORMATION ☎ 01244 402111
TOWN HALL, NORTHGATE STREET,
CHESTER, CHESHIRE, CH1 2HJ

HOSPITAL A & E ☎ 01244 365000
COUNTESS OF CHESTER HOSPITAL, HEALTH PK,
LIVERPOOL ROAD, CHESTER, CH2 1UL

COUNCIL OFFICE ☎ 01244 324324
THE FORUM,
CHESTER, CH1 2HS

Chester *Ches*. Population: 80110. City, county town and cathedral city on River Dee, 34m/54km SW of Manchester and 15m/24km SE of Birkenhead. Commercial, financial and tourist centre built on Roman town of Deva. Includes biggest Roman amphitheatre in Britain (English Heritage) and well preserved medieval walls (English Heritage). Castle, now county hall, includes 12c Agricola Tower (English Heritage). Cathedral with remains of original Norman abbey. Famed for Tudor timber-framed buildings which include Chester Rows, two-tier galleried shops and Bishop Lloyd's House, with ornate 16c carved façade. Eastgate clock built to commemorate Queen Victoria's diamond jubilee in 1897. Racecourse 1m/2km SW of city centre; zoo 3m/4km N of city centre.

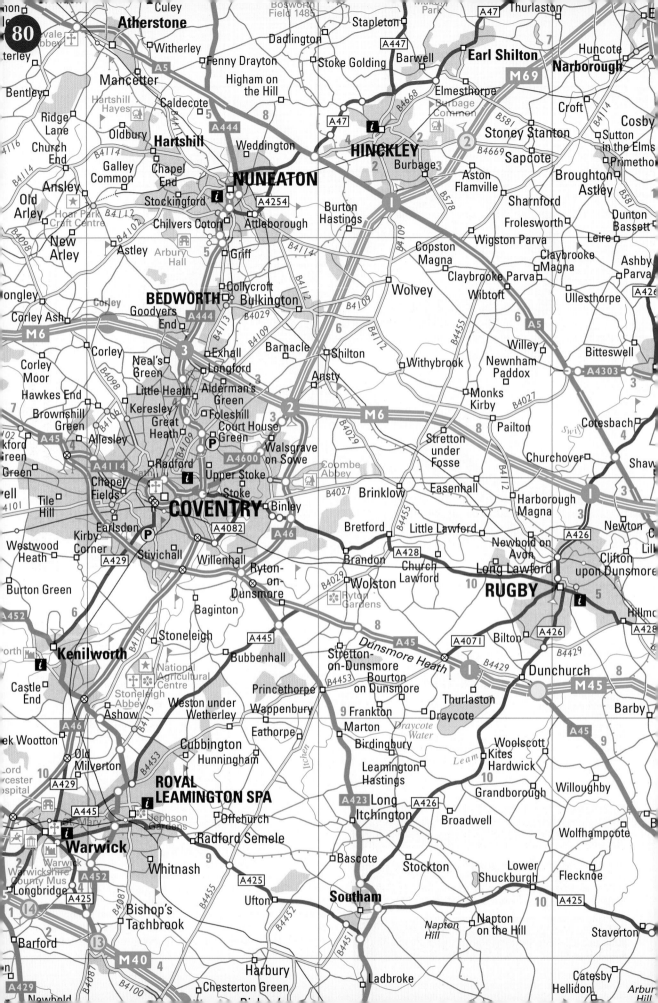

Area Code 024

West Midlands

COVENTRY

WEB-SITE www.coventry.gov.uk

LOCAL RADIO BBC RADIO COVENTRY & WARWICKSHIRE 103.7 FM CLASSIC GOLD 1359 AM, KIX 96.2 FM, MERCIA FM 97 FM, HEART FM 100.7 FM

INDEX TO STREET NAMES

TOURIST INFORMATION ☎ 024 7622 7264
BAYLEY LANE, COVENTRY,
WEST MIDLANDS, CV1 5RN

HOSPITAL A & E ☎ 024 7622 4055
COVENTRY & WARWICKSHIRE HOSPITAL,
STONEY STANTON ROAD, COVENTRY, CV1 4FH

COUNCIL OFFICE ☎ 024 7683 3333
COUNCIL HOUSE, EARL STREET,
COVENTRY, CV1 5RR

Coventry *W.Mid.* Population: 299,316. City, 17m/27km E of Birmingham. St. Michael's cathedral built 1954-62 beside ruins of medieval cathedral destroyed in air raid in 1940. The centre of the city was rebuilt in the 1950s and 1960s following WW II bombing, but some old buildings remain, including Bonds Hospital and the medieval Guildhall. A town rich from textile industry in middle ages, Coventry is now known for its motor car industry; other important industries are manufacturing and engineering. Museum of British Road Transport. Herbert Art Gallery and Museum. Universities. Civil airport at Baginton to S. Coventry Canal runs N to Trent and Mersey Canal at Fradley Junction near Lichfield.

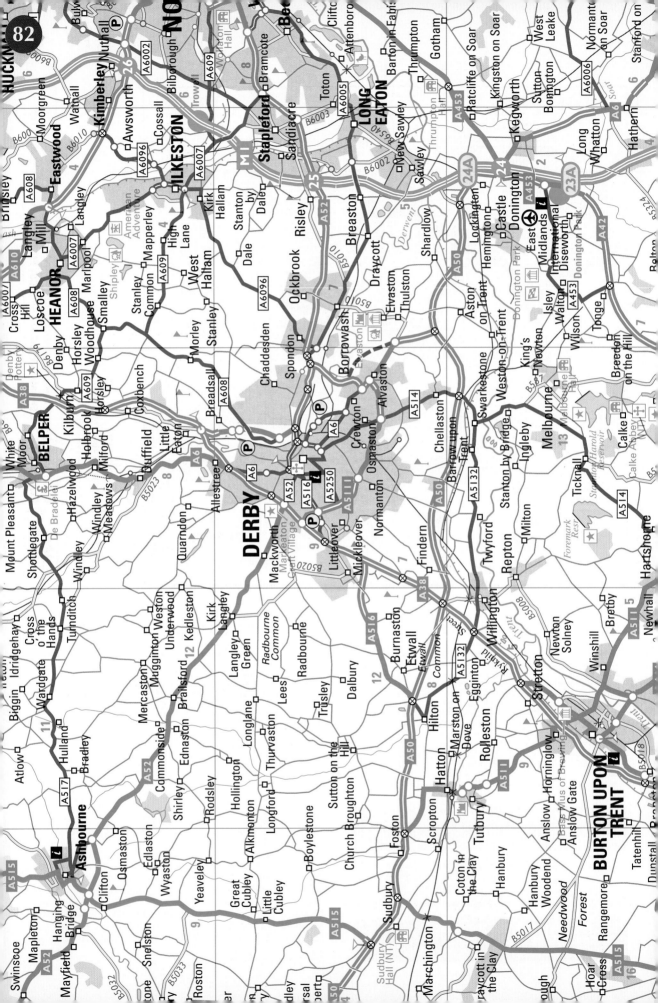

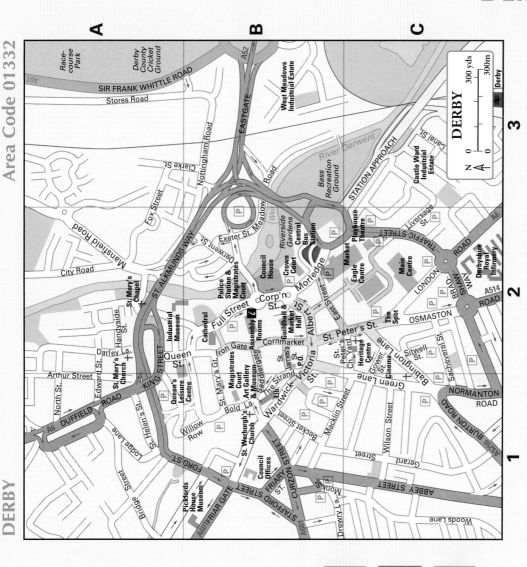

INDEX TO STREET NAMES

Abbey Street	C1	Fox Street	C1
Albert Street	B2	Friar Gate	B2
Arthur Street	A1	Friary Street	B1
Babington Lane	C1	Full Street	B2
Becket Street	B2	Gerard Street	C1
Bold Lane	B1	Gower Street	B1
Bradshaw Way	C2	Green Lane	C2
Bridge Street	A1	Handyside Street	A2
Burton Road	C1	Iron Gate	B2
Canal Street	C3	King Street	A1
City Road	A2	Liversage Street	C2
Clarke Street	B3	Lodge Lane	A1
Cornmarket	B2	London Road	C2
Corporation Street	B2	Macklin Street	B1
Curzon Street	B1	Mansfield Road	A2
Darley Lane	A2	Market Place	B2
Derwent Street	B2	Meadow Road	B2
Drewry Lane	B1	Monk Street	B1
Duffield Road	A1	Morledge	B2
Eastgate	B3	Normanton Road	C1
East Street	B2	North Street	A1
Edward Street	A1	Nottingham Road	B3
Exeter Street	B2	Osmaston Road	C2
Ford Street	B1	Queen Street	A2

Sacheverel Street	C1
Saddlergate	B2
St. Alkmunds Way	A2
St. Helen's Street	A1
St. James Street	B2
St. Mary's Gate	B1
St. Peter's Church	C2
Yard	
St. Peter's Street	B2
Sir Frank Whittle	A3
Road	
Sitwell Street	C2
Stafford Street	B1
Station Approach	B3
Stores Road	A3
The Strand	B1
Traffic Street	C2
Victoria Street	B1
Wardwick	B1
Willow Row	B1
Wilson Street	C1
Woods Lane	C1

WEB-SITE

www.derby.gov.uk

LOCAL RADIO

BBC RADIO DERBY 104.5 FM

CLASSIC GOLD GEM 945 AM, RAM FM 102.8 FM

TOURIST INFORMATION ☎ 01332 255802
ASSEMBLY ROOMS, MARKET PLACE,
DERBY, DE1 3AH

HOSPITAL A & E ☎ 01332 347141
DERBYSHIRE ROYAL INFIRMARY,
LONDON ROAD, DERBY, DE1 2QY

COUNCIL OFFICE ☎ 01332 293111
THE COUNCIL HOUSE, CORPORATION STREET,
DERBY, DE1 2FS

Derby Population: 223,836. City, industrial city and county town on River Derwent, 35m/56km NE of Birmingham. Shopping and entertainment centre. Cathedral mainly by James Gibbs, 1725. Both manufacturing and engineering are important to local economy. Derby Industrial Museum charts city's industrial history with emphasis on Rolls Royce aircraft engineering. Tours at Royal Crown Derby porcelain factory. University.

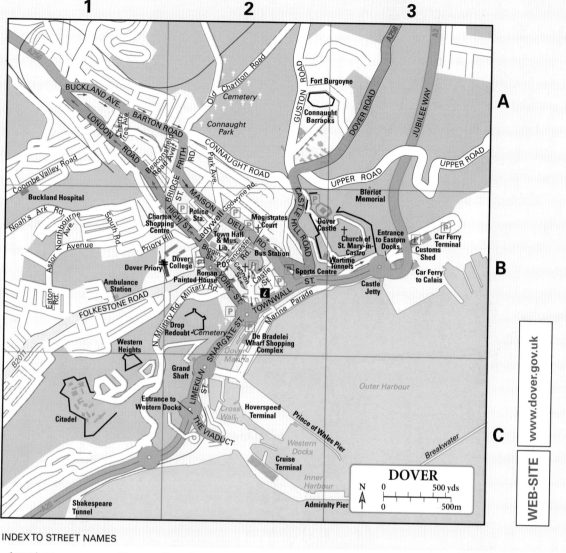

WEB-SITE www.dover.gov.uk

LOCAL RADIO BBC RADIO KENT 102.4 FM · NEPTUNE RADIO 106.8 FM, INVICTA FM 97 FM

INDEX TO STREET NAMES

TOURIST INFORMATION ☎ 01304 205108
TOWNWALL STREET,
DOVER, KENT, CT16 1JR

HOSPITAL A & E ☎ 01227 766877
KENT & CANTERBURY HOSPITAL,
ETHELBERT ROAD, CANTERBURY, CT1 3NG

COUNCIL OFFICE ☎ 01304 821199
WHITE CLIFFS BUSINESS PARK,
DOVER, CT16 3PJ

Dover *Kent* Population: 34,179. Town, cinque port, resort and Channel port on Strait of Dover, 15m/24km SE of Canterbury, with large modern docks for freight and passengers. Dominated by high white cliffs and medieval castle (English Heritage) enclosing the Pharos, 50AD remains of Roman lighthouse. Remains of 12c Knights Templar Church (English Heritage) across valley from castle. Sections of moat of 19c fort at Western Heights (English Heritage), above town on W side of harbour. White Cliffs Experience re-creates Roman and wartime Dover.

DUNDEE

St Andrews

Carnoustie
Monifieth
Broughty Ferry
Tayport
Newport-on-Tay
Newburgh
Coupar Angus
Blairgowrie
Rattray

Denhead
Arbirlot
Arbi
Guynd
Carmyllie
Bennyton
Salmon
Mu
Panbride
Barry Mill (NTS)
Barry Links
Buddon Ness

Mosston
Greystone
Crombie Mill
Upper Muirdrum
Victoria
Barry
Buddon
Barry Links
Tentsmuir Point

Lochlair
Hayhillock
Kirkton of Monikie
Craigton
Newton of Affleck
Newbigging
Mains of Ardestie
Tentsmuir Forest
Out Head
British Andrews Golf Museum
St Andrews Bay

Whigstreet
Inverarity
Kirkbuddo
Greenburn
Affleck
Monikie
Laws
Broughty
Eden Mouth

Carrot
Carrot Hill
Wellbank
Bucklerheads
Drumsturdy
Murroes
Baldovie
Broughty Castle
Earlshall
RAF Memorial
Pickletillem
Guardbridge

Hill
Kincaldrum
Gateside
Gallowfauld
Todhills
Newbigging
East March
Kellas
Burnside of Duntrune
Douglas and Angus
Tay Road Bridge
Newport-on-Tay
Woodhaven
Carrick
Leuchars
Kincaple

Balgray
Kirkton of Tealing
Kirkton of Strathmartine
Downfield
Toll
Discovery Point & R.R.S. Discovery
Cuivie
Lucklawhill
Balmullo
Logie
Dairsie

Milton
Glen Ogilvy
Gallow Hill
Craigowl Hill 455
Dovecot & Earth House
Clatto
Tay Bridge
Wormit
Kirkton
Bottomcraig
Gauldry
Forret Hill
Craigsanquhar

Kirkton of Auchterhouse
Leoch
Muirhead
Lochee
Denhead
DUNDEE
Kingoodie
Dundee
Balmerino
Coultra
Hazelton Walls
Rathillet
Moonzie

Eassie and Nevay
Ark Hill
Nether Handwick
Kinpurney Hill
Auchterhouse Hill
Bonnyton
Auchterhouse
Dronley
Birkhill
Liff
Camperdown
Benvie
Invergowrie
Longforgan
Balhelvie
Abbey (NTS)
Brunton
Creich
Luthrie
Balhelvie

Balkeerie
Kirkinch
Newbigging
Newtyle
Thriepley
Fowlis
Lundie
Knapp
Rossie Priory
Inchture
Norman's Law 285
Norman's Hill

Meigle
Arthurstone
Auchtertyre
Long Loch
Blacklaw Hill
Littleton
Abernyte
Ballindean
Craigdallie
Glenduckie Hill
Glenduckie
Dunbog

Leitfie
Kinloch
Ardler
Keillor
Pitcur
Leys
King's Seat
Hallyburton Forest
Pitmiddle Wood
Kinnaird
Grange
Megginch Castle
Errol
Port Allen
Mugdrum Island
Lindores Abbey
Lindores

Coupar Angus
Keithick
Woodside
Campmuir
Burrelton
Springfield
Saucher
Collace
Kirkton of Collace
Kilspindie
Pitroddie
Rait
Glencarse
Kinfauns Forest
Chapelhill
Pole Hill
Inchyra

Stormont Loch
Balbeggie
Mencarse

A90 A92 A94 A913 A919 A91 A914 A923 A928 A984 A953 A85 B954 B961 B945 B946 B953 B9127 B9128

Area Code 01382

WEB-SITE www.dundeecity.gov.uk

LOCAL RADIO

BBC RADIO SCOTLAND 810 AM/92.4-94.7 FM
TAY AM 1161 AM, WAVE 102 FM, TAY FM 102.8 FM

INDEX TO STREET NAMES

Albany Terrace	A1	Dens Road	A2
Albert Street	B3	Douglas Street	B1
Alexander Street	A2	Dudhope Street	B2
Ann Street	A1	Dudhope Terrace	A3
Arbroath Road	B3	Dundonald Street	A3
Arklay Street	A3	Dura Street	B3
Arthurstone	B3	East Dock Street	B3
Terrace		East Marketgait	B2
Barrack Road	B1	Guthrie Street	B1
Blackness Road	B1	Hawkhill	B1
Blackscroft	B3	High Street	B1
Blinshall Street	B1	Hill Street	C2
Brook Street	B1	Hilltown	A2
Broughty Ferry	B3	Kenmore Terrace	A2
Road		Killin Avenue	A1
Brown Street	B1	Kinghorne Road	A1
Bruce Street	A1	King Street	B2
Byron Street	A1	Larch Street	B1
Canning Street	A2	Law Crescent	A1
City Square	C2	Lawside Avenue	A1
Constitution Road	B2	Leng Street	A2
Constitution Street	A2	Lochee Road	B1
Court Street	A3	Mains Road	A2
Cowgate Street	B2	Main Street	B2

Meadowside	B2
Nelson Street	B2
Nethergate	C1
North Marketgait	B1
Perth Road	C1
Princes Street	B3
Roseangle	C1
Riverside Drive	C1
Seagate	B2
South Marketgait	C2
South Tay Street	C1
Strathmartine	A2
Road	
Tay Road Bridge	C2
Trades Lane	B2
Upper Constitution	A1
Street	
Victoria Road	B2
Victoria Street	B3
Ward Road	B1
West Marketgait	B1
West Port	B1

TOURIST INFORMATION ☎ 01382 527527
21 CASTLE STREET,
DUNDEE, DD1 3BA

HOSPITAL A & E ☎ 01382 660111
NINEWELLS HOSPITAL, NINEWELLS ROAD,
DUNDEE, DD1 9SY

COUNCIL OFFICE ☎ 01382 434000
CITY CHAMBERS, 21 CITY SQUARE,
DUNDEE, DD1 3BY

Dundee Population: 158,981. City, Scotland's fourth largest city, commercial and industrial centre and port, 18m/29km E of Perth on N side of Firth of Tay, crossed here by a 1m/2km road bridge and a 2m/3km railway bridge. Robert the Bruce declared King of the Scots in Dundee in 1309. Sustained severe damage during Civil War and again prior to Jacobite uprising. City recovered in early 19c and became Britain's main processor of jute. One of largest employers in Dundee today is D.C. Thomson, publisher of The Beano and The Dandy. Many museums and art galleries. Cultural centre, occasionally playing host to overflow from Edinburgh Festival. Episcopal cathedral on site of former castle. Universities. Ship 'Discovery' in which Captain Scott travelled to Antarctic has returned to Victoria dock, where she was built.

SUNDERLAND
SEAHAM
WASHINGTON
CHESTER-LE-STREET
STANLEY
CONSETT
DURHAM
HOUGHTON LE SPRING
Hetton-le-Hole
Peterlee
Easington
Spennymoor
Willington
Crook
Ferryhill
Bishop Auckland
Tow Law

Ryhope
New Silksworth
Silksworth
Herrington
Penshaw
Fatfield
Shiney Row
Bournmoor
Colliery Row
Fence Houses
Pelton
Ouston
Newfield
Waldridge
Pity Me
Plawsworth
Great Lumley
Little Lumley
Lumley
East Rainton
West Rainton
Colliery Row
Easington Lane
South Hetton
Murton
Hawthorn
Cold Hesledon
Dalton-le-Dale
Seaton
Nose's Point
Horden
Blackhall
Blackhall Colliery
Easington Colliery
Little Thorpe
Shotton
Shotton Colliery
Wheatley Hill
Wingate
Station Town
South Wingate
Castle Eden
Hutton Henry
Sheraton
Elwick
Hart
Crimdon
Hesleden
Fishburn
Sedgefield
Trimdon
Trimdon Grange
Trimdon Colliery
Kelloe
Coxhoe
Cassop
Quarrington Hill
Thornley
Ludworth
Haswell
Littletown
Shadforth
Sherburn
Pittington
Carrville
Shincliffe
Bowburn
Hett
Cornforth
Bishop Middleham
Chilton
Rushyford
Coundon
Coundon Grange
Kirk Merrington
Middlestone Moor
Westerton
Byers Green
Newfield
Hunwick
Witton Park
High Grange
Howden-le-Wear
Fir Tree
Billy Row
Sunniside
Thornley
Hamsterley
Bedburn
St Johns Hall
Witton-le-Wear
Low Etherley
High Etherley
Croxdale
Sunderland Bridge
Dean Bank
Tudhoe
Brandon
Brancepeth
Oakenshaw
Langley Moor
Deerness Valley Walk
Esh Winning
Ushaw Moor
Bearpark
Langley Park
Esh
Quebec
Cornsay
Cornsay Colliery
Waterhouses
East Hedleyhope
Satley
Butsfield
Knitsley
Lanchester
Greencroft
Iveston
Leadgate
Delves
Medomsley
Dipton
Hobson
Tantobie
Tanfield
Annfield Plain
South Moor
Beamish
Grange Villa
Craghead
Newfield
Holmside
Edmondsley
Kimblesworth
Sacriston
Witton Gilbert
Burnhope
Maiden Law
Ebchester
Shotley Bridge
Rowley
Knitsley
Framwellgate Moor
Finchale
Nevilles Cross
Cathedral
Botanic Garden
Beamish Open Air Museum
Consett & Sunderland Rly Path
Derwent Walk
Lanchester Valley Walk
Brandon to Bishop Auckland Walk

A19 A690 A691 A692 A693 A694 A695 A167 A177 A179 A181 A182 A183 A195 A688 A689 A68 A177 A1(M)
B1287 B1286 B1285 B1284 B1283 B1282 B1280 B1279 B1278 B1404 B1432 B1052 B6532 B6313 B6168 B6299 B6301 B6300 B6302 B6076 B6286 B6287 B6288 B6281 B6282 B6296 B6297

Wear
Browney
Skerne
Crookfoot Resr
Tunstall Resr
Derwent
Team
Dene Mouth

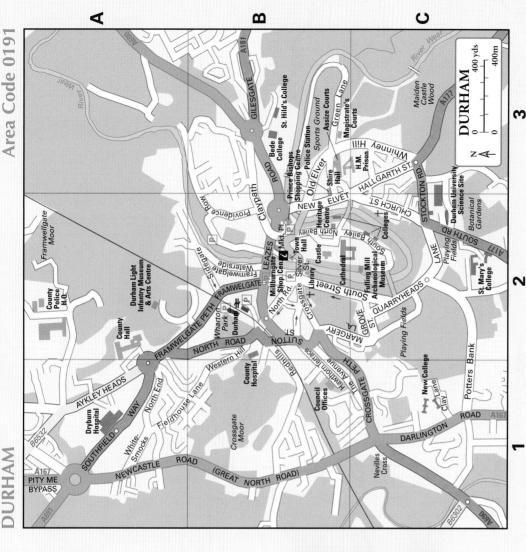

DURHAM

N

0   400 yds
0   400m

INDEX TO STREET NAMES

Aykley Heads	A1	New Elvet	B2
Church Street	C2	North Bailey	B2
Clay Lane	C1	North End	A1
Claypath	B2	North Road	B2
Crossgate	B2	Old Elvet	B3
Crossgate Peth	C1	Pity Me Bypass	A1
Darlington Road	C1	Potters Bank	C1
Fieldhouse Lane	A1	Quarryheads Lane	C2
Framwelgate	B2	Providence Row	B2
Framwelgate Peth	A2	Redhills	B1
Framwelgate Waterside	B2	Sidegate	B2
Gilesgate	B3	Silver Street	B2
Great North Road	A1	South Bailey	C2
Green Lane	B3	South Road	C2
Grove Street	C2	South Street	A1
Hallgarth Street	C3	Southfield Way	C2
Hawthorn Terrace	B1	Stockton Road	B2
Leazes Road	B2	Sutton Street	C1
Margery Lane	C2	The Avenue	B1
Market Place	B2	Western Hill	B2
Millburngate Bridge	B2	Whinney Hill	C3
Newcastle Road	A1	Whitesmocks	A1

TOURIST INFORMATION ☎ 0191 384 3720
MARKET PLACE, DURHAM,
COUNTY DURHAM, DH1 3NJ

HOSPITAL A & E ☎ 0191 333 2333
DRYBURN HOSPITAL, NORTH ROAD,
DURHAM, DH1 5TW

COUNCIL OFFICE ☎ 0191 386 4411
COUNTY HALL,
DURHAM, DH1 5UB

WEB-SITE | www.durhamcity.gov.uk

LOCAL RADIO | BBC RADIO NEWCASTLE 95.4 FM
SUN FM 103.4 FM, GALAXY 105-106 105.3, 105.6, 105.8 & 106.4 FM

Durham *Dur.* Population: 36,937. Cathedral city on narrow bend in River Wear, 14m/22km S of Newcastle upon Tyne. Norman-Romanesque cathedral founded in 1093 on site of shrine of St. Cuthbert is World Heritage Site. England's third oldest University founded in 1832. Motte-and-bailey castle dating from 1072 now part of the University. Collection in Fulling Mill Museum of Archaelogy illustrates history of city. Museum of Oriental Art. Light Infantry Museum. Art Gallery. Universtiy Botanic Garden S of city.

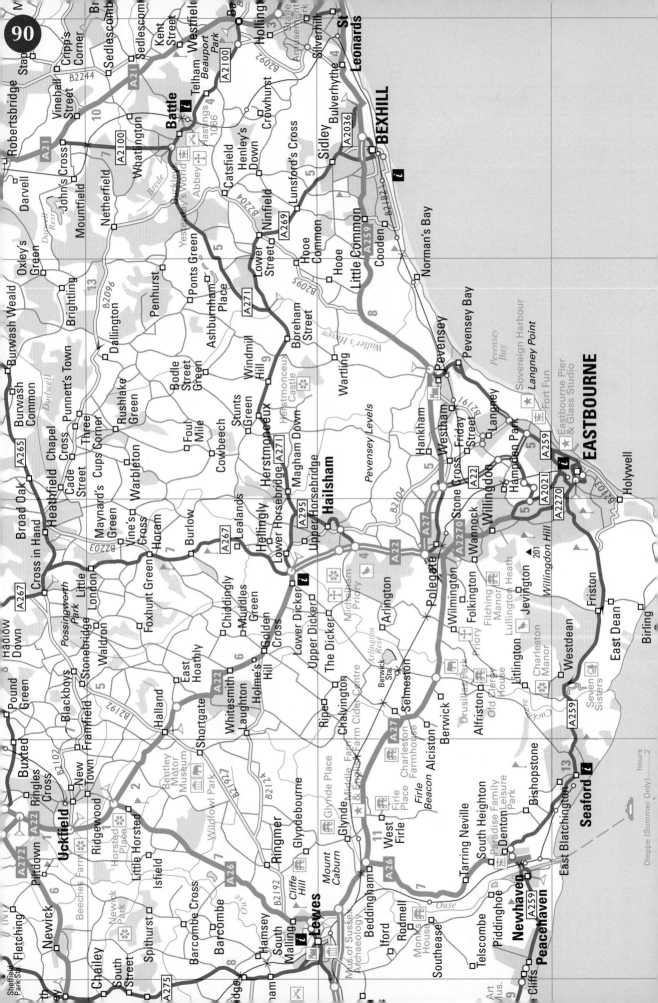

EASTBOURNE East Sussex

Area Code 01323

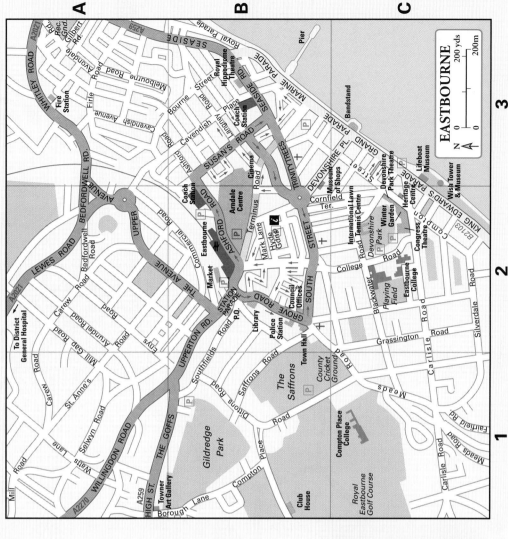

EASTBOURNE

N

0   200 yds
0   200m

WEB-SITE   www.eastbourne.gov.uk

LOCAL RADIO

BBC SOUTHERN COUNTIES RADIO 104.5 FM, 1161 AM
SOVEREIGN RADIO 107.5 FM

INDEX TO STREET NAMES

Arundel Road	A2	Langney Road	B3
Ashford Road	B2/B3	Lewes Road	A2
Avondale Road	A3	Marine Parade	B3
Bedfordwell Road	A2	Mark Lane	B2
Blackwater Road	C2	Meads Road	C1
Borough Lane	A1	Melbourne Road	A3
Bourne Street	B3	Mill Gap Road	A1
Carew Road	A1/A2	Mill Road	A1
Carlisle Road	C1	Royal Parade	B3
Cavendish Avenue	A3	Saffrons Road	B1
Cavendish Place	B3	St. Anne's Road	A1
College Road	C2	Seaside	B3
Commercial Road	B2	Seaside Road	B3
Compton Place Road	B1	Selwyn Road	A1
Compton Street	C2	Silverdale Road	C2
Cornfield Terrace	B2	South Street	B2
Devonshire Place	B2	Southfields Road	B1
Dittons Road	B1	Station Parade	B2
Enys Road	A2	Susan's Road	B3
Fairfield Road	C1	Terminus Road	B2
Firle Road	A3	The Avenue	B2
Gilbert Road	A1	The Goffs	A1
Grand Parade	C3	Trinity Trees	B3
Grassington Road	C2	Upper Avenue	A2
Grove Road	B2	Upperton Road	A1
High Street	A1	Watts Lane	A1
Hyde Gardens	B2	Whitley Road	A1
King Edward's Parade	C2	Willingdon Road	C2

TOURIST INFORMATION ☎ 01323 411400
3 CORNFIELD ROAD,
EASTBOURNE, BN21 4QL

HOSPITAL A & E ☎ 01323 417400
EASTBOURNE DISTRICT GENERAL HOSPITAL, KING'S DRIVE,
EASTBOURNE, BN21 2UD

COUNCIL OFFICE ☎ 01323 410000
EASTBOURNE BOROUGH COUNCIL, TOWN HALL,
GROVE ROAD, EASTBOURNE BN21 4UG,

Eastbourne E.Suss. Population: 94,793. Town, coastal resort and conference centre, 19m/31km E of Brighton. Towner Art Gallery in 18c manor house shows a contemporary collection of work. South Downs Way begins at Beachy Head, the 163m/536ft chalk cliff on the outskirts of the town. Eastbourne hosts an International Folk Festival and international tennis at Devonshire Park.

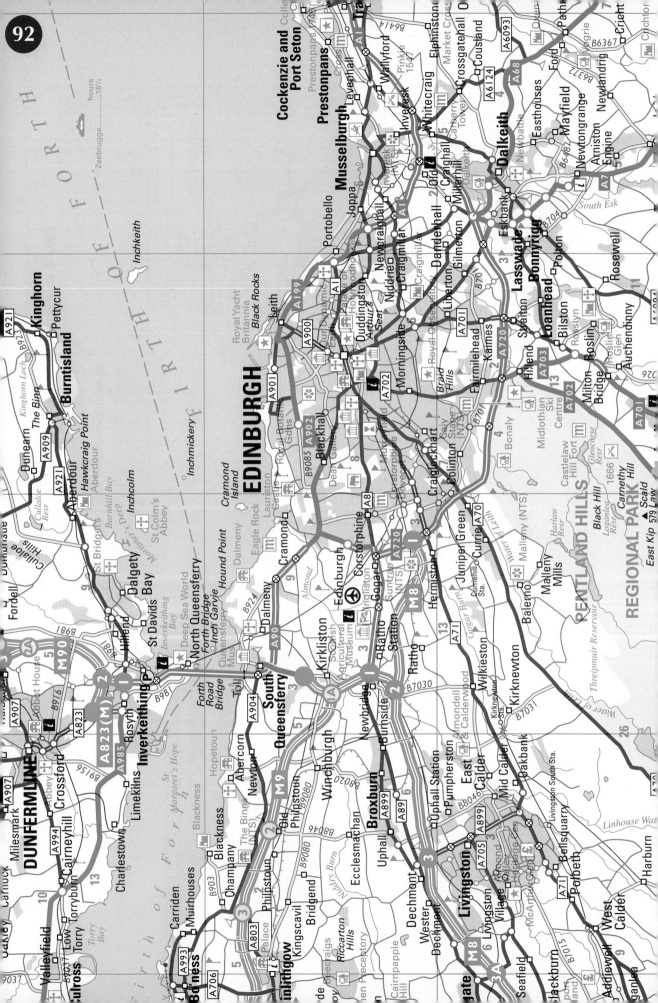

Area Code 0131

EDINBURGH

WEB-SITE www.edinburgh.gov.uk

LOCAL RADIO BBC RADIO SCOTLAND 810 AM & 92.4-94.7 FM
FORTH 2 1548 AM, FORTH 1 97.3 FM, REAL RADIO 101.1 FM

INDEX TO STREET NAMES

TOURIST INFORMATION ☎ 0131 473 3800
INFORMATION CENTRE, 3 PRINCES STREET,
EDINBURGH, EH2 2QP

HOSPITAL A & E ☎ 0131 536 1000
ROYAL INFIRMARY OF EDINBURGH,
1 LAURISTON PLACE, EDINBURGH, EH3 9YW

COUNCIL OFFICE ☎ 0131 200 2000
COUNCIL HEADQUARTERS, 10 WATERLOO PLACE,
EDINBURGH, EH1 3EG

Edinburgh *Edin.* Population: 401,910. City, historic city and capital of Scotland, built on a range of rocky crags and extinct volcanoes, on S side of Firth of Forth, 41m/66km E of Glasgow. Administrative, financial and legal centre of Scotland. Medieval castle (Historic Scotland) on rocky eminence overlooks central area and was one of main seats of Royal court, while Arthur's Seat (largest of the volcanoes) guards eastern approaches. Three universities. Port at Leith, where Royal Yacht Britannia is now docked and open to public. Important industries include brewing, distilling, food and electronics. Palace of Holyroodhouse (Historic Scotland) is chief royal residence of Scotland. Old Town typified by Gladstone's Land (Historic Scotland), 17c six-storey tenement with arcaded front, outside stair and stepped gables. Numerous literary associations including Sir Arthur Conan Doyle who was born here. Many galleries and museums including National Gallery of Scotland. Annual arts festival attracts over a million visitors each year and is largest such event in the world.

Honiton

Combe Raleigh
Monkton
Broadhembury
Godford Cross
Awliscombe
Buckerell
Upton
Payhembury
Higher Cheriton
Gittisham
Hamlet
Offwell
Church Green
Putts Corner
Farway
Northleigh
Broad Down
Old Bakery
Weston
Branscombe
Donkey Sanctuary
Salcombe Regis
Sidbury
Sidford
Sidmouth
Harcombe
Sand

Fenny Bridges
Alfington
Ottery St Mary
Wiggaton
Fairmile
Cadhay
Fenny Bridges
A375
B3174
A30
Feniton
Colestocks
Talaton
Whimple
Fenwood
West Hill
Tipton St John
Venn Ottery
Harpford
Newton Poppleford
Bowd
Pinn
Fairlynch Arts Centre & Museum
Budleigh Salterton

Colliton
Luton
Norman's Green
Higher Tale
Aunk
Clyst St Lawrence
Rockbeare
Marsh Green
Half Way Inn
Hawkerland
Colaton Raleigh
Bicton Park
Otterton
James Countryside Collection
East Budleigh
Knowle
Exmouth
Littleham

Mutterton
Westcott
Langford
Plymtree
Clyst Hydon
Clyst St Lawrence
Westwood
Budlake
Broadclyst
Clyst Honiton
Sowton
Crealy Park
Clyst St Mary
Aylesbeare
White Cross
Woodbury Salterton
Cyst St George
Woodbury
Yettington
Black Hill
A3052
B3184
B3180
B3179
A La Ronde

Bradninch
Hele
Silverton
Ravenshayes
A396
Killerton
M5
Broadclyst
Dog Village
Poltimore
Pinhoe
Whipton
Exeter
Countess Wear
Topsham
Ebford
Exton
Powderham
Lympstone
Withycombe Raleigh
EXMOUTH
Dawlish Warren
Starcross
A376
A379

Thorverton
Up Exe
Brampford Speke
Nether Exe
Stoke Canon
Rewe
Upton Pyne
A396
A377
Newton St Cyres
Cowley
Exwick
EXETER
Ide
Pocombe Bridge
Alphington
Shillingford St George
Exminster
Kennford
Kenn
Kenton
Mamhead
Ashcombe
Langdon House
A38
A380

Cadbury
Stockleigh Pomeroy
Efford
Shobrooke
Crediton
Upton Hellions
Sandford
Creedy Park
A3072
A377
Whitestone
Longdown
Tedburn St Mary
Pathfinder Village
Oldridge
Dunsford
Bridford
Christow
Coombe
Dunchideock
Boddiscombsleigh
Higher Ashton
Lower Ashton
Bickham House
Great Haldon
Devon and Exeter Falls
Trusham
Canonteign Falls
Chudleigh
Ideford
Bovey Tracey
Devon Guild of Craftsmen
Hennock
Bridford
B3193
A382
A38
A380

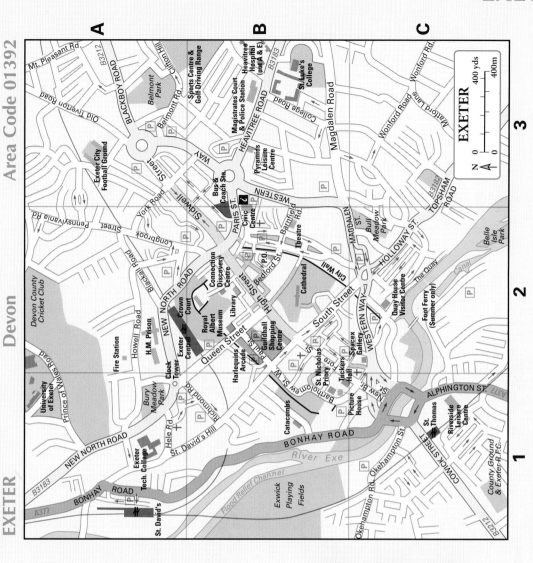

EXETER

400 yds
400m

N

TOURIST INFORMATION ☎ 01392 265700
CIVIC CENTRE, PARIS STREET,
EXETER, EX1 1RP

HOSPITAL A & E ☎ 01392 411611
ROYAL DEVON & EXETER HOSPITAL (WONFORD),
BARRACK ROAD, EXETER, EX2 5DW

COUNCIL OFFICE ☎ 01392 277888
CIVIC CENTRE, PARIS STREET,
EXETER, EX1 1JN

Exeter *Devon* Population: 94,717. City, county capital on River Exe, 64m/103km SW of Bristol. Major administrative, business and financial centre on site of Roman town Isca Dumnoniorum. Cathedral is Decorated, with Norman towers and façade with hundreds of stone statues. 15c guildhall. Modern buildings in centre built after extensive damage from World War II. Beneath the city lie remains of medieval water-supply system built in 14c to supply fresh water to city centre. Royal Albert Memorial Museum and Art Gallery. Early 16c mansion of Bowhill (English Heritage), with preserved Great Hall, 2m/3km SW. University 1m/2km N of city centre. Airport 5m/8km E at Clyst Honiton.

WEB-SITE www.exeter.gov.uk

LOCAL RADIO
BBC RADIO DEVON 95.8 FM
CLASSIC GOLD 666 AM, GEMINI FM 97 & 103 FM

STRAIT OF DOVER

DEAL
DOVER
FOLKESTONE
ASHFORD

Walmer Castle & Garden
Deal
Walmer
Kingsdown
Ringwould
St Margaret's at Cliffe
St Margaret's Bay
The Pines
South Foreland

Worth
Hacklinge
Sholden
Northbourne
Great Mongeham
Ripple
Sutton
West Cliffe
Martin Mill Sta.
De Bradelei Wharf
Channel Tunnel
Knights Templar Church

Ham
Finglesham
Betteshanger
East Studdal
Ashley
West Langdon
East Langdon
Guston
Whitfield
Buckland
Maxton
Farthingloe
East Wear Bay

Eastry
Knowlton
Tilmanstone
Elvington
Eythorne
Shepherdswell (Sibertswold)
Coldred
Temple Ewell
Ewell Minnis
Alkham
St Radigund's Abbey
Drellingore
West Hougham
Capel le Ferne
Rotunda Amusement Park
Sandgate

Goodnestone
Goodnestone Park
Chillenden
Nonington
Easole Street
Barfrestone
Woollage Green
Lydden
Swingfield Minnis
Densole
Hawkinge
Cheriton

Aylesham
Womenswold
Wootton
Selstead
Denton
Lyddon

Bekesbourne
Patrixbourne
Adisham
Barham
Breach
Bladbean
Elham
Acrise Place
Paddlesworth
Etchinghill
Newington
Hythe

Kingston
Bishopsbourne
Derringstone
Wingmore
Ottinge
Lyminge
Beachborough
Saltwood
West Hythe

Nackington
Lower Hardres
Bossingham
Stelling Minnis
Rhodes Minnis
Newbarn
Postling
Stanford
Lympne
Court-at-Lympne
Port Lympne

Chartham
Street End
Petham
Upper Hardres Court
Sixmile Cottages
Stone Street
Stowting
Sellindge
Stanford
Aldington
Burmarsh
Dymchurch
Martello Tower

Waltham
Bodsham Green
Lymbridge Green
Brabourne
Brabourne Lees
Smeeth
Stonestreet Green
Bonnington
Newchurch

Hassell Street
National Nature Trails
Hastingleigh
Wye
Brook
Willesborough Lees
Hinxhill
Mersham
Kingsnorth
Cheeseman's Green
Swanton
Bilsington
Ruckinge
St Mary in the Marsh
Snave

Romney Marsh

Shalmsford Street
Old Wives Lees
Crundale
Godmersham
Boughton Aluph
Kennington
Willesborough
Sevington

Selling
Shottenden
Chilham
Chilham Castle
Bilting
Molash
Challock
Eastwell Park
Boughton Lees
Kingsnorth

Badlesmere
Leaveland
Sheldwich

Great Stour
Lyminge Forest
Roman Road
Romney, Hythe & Dymchurch Railway

A2
A28
A20
A256
A258
A260
A261
A252
A251
A250
A2050
A2070
A259
B2046
B2068
B2067
M20

Channel Tunnel Terminal
Westenhanger Sta.
Port Lympne

Calais........1½–1¾
Oostende........2
Zeebrugge........4½
hours

FOLKESTONE   Kent   Area Code 01303

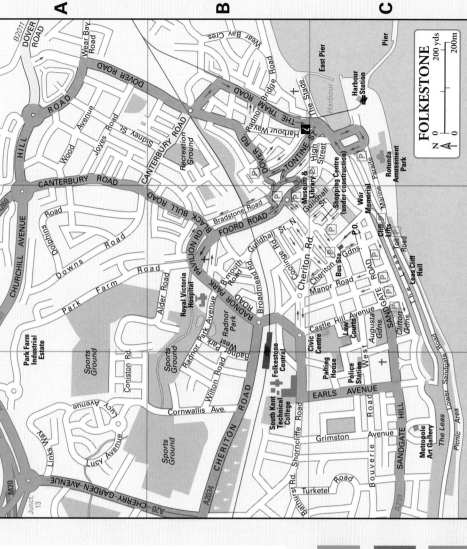

INDEX TO STREET NAMES

Alder Road	B2	Hill Road	A3
Bathurst Road	B1	Joyes Road	A3
Black Bull Road	B2	Links Way	A1
Bournemouth Road	B2	Lower Sandgate Road	C1
Bouverie Road West	C1	Lucy Avenue	A1
Bradstone Road	B2	Manor Road	C2
Broadmead Road	B2	Marine Parade	C2
Canterbury Road	A3	Park Farm Road	A2
Castle Hill Avenue	C2	Pavilion Road	B2
Cheriton Gardens	C2	Radnor Bridge Road	B3
Cheriton Road	B1	Radnor Park Avenue	B1
Cherry Garden Avenue	A1	Radnor Park Road	B2
Churchill Avenue	A2	Radnor Park West	B1
Coniston Road	C1	Sandgate Hill	C1
Coolinge Road	C2	Sandgate Road	B2
Cornwallis Avenue	B1	Shorncliffe Road	B1
Dolphins Road	A2	Sidney Street	B3
Dover Road	A3	The Leas	C2
Downs Road	A2	The Stade	C3
Earles Avenue	C1	The Tram Road	B3
Foord Road	B2	Tontine Street	B3
Grimston Avenue	C1	Turketel Road	C1
Guildhall Street	B2	Wear Bay Crescent	B3
Guildhall Street North	B2	Wear Bay Road	A3
Harbour Way	B3	Wood Avenue	A3
High Street	B2	Wilton Road	B1

TOURIST INFORMATION ☎ 01303 258594
HARBOUR STREET, FOLKESTONE,
KENT, CT20 1QN

HOSPITAL A & E ☎ 01233 633331
WILLIAM HARVEY HOSPITAL, KENNINGTON RD,
WILLESBOROUGH, ASHFORD, TN24 0LZ

COUNCIL OFFICE ☎ 01303 850388
CIVIC CENTRE, CASTLE HILL AVENUE,
FOLKESTONE, CT20 2QY

Folkestone *Kent* Population: 45,587. Town, Channel port and resort, 14km/22km E of Ashford. Russian submarine docked in harbour is open to the public. The Lear marine promenade accessed by Victorian cliff lift. Ornate Victorian hotels. Martello tower on East Cliff. Kent Battle of Britain Museum at Hawkinge airfield 3m/5km N. Channel Tunnel terminal on N side.

WEB-SITE   www.shepway.gov.uk

LOCAL RADIO   BBC RADIO KENT 97.6 FM
INVICTA FM 97 FM

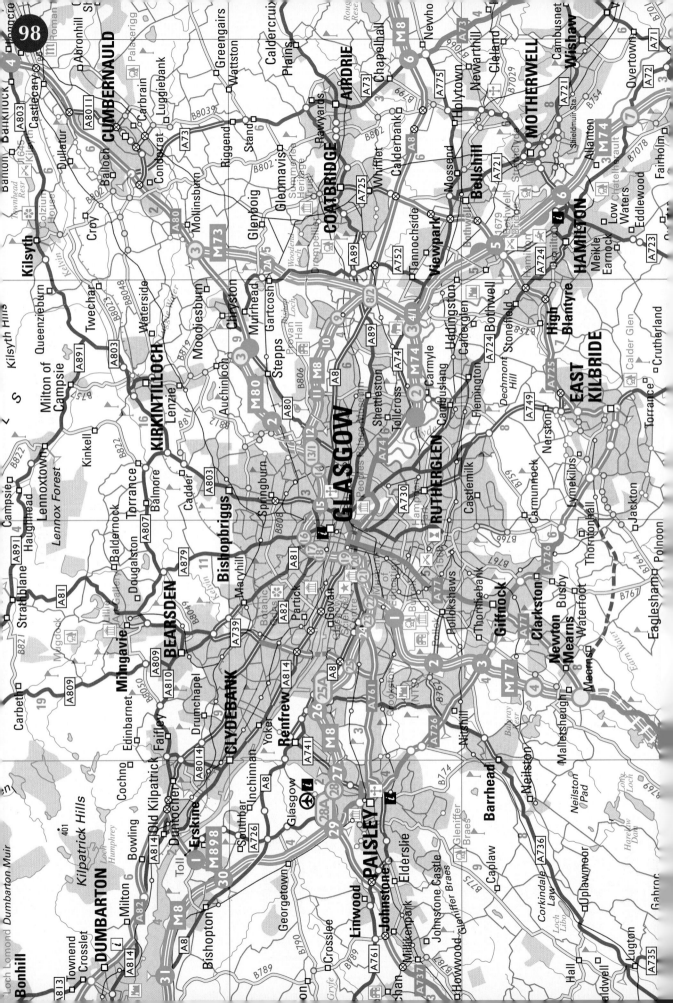

Area Code 0141

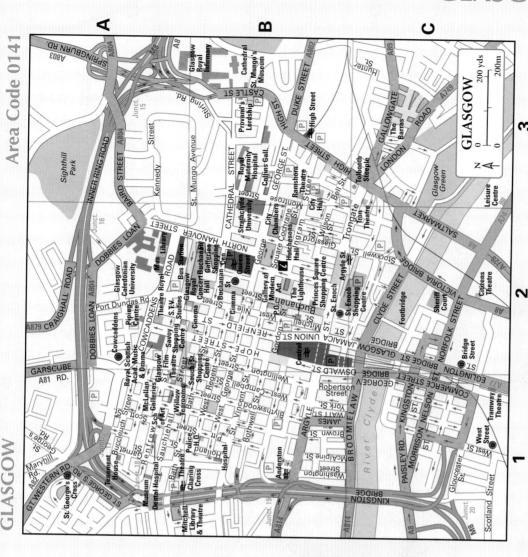

INDEX TO STREET NAMES

Street	Grid
Argyle Street	B1
Baird Street	A3
Bath Street	A1/B1
Bell Street	B3
Blythswood Street	B1
Bothwell Street	B1
Bridge Street	C2
Broomielaw	C1
Brown Street	B1
Buccleuch Street	A1
Buchanan Street	B2
Castle Street	B3
Cathedral Street	B2
Clyde Street	C2
Cochrane Street	B2
Commerce Street	C1
Cowcaddens Road	A2
Craighall Road	A2
Dobbie's Loan	A2
Duke Street	B3
Eglinton Street	C1
Gallowgate	C3
Garnet Street	A1
Garscube Road	A1
George Square	B2
George Street	B3
George V Bridge	C1
Glasgow Bridge	C2

Street	Grid
Glassford Street	B2
Gloucester Street	C1
Gordon Street	B2
Great Western	A1
Road	
High Street	B3
Holland Street	B1
Hope Street	B2
Hunter Street	C3
Ingram Street	B2
Inner Ring Road	A3
Jamaica Street	C2
James Watt Street	B1
Kennedy Street	B3
Kingston Bridge	C1
Kingston Street	C1
London Road	C3
Maryhill Road	A1
McAlpine Street	B1
Mitchell Street	B2
Montrose Street	B3
Morrison Street	C1
Nelson Street	C1
Norfolk Street	C2
North Hanover	B2
Street	
Oswald Street	C1
Paisley Road	C1

Street	Grid
Pitt Street	B1
Port Dundas Road	A2
Renfield Street	B2
Renfrew Street	A1
Robertson Street	B1
Saltmarket	C2
Sauchiehall Street	A1
Scotland Street	C1
Scott Street	A1
Springburn Road	A3
St. George's Road	B1
St. Mungo Avenue	B3
St. Vincent Street	B1
Stirling Road	B3
Stockwell Street	C2
Trongate	B2
Union Street	B2
Victoria Bridge	C2
Washington Street	B1
Wellington Street	B1
West Campbell	B1
Street	
West George Street	B1
West Nile Street	B2
West Regent Street	B2
West Street	C1
Wilson Street	B2
York Street	B1

TOURIST INFORMATION ☎ 0141 204 4400
11 GEORGE SQUARE, GLASGOW, G2 1DY

HOSPITAL A & E ☎ 0141 211 2000
WESTERN INFIRMARY, DUMBARTON ROAD, GLASGOW, G11 6NT

COUNCIL OFFICE ☎ 0141 287 2000
CITY CHAMBERS, GEORGE SQUARE, GLASGOW, G2 1DU

Glasgow *Glas.* Population: 662,954. City, largest city in Scotland. Port and commercial, industrial, cultural and entertainment centre on River Clyde, 41m/66km W of Edinburgh and 346m/557km NW of London. Major industrial port and important trading point with America until War of Independence. During industrial revolution, nearby coal seams boosted Glasgow's importance and its population increased ten-fold between 1800 and 1900. By beginning of 20c shipbuilding dominated the city, although industry went into decline in 1930's. Glasgow is now seen to be a city of culture and progress. It has a strong performing arts tradition and many museums and galleries including Burrell Collection (set in Pollok Country Park). Cathedral is rare example of an almost complete 13c church. Early 19c Hutcheson's Hall (National Trust for Scotland) in Ingram Street is one of city's most elegant buildings; Tenement House (National Trust for Scotland) is late Victorian tenement flat retaining many original features. Three universities. Airport 7m/11km W.

WEB-SITE www.glasgow.gov.uk

LOCAL RADIO BBC RADIO SCOTLAND 810 AM & 92.4-94.7 FM
CLYDE 1 102.5 FM, CLYDE 2 1152 AM, REAL RADIO 100.3 FM

Sudeley
War...
Gt...
Fam...
i
Winchcombe 10
Cleve Hill
Langley Hill
Isbourne
Belas Knap Long Barrow
Roman Villa
330
Southam
Charlton Abbots
Hawling
Charlton Kings Common
Brockhampton
Sevenhampton
Syreford
Whittington
Dowdeswell
Andoversford
Kilkenny
Shipton
Syreford
Compton Abdale
Chedworth Roman Villa
Withington
Withington Woods
Chedworth
Chedworth Wood
Fossebr...
Foss Cross
Calmsden
St John's Bapt Church
Barns...
Barns
Colesbourne
Rendcomb
North Cerney
A435
A429
A436
A40
Churn
Coberley
Upper Coberley
Elkstone
Seven Springs
A436
A417
Corinium
Cirencester i
Stratton
Baunton
Daglingworth
Duntisbourne Rouse
Sapperton
Frampton Mansell
COTSWOLD HILLS
Bishop's Cleve 7
Gotherington
Woodmancote
Woodmancote
Bishop's Cleve
Swindon Village
Prestbury
Whittington
A4632
Cheltenham Race
P
CHELTENHAM
i
Charlton Kings
Pilley
295
Ullenwood
Coberley
Cowley
Birdlip
297
Crickley Hill
Roman Road
Brimpsfield
Syde
Winstone
The Camp
Whiteway
Miserden Park Gardens
Duntisbourne Abbots
Duntisbourne Leer
Woodmancote
Sudgrove
Edgeworth
Bisley
Bournes Green
Oakridge Lynch
Chalford
Eastcombe
Bussage
Stad
Sheepscombe
Winstone
STROUD
i
A46
Rodborough
Thrupp
Leonard Stanley
King's Stanley
Woodchester
M5
Stoke Orchard
Elmstone Hardwicke
Uckington
Swindon Village
A4019
A4019
Golden Valley
Up Hatherley
Hatherley
Leckhampton
Shurdington
Bentham
Little Witcombe
Great Witcombe
Cranham
Prinknash Abbey
Cranham Pottery
Prinknash Park
Painswick
Sheepscombe
Rococo
Edge
Pitchcombe
Stroud Green
Whiteshill
Randwick
Stonehouse
Eastington
Frocester
A38
Hardwicke
Coombe Hill
The Leigh
Norton
Staverton
Staverton Bridge
Hatherley
Twigworth
Innsworth
Churchdown
Badgeworth
Brockworth
Upton St Leonards
Matson
Hucclecote
Brookthorpe
Whaddon
Haresfield
Harescombe
Edge
A4173
Pitchcombe
Tredington
Hardwicke
Coombe Hill
Poddington
A38
A38
Down Hatherley
Norton
Longford
Barnwood
Huccleote
Hempsted
Tuffley
Robinswood Hill
A430
A38
A430
Whaddon
M5 10
Whitminster
Moreton Valence
Putloe
Standish
Eastington
A419
Leonard Stanley
A38
Tredington 12
Hardwicke
Lower Apperley
Apperley
Tirley
Odda's Chapel
Deerhurst
Ashleworth Tithe Barn (NT)
Nature in Art
Sandhurst
Longford
A38
St Oswald's Priory
i
m
GLOUCESTER
National Waterways Mus
A40
A48
Quedgeley
Hardwicke
Elmore
Elmore Back
Farleys End
Longney
Saul
Wheatenhurst
Frampton on Severn
The Noose
New Grounds
Slimbridge
Cambridge
Slimbridge
Sharpness
A38
Lawn
Staunton
Corse
A417 12
Hasfield
Tirley
Hartpury
Ashleworth End
White End
Nup End
Blackwells End
Maisemore
Highleadon
B4215
Highnam
Over
Churcham
Minsterworth
Lassington
Rudford
Tibberton
B4213
Newent i
Kent's Green
Taynton
Glasshouse Hill
Oxenhall
Taynton
Huntley
Birdwood
A40
Oakle Street
Northwood Green
Westbury-on-Severn
Boxbush
Westbury Court (NT)
Rodley
Upper Framilode
Arlingham
Newnham
Framilode
Elton
Flaxley
Blaisdon
Longhope
A4136
Mitcheldean
Drybrook
May Hill
296
Harts Barn Craft Centre
Poolhill
Brand Green
Upleadon
Botloe's Green
Newent i
Clifford's Mesne
Kilcot
Aston Ingham
Lea
Longhope
B4215
B4216
B4221
B4224
Kempley 7
Kempley Green
M50
Upton Bishop
Ashley Crews
Little Gorsley
Gorsley Common
Gorsley
Gorsley
Brook
Mitcheldean
Drybrook
Littledean
Ruspidge
Dean Heritage Centre
Upper Soudley
Cinderford
A4151
Littledean
Ruspidge
A48
Viney Hill
Blakeney
Nibley
Awre
Purton
Sharpness
VALE
VALE OF BERKELEY
Severn
Leadon

GLOUCESTER   **Gloucestershire**   **Area Code 01452**

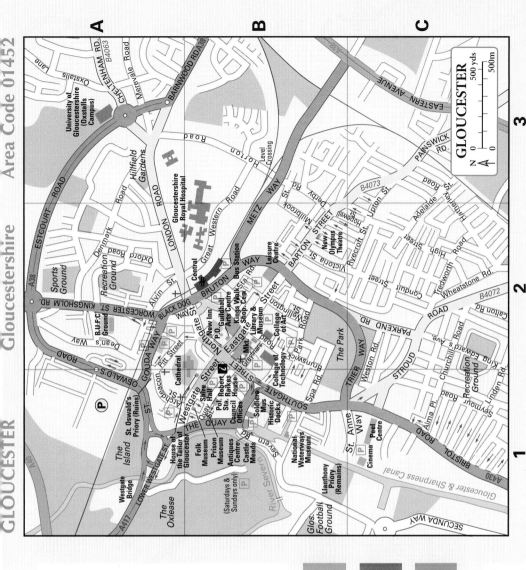

INDEX TO STREET NAMES

TOURIST INFORMATION ☎ 01452 421188
28 SOUTHGATE STREET, GLOUCESTER,
GLOUCESTERSHIRE, GL1 2DP

HOSPITAL A & E ☎ 01452 528555
GLOUCESTER ROYAL HOSPITAL
GREAT WESTERN RD, GLOUCESTER, GL1 3NN

COUNCIL OFFICE ☎ 01452 522232
COUNCIL OFFICES, NORTH WAREHOUSE,
THE DOCKS, GLOUCESTER, GL1 2EP

Gloucester *Glos.* Population: 114,003. City, industrial city on River Severn, on site of Roman town of Glevum, 32m/52km NE of Bristol. Norman era saw Gloucester grow in political importance, from here William the Conqueror ordered survey of his Kingdom which resulted in Domesday Book of 1086. City became a religious centre during middle ages. Cathedral built in mixture of Norman and Perpendicular styles, has cloisters and England's largest stained glass window, dating from 14c. Remains of 15c–16c Franciscan friary, Greyfriars, (English Heritage). Historic docks, now largely redeveloped, on Gloucester and Sharpness Canal. Three Choirs Festival held every third year.

WEB-SITE
www.glos-city.gov.uk

LOCAL RADIO
BBC RADIO GLOUCESTERSHIRE 104.7 FM
CLASSIC GOLD 774 AM, SEVERN SOUND FM 102.4 & 103 FM

Surrey   Area Code 01483

GUILDFORD

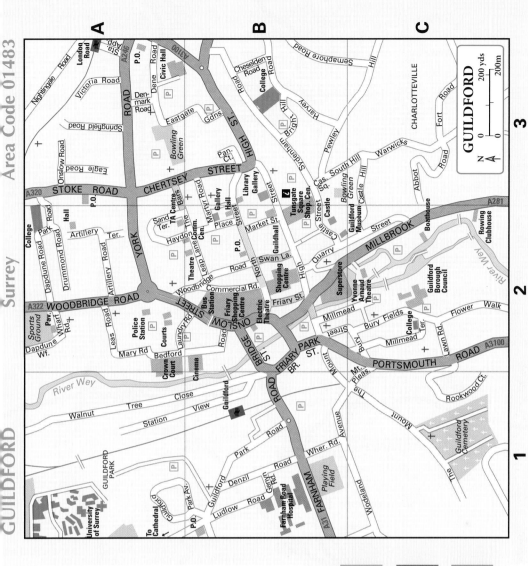

TOURIST INFORMATION ☎ 01483 444333
14 TUNSGATE,
GUILDFORD, GU1 3QT

HOSPITAL A & E ☎ 01483 571122
ROYAL SURREY COUNTY HOSPITAL, EGERTON ROAD,
GUILDFORD, GU2 5XX

COUNCIL OFFICE ☎ 01483 505050
GUILDFORD BOROUGH COUNCIL, MILLMEAD HOUSE,
MILLMEAD, GUILDFORD, GU2 4BB

Guildford *Surr.* Population: 65,998. County town and former weaving centre on River Wey, 27m/43km SW of London. High Street lined with Tudor buildings, the Guildhall the most impressive. Remains of Norman castle keep built c.1173, on an 11c motte, used as county gaol for 400 years. Cathedral consecrated in 1961 and built of red brick, the interior is designed in a modern gothic style. University of Surrey. Royal Grammar School noted for its chained library

WEB-SITE www.guildford.gov.uk

LOCAL RADIO
BBC SOUTHERN COUNTIES RADIO 104.6 FM
THE EAGLE 96.4 FM, COUNTY SOUND 1566 AM

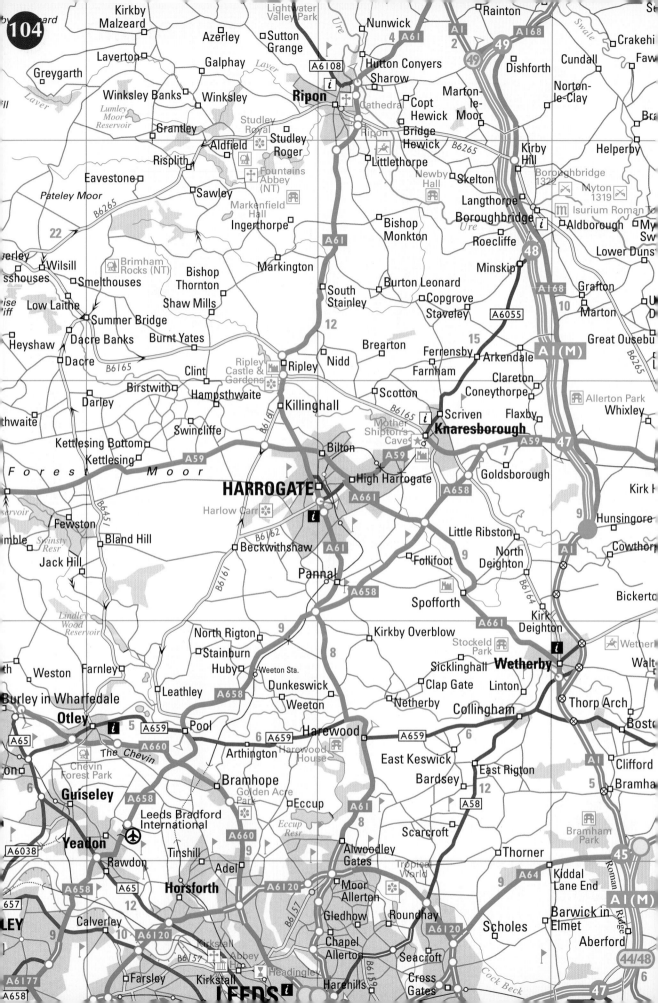

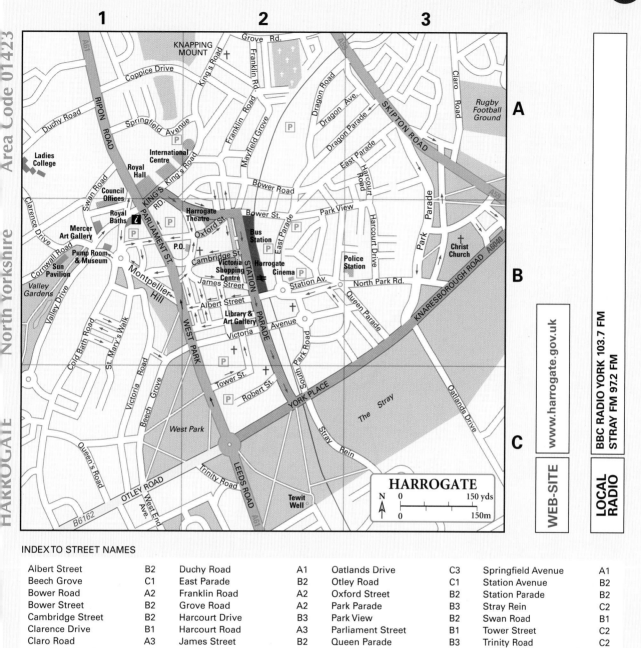

WEB-SITE www.harrogate.gov.uk

LOCAL RADIO BBC RADIO YORK 103.7 FM / STRAY FM 97.2 FM

HARROGATE

N   0   150 yds
0   150m

INDEX TO STREET NAMES

TOURIST INFORMATION ☎ 01423 537300
ROYAL BATHS ASSEMBLY ROOMS, CRESCENT RD,
HARROGATE, NORTH YORKSHIRE, HG1 2RR

HOSPITAL A & E ☎ 01423 885959
HARROGATE DISTRICT HOSPITAL,
LANCASTER PARK ROAD, HARROGATE, HG2 7SX

COUNCIL OFFICE ☎ 01423 500600
COUNCIL OFFICES, CRESCENT GARDENS
HARROGATE, HG1 2SG

Harrogate *N. Yorks.* Population: 66,178. Town, spa town and conference centre, 12m/21km N of Leeds. Fashionable spa town of 19c with many distinguished Victorian buildings, extensive gardens and pleasant tree-lined streets. Royal Baths Assembly Rooms (1897) open for Turkish baths. Royal Pump Room (1842) now a museum. The Stray park and gardens are S of town centre. The Valley Gardens to the SW are the venue for band concerts and flower shows. Harlow Carr Botanical Gardens and Museum of Gardening 2m/3km SW. Mother Shipton's cave, reputed home to the 16c prophetess, near Knaresborough, 4m/6km NW.

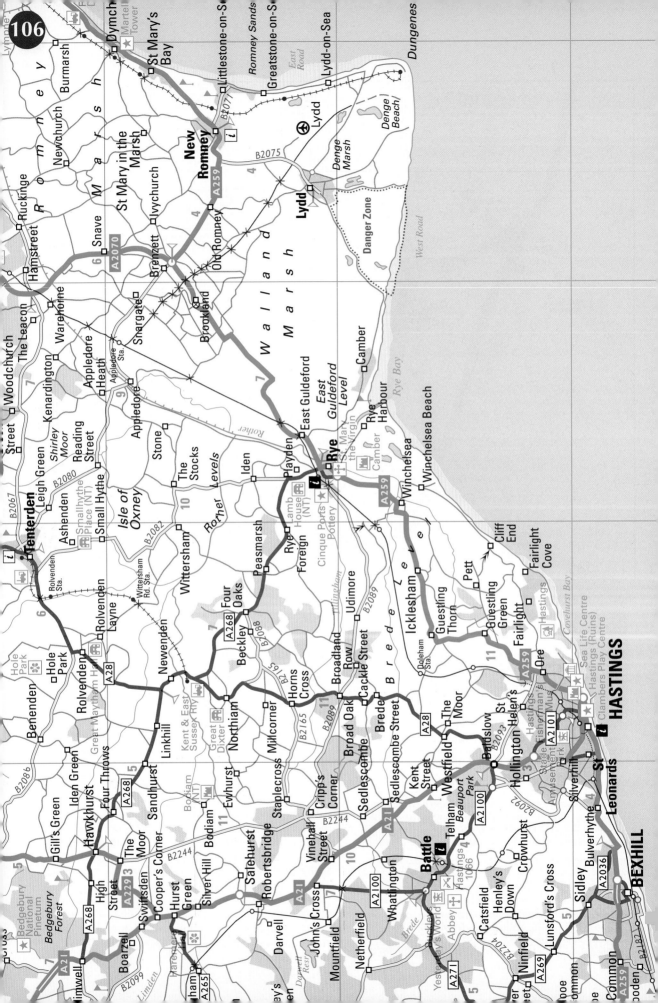

Hastings | East Sussex | Area Code 01424

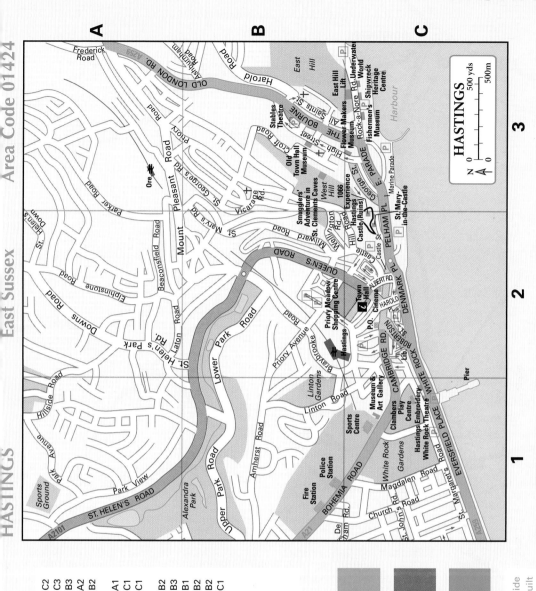

INDEX TO STREET NAMES

Albert Road	C2	George Street	C2
All Saints Street	B3	Harold Place	C2
Amherst Road	B1	Harold Road	B3
Ashburnham Road	B3	High Street	B3
		Hillside Road	A1
Beaconsfield Road	A2	Laton Road	A2
		Linton Road	B1
Bohemia Road	B1	Lower Park Road	B1
Braybrooke Road	B2	Magdalen Road	B2
Cambridge Road	C1	Marine Parade	C1
Castle Hill Road	C2	Milward Road	B2
Castle Street	C2	Mount Pleasant Road	A2
Church Road	C1		
Croft Road	B3	Old London Road	B3
De Cham Road	C1	Park Avenue	A1
Denmark Place	C2	Park View	A1
Downs Road	A2	Parker Road	A2
East Parade	C3	Pelham Place	C2
Elphinstone Road	A2	Priory Avenue	B2
Eversfield Place	C1	Priory Road	B3
Frederick Road	A3	Queen's Road	B2
Robertson Street	C3	St. Helen's Road	A1
Rock-a-Nore Road	C3	St. John's Road	C1
St. George's Road	B3	St. Margaret's Road	C1
St. Helen's Down	A2	St. Mary's Road	B2
St. Helen's Park Road	B2	The Bourne	B3
		Upper Park Road	B1
		Vicarage Road	B2
		Wellington Road	B2
		White Rock	C1

TOURIST INFORMATION ☎ 01424 781111
QUEENS SQUARE, PRIORY MEADOW,
HASTINGS, TN34 1TL

HOSPITAL A & E ☎ 01424 755255
CONQUEST HOSPITAL, THE RIDGE,
ST. LEONARDS-ON-SEA, TN37 7RD

COUNCIL OFFICE ☎ 01424 781066
HASTINGS BOROUGH COUNCIL, TOWN HALL,
QUEENS ROAD, HASTINGS, TN34 1QR

Hastings *E.Suss.* Population: 84,139. Town, Cinque port and seaside resort 32m/52km E of Brighton. Remains of Norman castle built 1068-1080 on hill in town centre, houses the 1066 exhibition which relates the history of castle and Norman invasion. Battle of 1066 fought at Battle, 6m/9km NW. Former smugglers caves have a display on smuggling, once a vital part of the towns economy.

WEB-SITE www.hastings.gov.uk

LOCAL RADIO BBC SOUTHERN COUNTIES RADIO 104.5 FM, 1161 AM
ARROW FM 107.8 FM

Kingsland
Eyton
Cobnash
Cholstrey
Shirl Heath
Lawton
Shland
Burton Court
wood
Stretford Court
Monkland
Ivington
Sollers Dilwyn
Ivington Green
Brierley
Dilwyn
Aulden
Upper Hill
Dilwyn Common
Birley
Knapton Green
gemoor
Weobley Marsh
King's Pyon
Bush Bank
Westhope
Queenswood
Dinmore Manor
Canon Pyon
Wormsley
Yarsop
Foxley
Tillington Common
Wellington
Wellington Marsh
Mansell Lacy
Tillington
Brinsop
Burghill
Marden
Sutton Walls
Moreton on Lugg
Sutton St Nicholas
Bishopstone
Credenhill
Stretton Sugwas
Holmer
Pipe and Lyde
Shelwick
Bridge Sollers
Kenchester
The Weir (NT)
Canon Bridge
Swainshill
Upper Breinton
Breinton
White Cross
HEREFORD
Lulham
Madley
Eaton Bishop
Belmont Abbey
Lower Bullingham
Tupsley
Clehonger
Grafton
Dinedor
Kingstone
Allensmore
Callow
Twyford Common
Thruxton
Whitfield
Didley
Dewsall Court
Aconbury
St. John Baptist
Kilpeck
Much Dewchurch
Wormelow Tump
Kingsthorne
Little Birch
Little Dewchurch
Much Birch
Howton
Kenderchurch
Orcop Hill
Hoarwithy
ontrilas
Bagwyllydiart
Llanwarne
Llandinabo
Harewood End
Garway Hill
Orcop
Pencoyd
Sandyway
Michaelchurch
angua
Kentchurch
Little Garway
St Weonards
Garway
St Owen's Cross
Tretire
Peterstow
Bridstow
Ross Spur
Ross-on-Wye
Craig Syfyddrin
Skenfrith (NT)
Broad
Llangarron
Pencraig
Glewstone
Hom Green
Hillcourt

Leominster
Kimbolton
Stockton
Whyle
Grafton
Hatfield
Bach Camp
Pudleston
Stoke Prior
Steen's Bridge
Docklow
Humber
Risbury
Grendon Green
Marston Stannett
Bredenbury
Bromyard Downs
Wharton
Hope under Dinmore
Bowley
Pencombe
Bromyard
Bodenham
Maund Bryan
Little Cowarne
Munderfield Row
Stan Bisl
Bodenham Moor
Ullingswick
Munderfield Stocks
Acton Beauc
Urdimarsh
The Vauld
Felton
Stoke Lacy
Walker's Green
Preston Wynne
Burley Gate
Moreton Jeffries
Bishop's Frome
Five Bridges
Westhide
Much Cowarne
Ocle Pychard
Castle Frome
Newtown
Lower Egleton
Canon Frome
Withington
Yarkhill
Stretton Grandison
Ashperton
Shucknall
Hagley
Weston Beggar
Stan
Muns
Lugwardine
Bartestree
Tarrington
Dormington
Prior's Frome
Checkley
Trumpet
Hampton Bishop
Aylton
Putley
Little Marcle
Mordiford
Fiddler's Green
Woolhope
Rushall
Holme Lacy
Fownhope
Sollers Hope
Bolstone
Ballingham
Brockhampton
Carey
How Capel Court
How Caple
Yatton Wood
St. Mary's Church
Hellen's
Much Marcle
Tillers
Penalt
Fawley Chapel
Foy
Old Gore
Kings Caple
Baysham
Sellack
Hole-in-the-Wall
Brampton Abbotts
Crow Hill
Upton Bishop
Kem Gree
Gorsle
Rudhall
Linton
Little Gor
Bromsash
Aston Crews
Weston under Penyard
Coughton
Pontshill
Lea

Road numbers: M1461, A4112, A4361, B4360, B4529, A44, B4361, A49, A4110, A480, A4103, A438, A465, A417, A4103, B4352, B4349, A49, B4399, B4224, A465, A466, A4137, A40, A4172, A449, B4215, B4221, A40, B4234, B4521, B4434, B4203

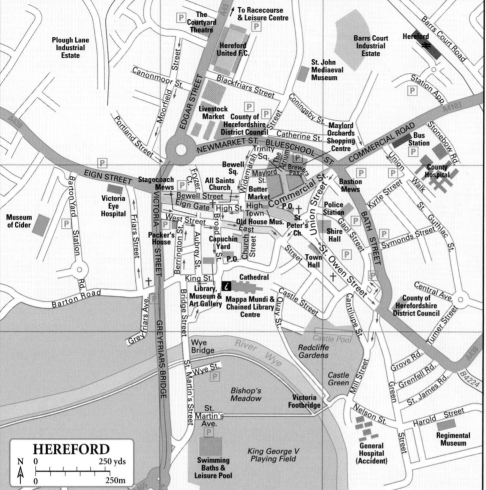

Area Code 01432

Herefordshire

HEREFORD

TOURIST INFORMATION ☎ 01432 268430
1 KING STREET,
HEREFORD, HR4 9BW

HOSPITAL A & E ☎ 01432 355444
HEREFORD GENERAL HOSPITAL,
NELSON STREET, HEREFORD, HR1 2PA

COUNCIL OFFICE ☎ 01432 260456
COUNCIL OFFICES, THE TOWN HALL,
HEREFORD, HR1 2PJ

WEB-SITE www.hereford.gov.uk

LOCAL RADIO BBC RADIO HEREFORD & WORCESTER 94.7 FM   WYVERN FM 96.7 FM

Hereford *Here.* Population: 54,326. City, county town and cathedral city on River Wye, 45m/72km SW of Birmingham. Many old buildings and museums, including Waterworks museum and City Museum and Art Gallery. 1621 Old House is a museum of local history. Medieval Wye Bridge. Cathedral includes richly ornamented Early English style Lady chapel. New building houses Chained Library of 1500 volumes and 1289 Mappa Mundi Map of the world. Three Choirs Festival every third year. Cider Museum and King Offa Distillery W of city centre depicts history of cider making.

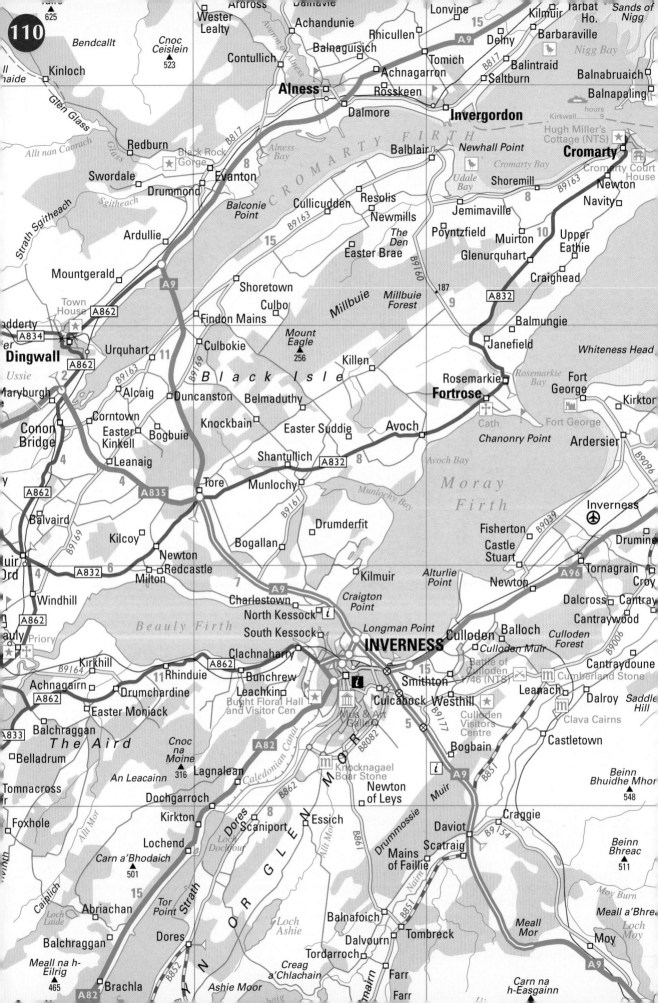

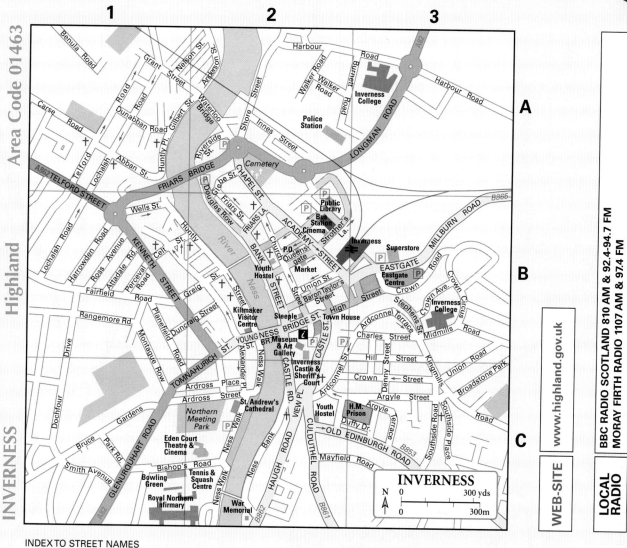

Area Code 01463

Highland

INVERNESS

INVERNESS

N 0 — 300 yds

0 — 300m

WEB-SITE www.highland.gov.uk

LOCAL RADIO

BBC RADIO SCOTLAND 810 AM & 92.4-94.7 FM
MORAY FIRTH RADIO 1107 AM & 97.4 FM

INDEX TO STREET NAMES

TOURIST INFORMATION ☎ 01463 234353
CASTLE WYND,
INVERNESS, IV2 3BJ

HOSPITAL A & E ☎ 01463 704000
RAIGMORE HOSPITAL, OLD PERTH ROAD,
INVERNESS, IV2 3UJ

COUNCIL OFFICE ☎ 01463 702000
COUNCIL OFFICES, GLENURQUHART ROAD,
INVERNESS, IV3 5NX

Inverness *High.* Population: 41,234. Town, at mouth of River Ness at entrance to Beauly Firth, 105m/169km NW of Aberdeen and 113m/181km NW of Edinburgh. Administrative, commercial and tourist centre. Caledonian Canal passes to W of town. Victorian castle in town centre used as law courts. Inverness Museum and Art Gallery depicts history of Highlands. Balnain House is a museum of Highland music and musical instruments. University of the Highlands and Islands. 1746 Culloden battle site 5m/8km E. Airport at locality of Dalcross, 7m/11km NE of town.

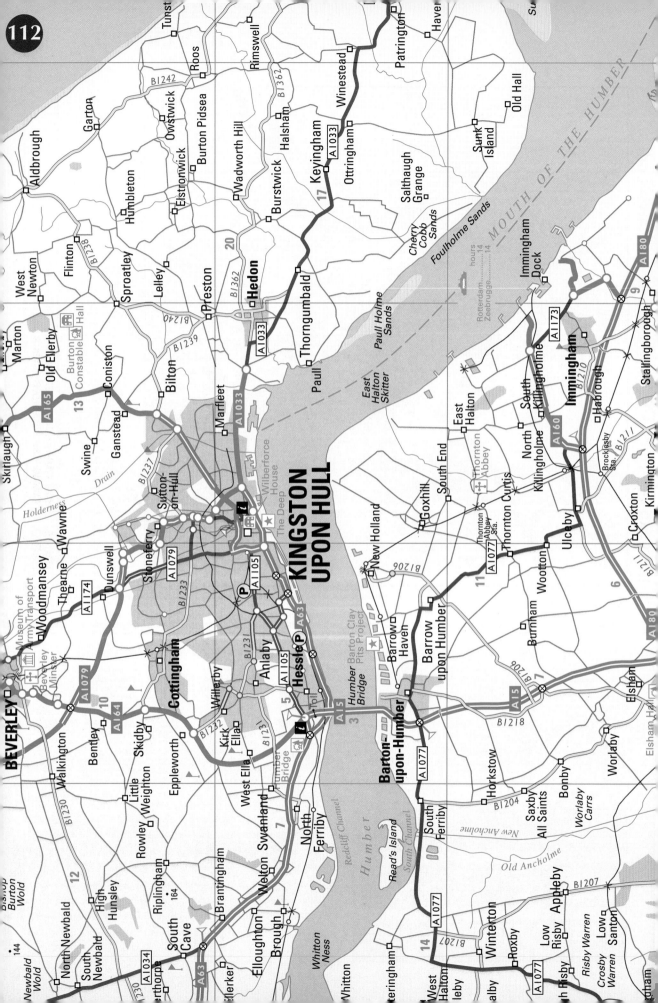

INDEX TO STREET NAMES

TOURIST INFORMATION ☎ 01482 223559
1 PARAGON STREET, KINGSTON UPON HULL, HU1 3NA

HOSPITAL A & E ☎ 01482 328541
HULL ROYAL INFIRMARY, ANLABY ROAD, KINGSTON UPON HULL, HU3 2JZ

COUNCIL OFFICE ☎ 01482 300300
GUILDHALL, ALFRED GELDER STREET, KINGSTON UPON HULL, HU1 2AA

Kingston upon Hull (Commonly known as Hull.) *Hull* Population: 310,636. City, port at confluence of Rivers Humber and Hull, 50m/80km E of Leeds. Much of town destroyed during bombing of World War II; town centre has been rebuilt. Formerly had a thriving fishing industry. Major industry nowadays is frozen food processing. Restored docks, cobble streeted Old Town and modern marina. Universities. Birthplace of William Wilberforce, slavery abolitionist, 1759. Wilberforce Museum covers history of slavery. Streetlife Transport Museum. Town Docks Museum explores city's maritime history. Famous for associations with poets Andrew Marvell, Stevie Smith and Philip Larkin.

WEB-SITE www.hullcc.gov.uk

LOCAL RADIO BBC RADIO HUMBERSIDE 95.9 FM / MAGIC 1161 AM, VIKING FM 96.9 FM

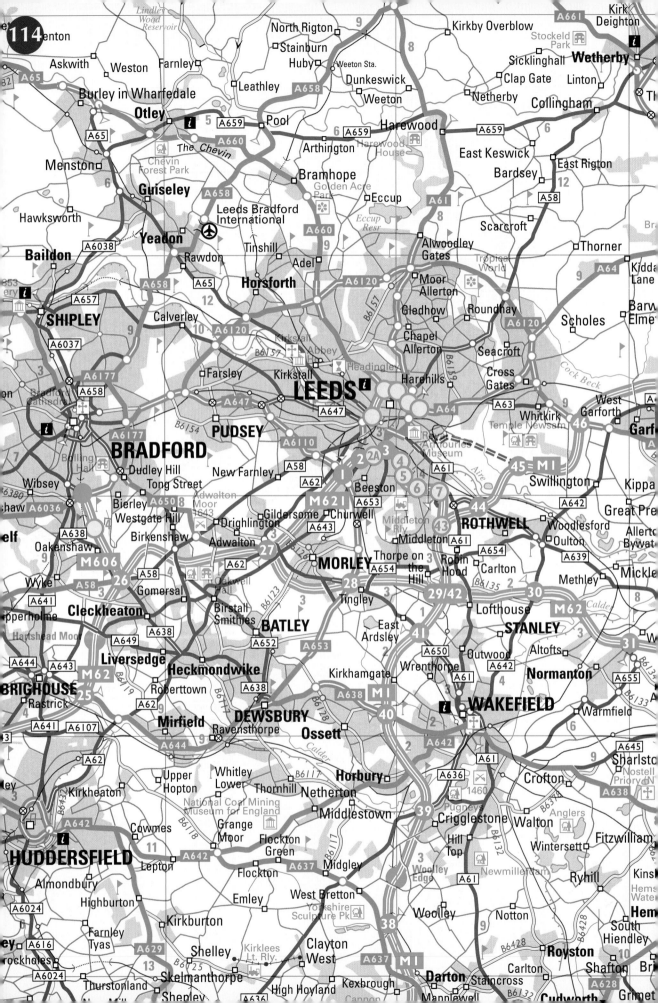

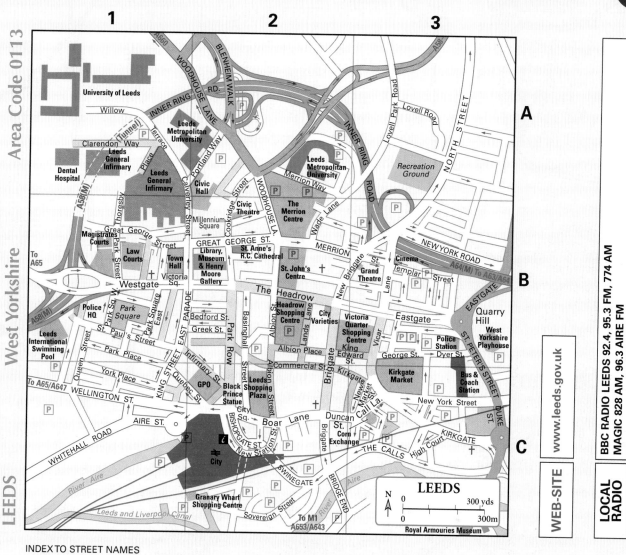

Area Code 0113

West Yorkshire

LEEDS

WEB-SITE www.leeds.gov.uk

LOCAL RADIO BBC RADIO LEEDS 92.4, 95.3 FM, 774 AM
MAGIC 828 AM, 96.3 AIRE FM

INDEX TO STREET NAMES

TOURIST INFORMATION ☎ 0113 242 5242
GATEWAY YORKSHIRE, THE ARCADE,
CITY STATION, LEEDS, LS1 1PL

HOSPITAL A & E ☎ 0113 243 2799
LEEDS GENERAL INFIRMARY,
GREAT GEORGE STREET, LEEDS, LS1 3EX

COUNCIL OFFICE ☎ 0113 234 8080
CIVIC HALL, CALVERLEY STREET,
LEEDS, LS1 1UR

Leeds *W. Yorks.* Population: 424,194. City, commercial and industrial city on River Aire and on Leeds and Liverpool Canal, 36m/58km NE of Manchester and 170m/274km NW of London. Previously important for textile industry. Prospered during Victorian period, the architecture of a series of ornate arcades containing some magnificent clocks reflecting the affluence of this time. City Art Gallery has a fine collection of 20c British Art. Edwardian Kirkgate Market is the largest in north of England. Royal Armouries Museum houses arms and armour collection from the Tower of London. Universities. Leeds Bradford International Airport at Yeadon, 7m/11km NW.

New Sawley
Shardlow
Sawley
Thrumpton
Gotham
Bradmore
Keyworth
Rushcliffe
Heritage Centre
Stanton-on-the-Wolds
Bunny
A606
A46
A50
Aston on Trent
Lockington
Hemington
Ratcliffe on Soar
Kingston on Soar
Costock
Widmerpool
Wysall
Hickling
Castle Donington
24
24A
M1
A453
Kegworth
A60
Willoughby-on-the-Wolds
Upper Broughton
A606
Donington Park
East Midlands International
Diseworth
Sutton Bonington
West Leake
East Leake
15
Rempstone
Isley Walton
A453
Donington Park
23A
Long Whatton
A6006
Normanton on Soar
Hoton
Prestwold
Wymeswold
Old Dalby
A42
A6
Soar
Hathern
6
Stanford on Soar
A60
B676
A6006
Belton
B5324
4
Cotes
Burton on the Wolds
Ragdale
Osgathorpe
Shepshed
8
A512
3
Thorpe Acre
A6004
LOUGHBOROUGH
Walton on the Wolds
Hoby
Thringstone
A512
23
A6004
Great Central Rly
Barrow upon Soar
Seagrave
Rotherby
Brooksby
Thrussington
Blackbrook Resr
B591
Woodthorpe
Nanpantan
Quorn
A6
Sileby
A46
15
Whitwick
Charnwood Forest
Beacon Hill
Woodhouse
Mountsorrel
Cossington
Ratcliffe on the Wreake
Rearsby
East Goscote
COALVILLE
5
Broombriggs Farm
Woodhouse Eaves
Swithland
Rothley
11
Syston
Queniborough
Snibston
Hugglescote
Bardon
Ulverscroft
Copt Oak
Cropston Resr
Cropston
Thurcaston
Wanlip
Watermead
South Croxto
Ellistown
5
Markfield
Bradgate Park
8
A607
Barkby
Barkby Thorpe
Ibstock
B585
22
Leicester
Stanton under Bardon
Newtown Linford
A46
Birstall
6
Thurmaston
Beeby
Bagworth
Thornton
Field Head
8
A50
Anstey
National Space Science Cen
A6
Belgrave
Keyham
Scraptoft
Nailstone
12
Thornton Resr
M1
Groby
8
A46
A607
A563
Humberston
Barlestone
B582
Ratby
Glenfield
Wygston's House
Belgrave Hall
Bushby
Osbaston
Botcheston
21A
Kirby Muxloe
Dane Hills
A50
Thurnby
Houg on th Hill
Newbold Verdon
Desford
Leicester Forest East
P
LEICESTER
A594
Stoneygate
A6030
B667
Ga
Cadeby
Kirkby Mallory
Peckleton
B582
Braunstone
A5460
A5199
Knighton
Leicester Farmworld
B582
Evington
Stoughton
Sutton Cheney
Mallory Park
12
A563
Aylestone
B5366
Little Str
Stapleton
A47
Thurlaston
7
21
A426
WIGSTON
Oadby
Great Glen
A447
Barwell
Huncote
Enderby
Glen Parva
South Wigston
Newton Harcourt
Burto Over
Earl Shilton
Narborough
Blaby
Whetstone
oke Golding
M69
Elmesthorpe
Burbage Common
B581
Croft
B4114
Cosby
Countesthorpe
Kilby
Kibworth Beauchamp
HINCKLEY
Burbage
2
B4669
Stoney Stanton
Sapcote
Sutton in the Elms
Primethorpe
Broughton Astley
Peatling Magna
10
Willoughby Waterleys
A5199
Arnesby
Fleckney
A5
Sharnford
B581
14
M1
Ashby
Saddingto

Area Code 0116

LEICESTER

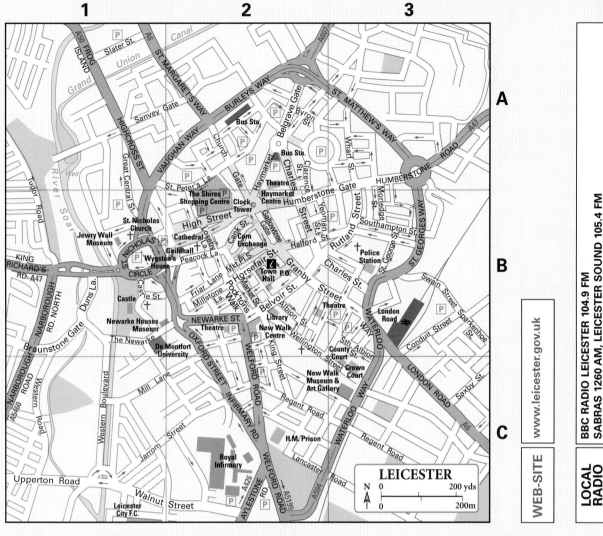

WEB-SITE www.leicester.gov.uk

LOCAL RADIO BBC RADIO LEICESTER 104.9 FM / SABRAS 1260 AM, LEICESTER SOUND 105.4 FM

INDEX TO STREET NAMES

TOURIST INFORMATION ☎ 0116 299 8888
7-9 EVERY STREET, TOWN HALL SQUARE,
LEICESTER, LE1 6AG

HOSPITAL A & E ☎ 0116 254 1414
LEICESTER ROYAL INFIRMARY,
INFIRMARY SQUARE, LEICESTER, LE1 5WW

COUNCIL OFFICE ☎ 0116 252 6480
COUNCIL OFFICES, NEW WALK CENTRE,
WELFORD PLACE, LEICESTER, LE1 6ZG

Leicester *Leic.* Population: 318,518. City, county town and commercial and industrial centre on River Soar, on site of Roman town of Ratae Coritanorum, 89m/143km NW of London. Industries include hosiery and footwear, alongside more modern industries. Universities. Many historic remains including Jewry Wall (English Heritage), one of largest surviving sections of Roman wall in the country, Roman baths and a medieval guildhall. Saxon Church of St. Nicholas. 11c St. Martin's Cathedral. Victorian clock tower. Newarke Houses Museum explores the city's social history. Home to England's second biggest street festival after Notting Hill Carnival. Joseph Merrick, the 'Elephant Man' born and lived here.

Gainsborough

kingham
Old Hall
B1433
A631
A631
A631
Street
Glentham
A6

Springthorpe
Harpswell
Caenby Corner
Normanby-by-Spital
Caenby
Toft

ndby
Bole
Heapham
Glentworth
Owmby-by-Spital

Wheatley
Upton
Kexby
Fillingham
Saxby

ey
Lea
Knaith
Willingham
Coates
Ingham
Spridlington

Sturton le Steeple
Gate Burton
Normanby by Stow
B1241
Cammeringham
Hackthorn
Cold Hanworth

verton thorpe
Littleborough
Marton
Stow
A1500
Brattleby
Welton
Ryland
Snarford

swell
South Leverton
A156
Sturton by Stow
Thorpe in the Fallows
Aisthorpe
Dunholme

Cottam
Brampton
Bransby
Scampton
Stainton by Lang

dbeck
Rampton
Torksey
Ingleby
Broxholme
North Carlton
Scothe

ast ton
Stokeham
Laneham
Fenton
B1241
South Carlton
70
B1398
Sudbrooke

Dunham
Laughterton
A1133
Kettlethorpe
Saxilby
A57
Burton
Nettleham
A158
Reepham
Cherry

Darlton
A57
Ragnall
Newton on Trent
Toll
Broadholme
A57
A158
Washingborough

North Clifton
Thorney
Skellingthorpe
LINCOLN
Cath
Canwick
Heighingto

South Clifton
A1133
Wigsley
Harby
Doddington
A46
B1378
B1003
B1308

Normanton on Trent
Spalford
Doddington Hall
Hartsholme
Boultham
Bracebridge
Branston

Weston
Grassthorpe
North Scarle
Eagle
Whisby
B1190
Swallow Beck
Bracebridge Heath
B1188

Sutton on Trent
Girton
Thorpe on the Hill
A1434
North Hykeham
A607
Waddington
B1178

Besthorpe
South Scarle
Fosse Way
Aubourn Hall
South Hykeham
A15

Carlton-on-Trent
A1133
Swinderby
Haddington
Aubourn
Harmston
B1178
Methering

Cromwell
Collingham
Thurlby
Coleby
B1202

A46
Bassingham
Boothby Graffoe
13

Holme
Norton Disney
Navenby
15

hley
North Muskham
Langford Brough
Danethorpe Hill
Carlton-le-Moorland
Wellingore
Sc

e Carlton
Muskham
Winthorpe
Stapleford
Brant
A607

A616
A17
A1
Coddington
Brant Broughton
Welbourn
Temple Bruer
A15

A617
A46
NEWARK-ON-TRENT
Beckingham
A17
Stragglethorpe
Leadenham
A17

Hawton
Balderton
B6326
Sutton
Fulbeck Hall
Cranwell

Thorpe
Barnby in the Willows
Fenton
Fulbeck
A607
B1429
Bl

Area Code 01522

Lincolnshire

LINCOLN

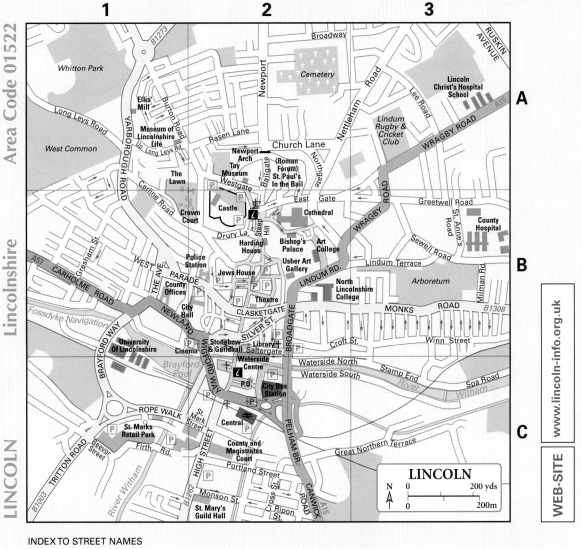

WEB-SITE www.lincoln-info.org.uk

LOCAL RADIO — BBC RADIO LINCOLNSHIRE 94.9 FM / LINCS FM 102.2 FM

INDEX TO STREET NAMES

TOURIST INFORMATION ☎ 01522 873213
9 CASTLE HILL, LINCOLN, LN1 3AA

HOSPITAL A & E ☎ 01522 512512
LINCOLN COUNTY HOSPITAL, GREETWELL ROAD, LINCOLN, LN2 5QY

COUNCIL OFFICE ☎ 01522 552222
COUNTY OFFICES, NEWLAND, LINCOLN, LN1 1YG

Lincoln *Lincs.* Population: 80,281. City, county town and cathedral city on River Witham, on site of Roman town of Lindum, 120m/193km N of London. City grew as a result of strategic importance in the wool trade. Many ancient monuments and archaeological features. Castle built by William I. 13c cathedral, is the third largest in Britain with its three towers on hilltop dominating the skyline. Carvings in the Angel Choir include the stone figure of the Lincoln Imp which is the city's emblem. Lincoln Bishop's Old Palace (English Heritage) is medieval building on S side of cathedral. 12c Jew's House. Museum of Lincolnshire Life. Universities.

LIVERPOOL

Merseyside

Area Code 0151

Liverpool street map (grid A–C / 1–3), showing streets including St. Anne Street, London Rd, Byrom Street, Vauxhall Road, Leeds Street, Pall Mall, Old Hall Street, Strand Street, Wapping, New Quay, River Mersey, Albert Dock, Canning Dock, Salthouse Dock, Prince's Dock, Graving Docks, and landmarks such as Coach Sta., Police Station, Liverpool John Moores University (JMU), Walker Art Gallery, Picton Library, St. George's Hall, Lime St. (Main Line and Underground), Empire Theatre, Royal Court Theatre, Playhouse, Neptune Theatre, Central Station, Cavern Club, Bluecoat Arts Centre, Town Hall, Cotton Exchange, Mercury Court, Conservation Centre, Queen Elizabeth II Crown Court, Fire Station, Police H.Q., Cunard Building, Port of Liverpool Building, Royal Liver Building, Georges Pierhead, Mersey Ferry Terminal, Museum of Liverpool Life, Tate Liverpool, Albert Dock Village, Maritime Museum & H.M. Customs Museum.

LIVERPOOL
N
200 yds
200m
0
0

INDEX TO STREET NAMES

Addison Street	A2	Gradwell Street	C2	Paradise Street	C2
Argyle Street	C2	Great Crosshall Street	A2	Park Lane	C2
Bath Street	A1	Great Howard Street	A1	Parker Street	B3
Berry Street	C3	Hanover Street	C2	Preston Street	B2
Bold Street	C3	Hartley Quay	C1	Princes Parade	B1
Brownlow Hill	B3	Hatton Garden	A2	Queens Square	B2
Brunswick Street	B1	Hawke Street	B3	Ranelagh Street	B3
Byrom Street	A3	Henry Street	C2	Renshaw Street	B3
Canning Place	C2	Hood Street	B2	Roe Street	B3
Castle Street	B2	Hunter Street	A3	Salthouse Quay	C1
Chapel Street	B1	James Street	B1	School Lane	B2
Cheapside	A2	King Edward Street	A1	Scotland Road	A3
Christian Street	A3	Leeds Street	A1	Seel Street	C2
Church Street	B2	Lime Street	B3	Sir Thomas Street	B2
Concert Street	C3	Liver Street	C2	Skelhorne Street	B3
Cook Street	B2	London Road	B3	Slater Street	C3
Copperas Hill	B3	Lord Nelson Street	B3	South John Street	B2
Crosshall Street	B2	Lord Street	B2	St. Anne Street	A3
Dale Street	B2	Marybone	A2	St. John's Lane	B3
Dawson Street	B2	Matthews Street	B2	The Strand	B1
Derby Square	C2	Midghall Street	A2	Tithebarn Street	A2
Duke Street	C2	Moorfields	B2	Vauxhall Road	A2
East Street	A1	Mount Pleasant	B3	Victoria Street	B2
Eaton Street	A1	Naylor Street	A2	Wapping	C2
Elliot Street	B3	New Quay	B1	Water Street	B1
Freemasons Row	A2	North John Street	B2	Waterloo Road	A1
Gascoyne Street	A1	Old Hall Street	A1	Whitechapel	B2
Gibraltar Row	A1	Old Haymarket	B2	William Brown Street	A3
Gilbert Street	C2	Paisley Street	A1		
Goree	B1	Pall Mall	A1		

TOURIST INFORMATION ☎ 09066 806886
MERSEYSIDE WELCOME CENTRE, CLAYTON SQ.
SHOPPING CEN, LIVERPOOL, L1 1QR

HOSPITAL A & E ☎ 0151 525 5980
UNIVERSITY HOSPITAL OF AINTREE, LOWER LANE,
FAZAKERLEY, LIVERPOOL, L9 7AL

COUNCIL OFFICE ☎ 0151 233 3000
MUNICIPAL BUILDINGS, DALE STREET,
LIVERPOOL, L69 2DH

Liverpool *Mersey.* Population: 481,786. City, major port and industrial city on River Mersey estuary, 178m/286km NW of London. Originally a fishing village it experienced rapid expansion during early 18c due to transatlantic trade in sugar, spice and tobacco and was involved in slave trade. Docks declined during 20c, now Albert Dock is home to shops, museums and Tate Liverpool. In 19c a multicultural city developed as Liverpool docks were point of departure for Europeans emigrating to America and Australia. Also became home to refugees from Irish potato famine of 1845. Present day Liverpool is home to variety of industries and many museums and art galleries. Also home of the Beatles, who performed at Liverpool's Cavern Club. Universities. Modern Anglican and Roman Catholic cathedrals. On Pier Head the famous Royal Liver Building is situated, topped by Liver Birds. Railway tunnel and two road tunnels under River Mersey to Wirral peninsula. Airport at Speke, 6m/10km.

WEB-SITE www.liverpool.gov.uk

LOCAL RADIO BBC RADIO MERSEYSIDE 95.8 FM
MAGIC 1548 AM, RADIO CITY 96.7 FM, JUICE 107.6 FM

Area Code 0161

Greater Manchester

MANCHESTER

MANCHESTER
N 0 — 400 yds
0 — 400m

WEB-SITE www.manchester.gov.uk

LOCAL RADIO
BBC RADIO GMR 95.1 FM
MANCHESTER'S MAGIC 1152 AM, CAPITAL GOLD 1458 AM, GALAXY 102 FM, KEY 103 FM

INDEX TO STREET NAMES

Street	Ref	Street	Ref	Street	Ref	Street	Ref	Street	Ref
Addington Street	A3	Corporation Street	A2	High Street	B2	New Quay Street	B1	Shudehill	A3
Albert Square	B2	Cross Street	B2	Irwell Street	B1	Newton Street	B3	Silk Street	A1
Aytoun Street	B3	Dale Street	B3	Jackson Crescent	C1	Oldham Road	A3	Southmill Street	B2
Blackfriars Road	A1	Dantzic Street	A2	John Dalton Street	B2	Oldham Street	B3	Spring Gardens	B2
Blackfriars Street	A2	Dawson Street	C1	King Street	B2	Oxford Road	C2	Store Street	B3
Bridge Street	B1	Deansgate	B2	King Street West	B2	Oxford Street	B2	Swan Street	A3
Bridge Viaduct	C1	Ducie Street	B3	Lever Street	B3	Peter Street	B2	Thomas Street	A3
Brook Street	C3	East Ordsall Lane	B1	Liverpool Road	B1	Piccadilly	B3	Thompson Street	A3
Byrom Street	B1	Egerton Street	C1	London Road	B3	Portland Street	B2	Trinity Way	A1
Cambridge Street	C2	Fairfield Street	C3	Lower Byrom Street	B1	Princess Street	B2/C3	Victoria Street	A2
Camp Street	B1	Fountain Street	B2	Lower Mosley Street	C2	Quay Street	B1	Water Street	C1
Cannon Street	A2	Gartside Street	B1	Lower Moss Lane	C1	Rochdale Road	A3	Whitworth Street	C2
Chapel Street	B1	George Street	B2	Mancunian Way	C1	Sackville Street	B3	Whitworth Street West	C1
Charles Street	C3	Great Jackson Street	C1	Market Street	B2	St. Ann's Square	B2	Withy Grove	A2
Chepstow Street	C2	Greengate	A1/A2	Medlock Street	C2	St. Ann Street	B2	York Street	B3
Chester Road	C1	Gt. Ancoats Street	A3	Miller Street	A2	St. Mary's Parsonage	B2		
Chorlton Street	B3	Gt. Bridgewater Street	C2	Mosley Street	B2	St. Peter's Square	B2		
Church Street	B3	Gt. Ducie Street	A2	Mount Street	B2	St. Simon Street	A1		
City Road East	C2	Hampson Street	B1	New Bailey Street	B1	St. Stephen Street	A1		

TOURIST INFORMATION ☎ 0161 234 3157/8
MANCHESTER VISITOR CENTRE, TOWN HALL EXTENSION, LLOYD ST, MANCHESTER, M60 2LA

HOSPITAL A & E ☎ 0161 276 1234
MANCHESTER ROYAL INFIRMARY, OXFORD ROAD, MANCHESTER, M13 9WL

COUNCIL OFFICE ☎ 0161 234 5000
TOWN HALL, ALBERT SQUARE, MANCHESTER, M60 2LA

Manchester *Gt.Man.* Population: 402,889. City, important industrial, business, cultural and commercial centre and port, 164m/264km NW of London. Access for ships by River Mersey and Manchester Ship Canal, opened in 1894. 15c cathedral, formerly parish church, has widest nave in England. Experienced rapid growth during industrial revolution. In 1750, Manchester was essentially still a village. During Victorian era, city was global cotton milling capital. Present day city is home to wide range of industries and is unofficial capital of nation's 'youth culture'. Major shopping centres include Arndale and Trafford Centres. Universities. International airport 9m/14km S of city centre.

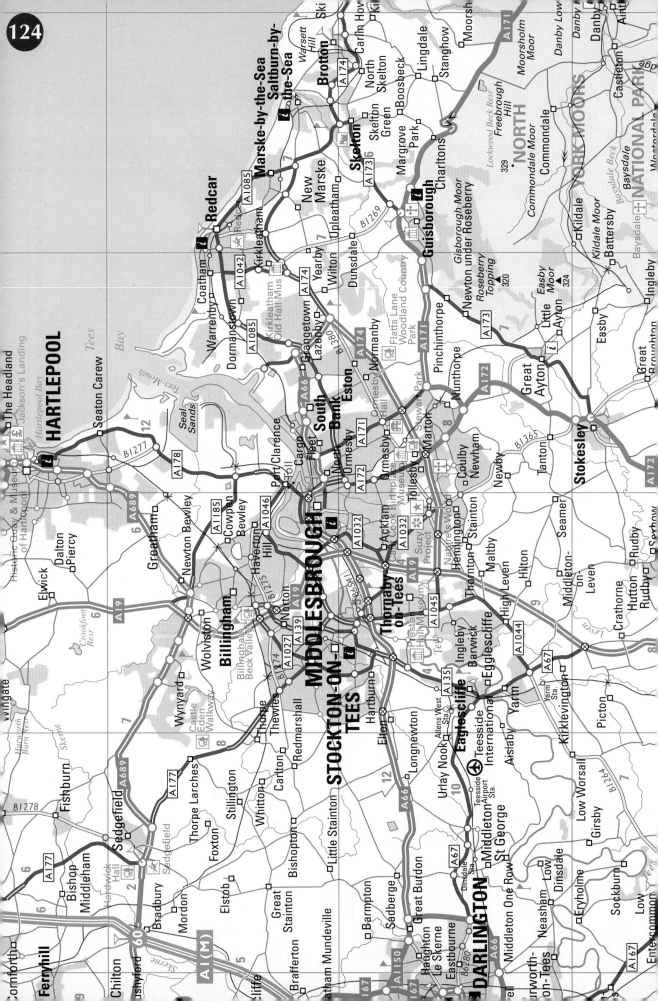

Area Code 01642

MIDDLESBROUGH

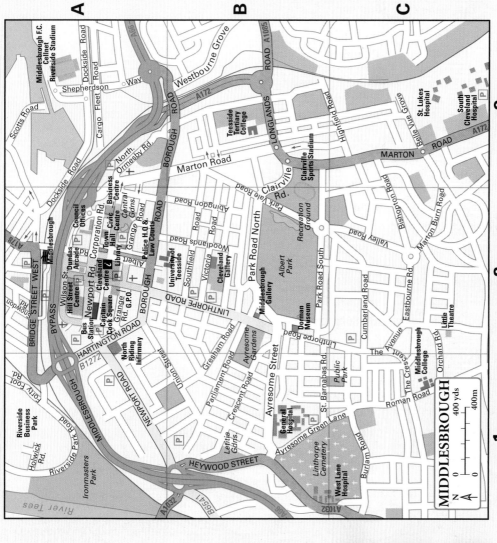

TOURIST INFORMATION ☎ 01642 358086/243425
99-101 ALBERT ROAD,
MIDDLESBROUGH, TS1 2PA

HOSPITAL A & E ☎ 01642 617617
NORTH TEES GENERAL HOSPITAL, HARDWICK ROAD,
STOCKTON-ON-TEES, TS19 8PE

COUNCIL OFFICE ☎ 01642 245432
MUNICIPAL BUILDINGS, PO BOX 99A, RUSSELL STREET,
MIDDLESBROUGH, TS1 2QQ

Middlesbrough *Middbro.* Population: 147,430. Town, port, with extensive dock area, on S bank of River Tees, forming part of Teesside urban complex. A former iron and steel town, its chief industries now involve oil and petrochemicals. Unusual 1911 transporter bridge over River Tees. University of Teesside. Captian Cook Birthplace Museum in Stewart Park at Marton.

WEB-SITE www.middlesbrough.gov.uk

LOCAL RADIO
BBC RADIO CLEVELAND 95 FM
MAGIC 1170 AM, TFM 96.6 FM, CENTURY FM 100.7 FM

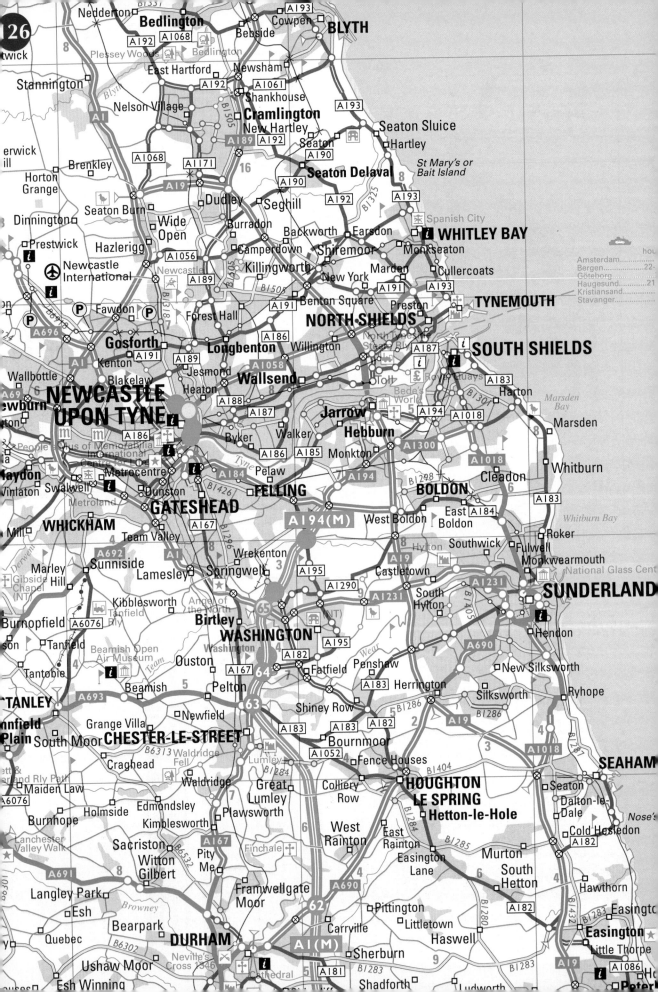

Area Code 0191

Tyne & Wear

NEWCASTLE

Map labels:

Royal Victoria Infirmary, Hancock Museum, Jesmond, Cemetery, University of Newcastle, Civic Centre, City Hall & Baths, University of Northumbria, Leazes Park, St. Mary's Pl., Laing Art Gallery & Museum, Newcastle United F.C., St James, Eldon Square Shopping Centre, Earl Grey Mon., St. N. Br. St., Library, Bus Station, Stanhope St., Blackett Monument, Cinema, Plummer Tower, Manors, Bus Sta., Markets, Theatre, Police Station, John George Joicey Museum, Newcastle Discovery Museum, People's Mus. of Memorabilia, St. Nicholas Cathedral, The Side, Quayside, Millennium Bridge, St. Marys R.C. Cath., Central, Castle Keep, River Tyne, Newcastle College, International Centre For Life, High Level Road/Rail Bridge, Gateshead Music Centre, Car Sleeper Loading Bay, Newcastle Arena

NEWCASTLE
N
0 — 400 yds
0 — 400m

WEB-SITE www.newcastle.gov.uk

LOCAL RADIO: BBC RADIO NEWCASTLE 95.4 FM MAGIC 1152 AM, METRO RADIO 97.1 FM, CENTURY RADIO 101.8 FM

INDEX TO STREET NAMES

TOURIST INFORMATION ☎ 0191 277 8000
128 GRAINGER STREET,
NEWCASTLE UPON TYNE, NE1 5AF

HOSPITAL A & E ☎ 0191 273 8811
NEWCASTLE GENERAL HOSPITAL, WESTGATE
ROAD, NEWCASTLE UPON TYNE, NE64 6BE

COUNCIL OFFICE ☎ 0191 232 8520
CIVIC CENTRE, BARRAS BRIDGE,
NEWCASTLE UPON TYNE, NE99 1RD

Newcastle upon Tyne T. & W. Population: 189,150. City, port on River Tyne about 11m/17km upstream from river mouth and 80m/129km N of Leeds. The 'new castle' of city's name started in 1080 by Robert Curthose, eldest son of William the Conqueror. 13c castle gatehouse known as 'Black Gate'. Commercial and industrial centre, previously dependent upon coalmining and shipbuilding. In its heyday, 25 percent of world's shipping built here. Cathedral dates from 14 to 15c. Bessie Surtees House (English Heritage) comprises 16c and 17c merchants' houses. Tyne Bridge, opened in 1928 and longest of its type at the time. Venerable Bede (AD 672-735) born near Jarrow. Catherine Cookson, writer, also born in Jarrow, Universities. Newcastle International Airport 5m/8km NW.

NORFOLK BROADS

THE BROADS

NORWICH

Sprowston

Wymondham

Attleborough

Potter Heigham, Catfield, Irstead, Bastwick, Repps, Clippesby, Billockby, Stokesby, Thrigby Hall, Tunstall, Damgate, Acle, Moulton St Mary, Halvergate, Freethorpe, Wickhampton, Freethorpe Common, Reedham, Lower Thurlton, Thurlton, Thorpe, Maypole Gn, Raveningham, Toft Monks

Ludham, Upper Street, Ranworth, Upton, Upton Green, South Walsham, North Burlingham, South Burlingham, Beighton, Southwood, Cantley, Limpenhoe, Hardley Street, Heckingham, Hales, Hales Hall, Stockton, Kirby Cane

Hickling, Sutton, Ashmanhaugh, Wroxham, Neatishead, Barton, Horning, Hoveton, Woodbastwick, Panxworth, Hemblington, Lingwood, Blofield, Brundall, Strumpshaw, Buckenham, Hassingham, Rockland St Mary, Ashby St Mary, Thurton, Langley Street, Loddon, Mundham, Sisland, The Laurels, Thwaite St Mary, Chedgrave

Belaugh, Crostwick, Rackheath, New Rackheath, Salhouse, Little Plumstead, Great Plumstead, Postwick, Surlingham, Bramerton, Claxton, Hellington, Bergh Apton, Brooke, Seething, Kirstead Green

Tunstead, Hautbois, Coltishall, Horstead, Frettenham, Newton St Faith, Horsham St Faith, Spixworth, Catton, Thorpe End Garden Village, Thorpe St Andrew, Kirby Bedon, Yelverton, Framingham Pigot, Poringland, Alpington, Howe, Shotesham

Waterloo, Hainford, Stratton Strawless, Hevingham, Horsford, Drayton, Hellesdon, New Costessey, Colney, Eaton, Caistor St Edmund, Trowse Newton, Framingham Earl, Dunston, Stoke Holy Cross, Saxlingham Nethergate, Saxlingham Thorpe, Hempnall

Swannington, Alderford, Felthorpe, Morton on the Hill, Attlebridge, Taverham, Costessey, Bowthorpe, Earlham, Cringleford, Keswick, Swardeston, Mulbarton, Swainsthorpe, Newton Flotman, Saxlingham Green, Forncett St Mary, Tasburgh

Whitwell, Brandiston, St Helena, Ringland, Weston Longville, Weston Green, Easton, Honingham, Marlingford, Bawburgh, Bawburgh, Great Melton, Little Melton, Hethersett, High Green, Wramplingham, East Carleton, Bracon Ash, Flordon, Hapton, Tharston, Thurston

Bawdeswell, Lyng, Lenwade, Primrose Green, North Tuddenham, East Tuddenham, Mattishall Burgh, Mattishall, South Green, Welborne, Barford, Colton, Barnham Broom, Coston, Runhall, Brandon Parva, Kimberley, Carleton Forehoe, Crownthorpe, Deopham, Hackford, Suton, Morley St Botolph, Spooner Row, Besthorpe

Elsing, Spatham, Hockering, Welborne, Kett's, Ashwellthorpe, Wreningham, Fundenhall, Tacolneston, Silfield, Bunwell Street, Micklewood

Dinosaur Adventure Park

Pettitts Animal Adventure Park

Pettitts Amusement Park

Norwich Airport

A47, A11, A140, A146, A143, A149, A1062, A1064, A1151, A1042, A1074, A1067, A1242, A140, B1150, B1145, B1140, B1152, B1332, B1108, B1113, B1135, B1527, B1172, B1114, B1149, B1354, B1351, B1136

Map labels (selected):
CLARENCE RD. · Cemetery · KETTS HILL · Gurney Road · B1140 · Mousehold Street · Silver Road · BARRACK STREET · BISHOP BRIDGE ROAD · Rosary Road · RIVERSIDE ROAD · THORPE ROAD · A1074 · Lt. Clarence Road · Leonards Street · River Wensum · Bishop Bridge · Bishopgate · Pulls Ferry · Magistrates and Crown Court · Norwich Puppet Theatre · Cathedral · WHITEFRIARS · BULLCLOSE ROAD · A1151 · MAGDALEN · CRISPIN'S ROAD · St. George's Street · Colegate · Fishergate · PALACE STREET · Elm Hill · WENSUM STREET · TOMBLAND · Playhouse Theatre · St. Andrew's · ST. Hall · St. Andrew's St. · Bridewell Museum · Bedford St. · St. Hall · MAGPIE Rd. · Edward St. · Pitt St. · ST. AUGUSTINE'S ST. · Sussex St. · Duke Street · Oak Street · Coslany St. · Strangers Hall · Maddermarket Theatre · St. Benedict's · St. Giles St. · Bethel St. · City Hall · Guildhall · Market · Castle Mall · Castle Museum · Mustard Shop · Chapelfield North · Chapelfield Theatre Gardens · Origins · Forum · Theatre Royal · Assembly House · City Wall · CHAPEL FIELD ROAD · GRAPES HILL · DEREHAM ROAD · A1074 (A47) · BARN ROAD · ST. MARTIN'S ROAD · A1067 · PITT ST. · Bakers Road · St. Martin's Road · Barker Street · Orchard · Heigham Street · EARLHAM ROAD · B1108 · R.C. Cathedral · Unthank Road · Newmarket Street · Vauxhall St. · Rupert St. · Trinity Street · Wessex St. · Brunswick Road · Norfolk & Norwich Hospital · Union Street · Brunswick St. · A11 · IPSWICH RD. · A1056 · NEWMARKET RD. · ST STEPHEN'S RD · Victoria St. · Surrey St. · Bus Station · All Saints Grn. · Ber Street · QUEENS ROAD · Southwell Road · Grove Wk. · Brazen Gate · GROVE ROAD · Hall Road · City Road · King Street · Rouen Road · ROUEN ROAD · The Julian Centre · Dragon Hall · Mountergate · Rose Lane · PRINCE OF WALES ROAD · Regimental Museum · BANK PLAIN · Foundry Bridge · Norwich Station · Yacht Station · Wherry Riverside · Riverside Cinema & Leisure Centre · Albion Way · Superstore · KOBLENZ AVENUE · Canary Way · CARROW ROAD · Norwich City F.C. · To A1146 · To A146

NORWICH · 400 yds · 400m · N

INDEX TO STREET NAMES

TOURIST INFORMATION ☎ 01603 666071
THE FORUM, MILLENNIUM PLAIN,
NORWICH, NR2 1TF

HOSPITAL A & E ☎ 01603 286286
NORFOLK & NORWICH HOSPITAL,
BRUNSWICK ROAD, NORWICH, NR1 3SR

COUNCIL OFFICE ☎ 01603 622233
CITY HALL, ST. PETER'S STREET,
NORWICH, NR2 1NH

Norwich *Norf.* Population: 171,304. City, county town and cathedral city at confluence of River Wensum and River Yare, 98m/158km NE of London. Middle ages saw Norwich become second richest city in country through exporting textiles. Medieval streets and buildings are well preserved. Sections of 14c flint city wall defences still exist, including CowTower (English Heritage). Current chief industries are high technology and computer based. Notable buildings include partly Norman cathedral with second highest spire in Britain, Norman castle with keep (now museum and art gallery), 15c guildhall, modern city hall, numerous medieval churches. University of East Anglia 2m/4km W of city centre. Airport 3m/5km N.

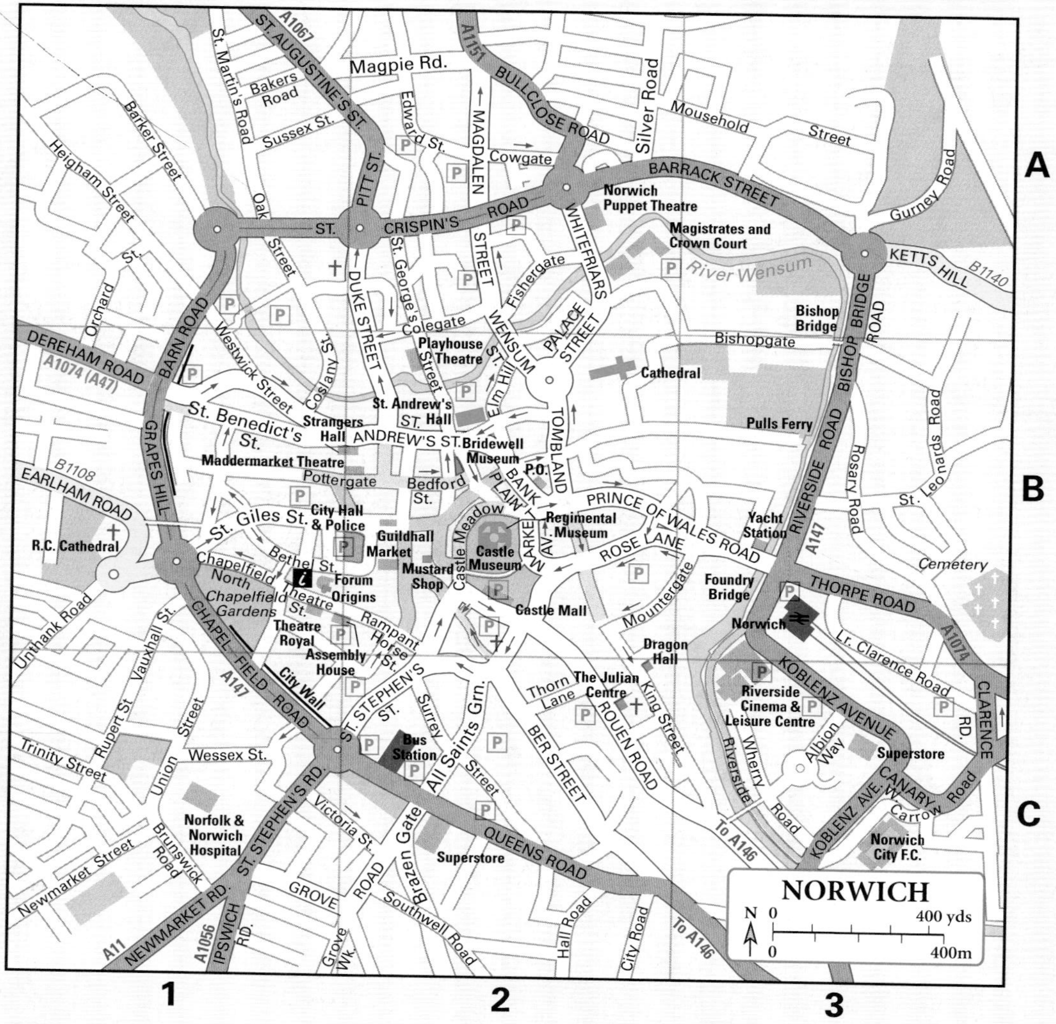

WEB-SITE | www.norwich.gov.uk

LOCAL RADIO | BBC RADIO NORFOLK 95.1 & 104.4 FM
CLASSIC GOLD AMBER 1152 AM, BROADLAND 102 102.4 FM

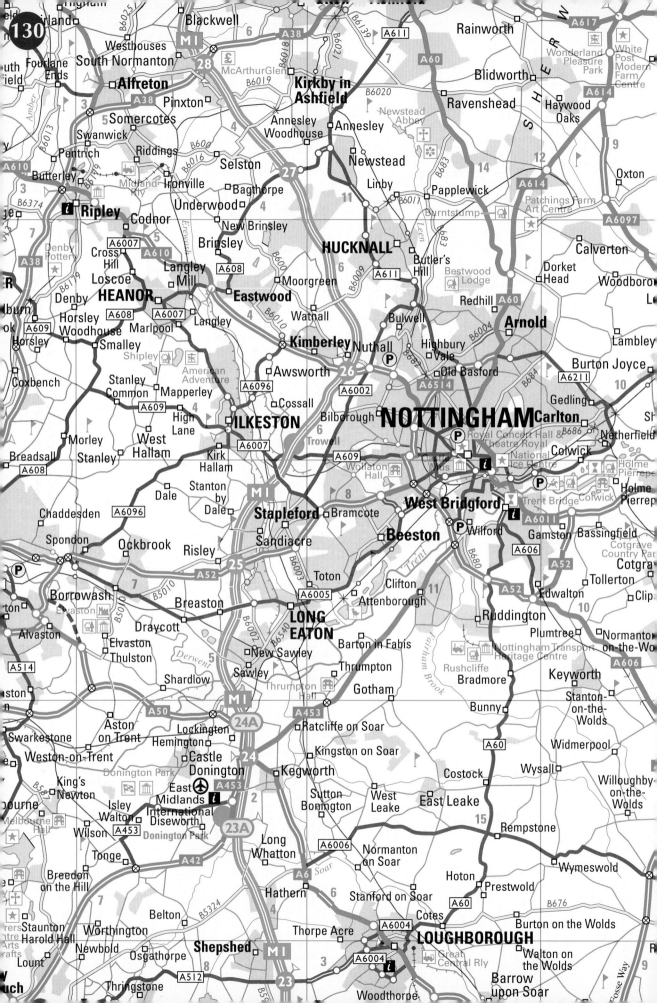

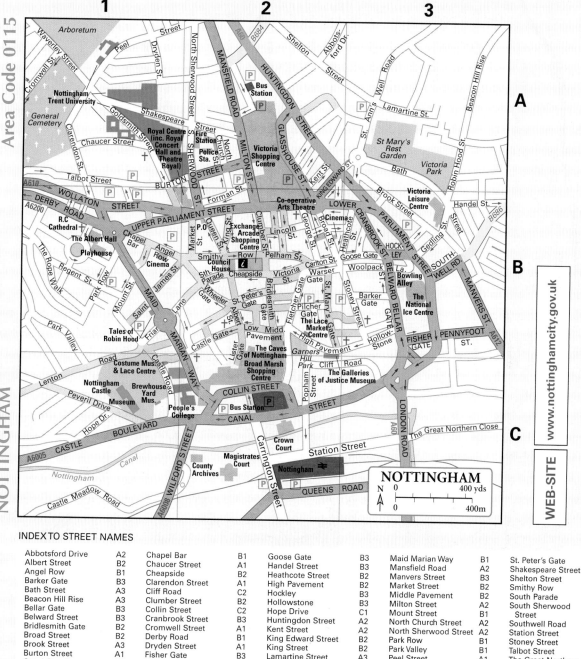

NOTTINGHAM

Area Code 0115

WEB-SITE www.nottinghamcity.gov.uk

LOCAL RADIO BBC RADIO NOTTINGHAM 103.8 FM
CENTURY FM 106 FM, CLASSIC GOLD GEM 999 AM, TRENT FM 96.2 FM

INDEX TO STREET NAMES

TOURIST INFORMATION ☎ 0115 915 5330
1-4 SMITHY ROW,
NOTTINGHAM, NG1 2BY

HOSPITAL A & E ☎ 0115 924 9924
QUEENS MEDICAL CENTRE, UNIVERSITY HOSP,
DERBY ROAD, NOTTINGHAM, NG7 2UH

COUNCIL OFFICE ☎ 0115 915 5555
THE GUILDHALL, SOUTH SHERWOOD STREET,
NOTTINGHAM, NG1 4BT

Nottingham *Nott.* Population: 270,222: City, on River Trent, 45m/72km NE of Birmingham. Originally Saxon town built on one of a pair of hills. In 1068, Normans built castle on other hill and both communities traded in valley between. Important commercial, industrial, entertainment and sports centre. Key industries include manufacture of lace, mechanical products, tobacco and pharmaceuticals. 17c castle, restored 19c, houses museum and art gallery. Two universities. Repertory theatre.

Westcott • Waddesdon Manor (N) • A4129 • Thame • A4012 • Sydenham • Postcombe • Weston Row • 6 • Path

Kingswood • Lower/Nether Winchendon • Cuddington • Chearsley • Notley Abbey (ruins) • A418 • B444 • Moreton • Tetsworth • Shirburn

Grendon Underwood • 16 • Wotton Underwood • Ashendon • Dorton • Chilton • Easington • Long Crendon • Shabbington • A329 • Bycote Chapel • 5 • A40 • Adwell • Lewknor • A40 • Pyrton • South Weston

Marsh Gibbon • Edgcott • Ludgershall • Brill • B4011 • 14 • Oakley • Worminghall • Ickford • Waterstock • A418 • Tiddington • Great Haseley • Little Haseley • Stoke Talmage • B480 • Easington • Chalgrove 1643

A41 • Blackthorn • Piddington • Upper Arncott • Boarstall • Duck Decoy (NT) • 13 • Stanton St John • Forest Hill • 7 • 8 • 8 • Great Milton • Denton • Little Milton • A329 • Stadhampton • 10 • Chalgrove • Newington

Launton • Blackthorn • B4011 • Merton • Horton-cum-Studley • Beckley • Holton • Wheatley • Horspath • Cuddesdon • B480 • Marsh Baldon • Chislehampton • Drayton St Leonard

Bicester • Chesterton • Ambrosden • Wendlebury • Fencott • Murcott • Oddington • Ot Moor • Noke • Islip • Elsfield • OXFORD • Marston • Shotover • Horspath • Garsington • Toot Baldon • A4074 • Nuneham Courtenay • Nuneham Park • Berinsfield

B4030 • M40 • 9 • B430 • Charlton-on-Otmoor • B4027 • Woodeaton • Water Eaton • Sunnymead • A40 • A4142 • Cowley • Iffley • Littlemore • Sandford-on-Thames • Radley • ABINGDON

Middleton Stoney • A4095 • Kirtlington • Weston-on-the-Green • Bletchingdon • A34 • 8 • Headington • St Mary's • University Colleges • Botanic Gardens • Cath Garden • Kennington • County Hall & Mus • Clifton Hampden

Northbrook • Nethercott • Tackley • Shipton-on-Cherwell • Thrupp • Hampton Poyle • Kidlington • Begbroke • A4260 • Yarnton • Cassington • A40 • Wolvercote • Wytham • A4165 • A4144 • Osney • Botley • North Hinksey • South Hinksey • Boars Hill • Wootton • Sunningwell • Shippon • A4183 • Abbey

Kiddington • Rousham Gap • Glympton • Oxfordshire County Mus • Woodstock • Bladon • Blenheim Palace • Evenlode • Swinford • Farmoor • Toll • Wytham • Cumnor • Chawley • Bessels Leigh • Cothill • Dry Sandford • Frilford • Marcham • A415 • A338

Over Kiddington • Ditchley • Wootton • Stonesfield • Combe • Long Hanborough • East End • Freeland • Church Hanborough • Eynsham • Farmoor Resr • West End • Stanton Harcourt • Northmoor • Appleton • Netherton • Fyfield • Tubney • A420 • A338 • Garford • Kingston • Garford

Fulwell • Charlbury • Fawler • Finstock • Ramsden • New Yatt • North Leigh • Barnard Gate • South Leigh • High Cogges • Ducklington • Hardwick • Standlake • Newbridge • Longworth • Kingston Bagpuize • Pusey House • Charney

Eastend • Taston • Spelsbury • Wychwood • Ditchley • Leafield • Crawley • Minster Lovell Hall & Dovecote (ruins) • Witney • A40 • Lew • Aston • Brighthampton • Cote • Shifford • Chimney • Shifford • Hinton Waldrist • Pusey • A420

Charlbury • B4022 • Evenlode • Roman Villa • Poffley End • A4095 • B4449 • Buckland Marsh • Carswell Marsh • B4508

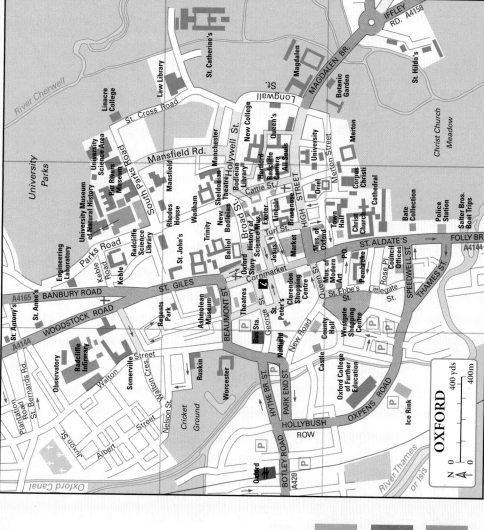

OXFORD

N
400 yds
400m
0
0

WEB-SITE | www.oxford.gov.uk

LOCAL RADIO | BBC RADIO OXFORD 95.2 FM
FOX FM 102.6 FM, FUSION 107.9 FM

INDEX TO STREET NAMES

Street	Grid
Albert Street	A1
Banbury Road	A2
Beaumont Street	B1
Botley Road	B1
Broad Street	B2
Cattle Street	B2
Cornmarket	B2
Folly Bridge	C2
George Street	B1
High Street	B2
Hollybush Row	B1
Holywell Street	B2
Hythe Bridge Street	B1
Iffley Road	C3
Juxon Street	A1
Keble Road	A2
Littlegate Street	C2
Longwall Street	B3
Magdalen Bridge	B3
Mansfield Road	A3
Merton Street	C2
Nelson Street	B1
New Road	B1
Oxpens Road	C1
Park End Street	B1
Parks Road	A2
Plantation Road	A1
Queen Street	B2
Rose Place	C2
St. Aldate's	C2
St. Bernards Road	A1
St. Cross Road	A3
St. Ebbe's Street	C2
St. Giles	A2
South Parks Road	A2
Speedwell Street	C2
Thames Street	B2
Turl Street	A1
Walton Crescent	A1
Walton Street	A1

TOURIST INFORMATION ☎ 01865 726871
15-16 BROAD STREET,
OXFORD, OX1 3AS

HOSPITAL A & E ☎ 01865 741166
JOHN RADCLIFFE HOSPITAL, HEADLEY WAY, HEADINGTON,
OXFORD, OX3 9DU

COUNCIL OFFICE ☎ 01865 249811
PO BOX 10,
OXFORD, OX1 1EN

Oxford *Oxon.* Population: 118,795. City, at confluence of Rivers Thames and Cherwell, 52m/84km NW of London. Began as Saxon settlement, flourished under Normans when it was chosen as royal residence. University dating from 13c, recognised as being among best in the world. Many notable buildings create spectacular skyline. Cathedral. Bodleian Library, second largest in UK. Ashmolean museum, oldest public museum in country. Tourist and commercial centre. Ancient St. Giles Fair held every September. Oxford Brookes University at Headington, 2m/4km E of city centre. Airport at Kidlington.

Area Code 01738

Perth & Kinross

PERTH

PERTH

N

0 — 300 yds

0 — 300m

To M.90

INDEX TO STREET NAMES

**TOURIST INFORMATION ☎ 01738 450600
LOWER CITY MILLS, WEST MILL STREET,
PERTH, PH1 5QP**

**HOSPITAL A & E ☎ 01738 623311
PERTH ROYAL INFIRMARY,
TAYMOUNT TERRACE, PERTH, PH1 1NX**

**COUNCIL OFFICE ☎ 01738 475000
PERTH & KINROSS COUNCIL,
2 HIGH STREET, PERTH, PH1 5PH**

Perth *P. & K.* Population: 41,453. City, ancient cathedral city (Royal Charter granted 1210) on River Tay, 31m/50km N of Edinburgh. Once capital of Medieval Scotland. Centre of livestock trade. Previously cotton manufacturing centre; now important industries include whisky distilling. St. John's Kirk founded 1126. 15c Balhousie Castle houses regimental headquarters and Museum of the Black Watch. Art Gallery and Museum. 16c Fair Maid's House. Gothic mansion Scone Palace 2m/3km N contains collections of furniture, needlework and porcelain with site of Coronation Stone of Destiny in its grounds. Airfield (Scone) to NE.

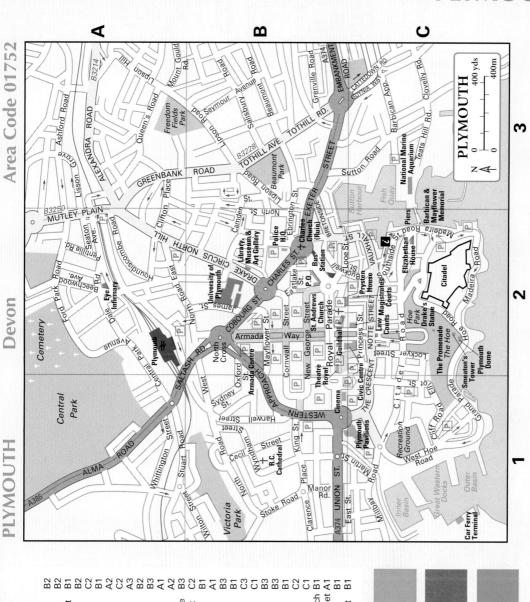

TOURIST INFORMATION ☎ 01752 264849
ISLAND HOUSE, 9 THE BARBICAN,
PLYMOUTH, PL1 2LS

HOSPITAL A & E ☎ 01752 777111
DERRIFORD HOSPITAL, DERRIFORD ROAD,
CROWNHILL, PLYMOUTH, PL6 8DH

COUNCIL OFFICE ☎ 01752 668000
CIVIC CENTRE, ARMADA WAY,
PLYMOUTH, PL1 2EW

Plymouth *Plym.* Population: 245,295. City, largest city in SW England, 100m/160km SW of Bristol. Port and naval base. Regional shopping centre. City centre rebuilt after bombing in World War II. Has strong commercial and naval tradition. In 1588 Sir Francis Drake sailed from Plymouth to defeat Spanish Armada. Captain Cook's voyages to Australia, South Seas and Antarctica all departed from here. University. Plymouth City Airport to N of city.

WEB-SITE www.plymouth.gov.uk

LOCAL RADIO BBC RADIO DEVON 103.4 FM
CLASSIC GOLD 1152 AM, PLYMOUTH SOUND FM 97 FM

Area Code 023

PORTSMOUTH

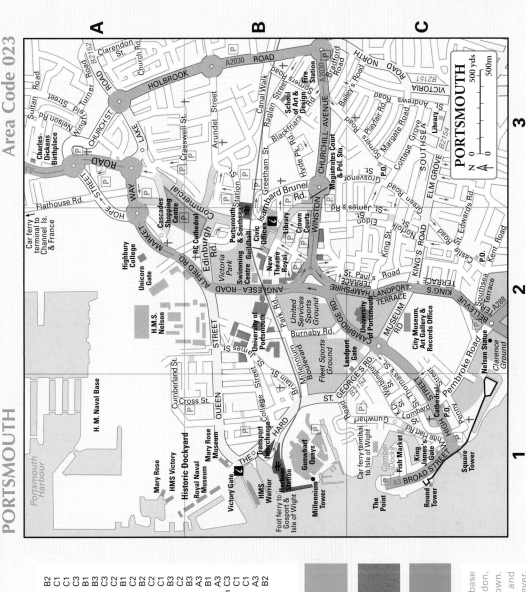

PORTSMOUTH

TOURIST INFORMATION ☎ 023 9282 6722
THE HARD,
PORTSMOUTH, PO1 3QJ

HOSPITAL A & E ☎ 023 9228 6000
QUEEN ALEXANDRA HOSPITAL, SOUTHWICK
HILL ROAD, COSHAM, PORTSMOUTH, PO6 3LY

COUNCIL OFFICE ☎ 023 9282 2251
CIVIC OFFICES, GUILDHALL SQUARE,
PORTSMOUTH, PO1 2BG

Portsmouth *Ports.* Population: 174,690. City, port and naval base (Portsmouth Harbour, on W side of city) 65m/105km SW of London, extending from S end of Portsea Island to S slopes of Ports Down. Various industries, including tourism, financial services and manufacturing. Partly bombed in World War II and now rebuilt; however, some 18c buildings remain. Boat and hovercraft ferries to Isle of Wight. University. Two cathedrals. Nelson's ship, HMS Victory, in harbour, alongside which are remains of Henry VIII's flagship, Mary Rose, which sank in 1545. King James's Gate and Landport Gate were part of 17c defences, and Fort Cumberland is 18c coastal defence at Eastney (all English Heritage). Royal Garrison Church (English Heritage) was 16c chapel prior to Dissolution. Museums, many with nautical theme.

WEB-SITE www.portsmouth.gov.uk

LOCAL RADIO
BBC RADIO SOLENT 96.1 FM
CAPITAL GOLD 1170 AM, OCEAN FM 97.5 FM, THE QUAY 107.4 FM, WAVE 105.2 FM

READING
MAIDENHEAD
WINDSOR
BRACKNELL
Wokingham
Woodley
Henley-on-Thames
Marlow
Wooburn
Burnham
Taplow
Cookham
Bourne End
Ascot
Sunninghill
Bagshot
Crowthorne
Sandhurst
Tilehurst
Theale
Pangbourne
Goring
Streatley
Wallingford
Cholsey
North Moreton
South Moreton
Aston Tirrold
Aston Upthorpe
Crowmarsh Gifford
Nettlebed
Nuffield
Hambleden
Skirmett
Stonor
Fawley
Medmenham
Hurley
Bisham
Wargrave
Twyford
Sonning
Caversham
Shinfield
Arborfield
Finchampstead
Eversley
Binfield
Winkfield
Warfield
Maiden's Green
Cranbourne
Burghfield
Mortimer
Stratfield Mortimer
Aldermaston
Padworth
Sulhamstead
Englefield
Bradfield
Yattendon
Upper Basildon
Ashampstead
Aldworth
Woodcote
Checkendon
Ipsden
Hailey
Moulsford
South Stoke
North Stoke
Cleeve
Whitchurch-on-Thames
Purley on Thames
Sulham
Calcot
Kidmore End
Sonning Common
Rotherfield Peppard
Rotherfield Greys
Greys Green
Lower Assendon
Middle Assendon
Bix
Maidensgrove
Park Corner
Highmoor Cross
Stoke Row
Exlade Street
Gallowstree Common
Cane End
Tokers Green
Mapledurham
Emmer Green
Shiplake
Lower Shiplake
Binfield Heath
Dunsden Green
Play Hatch
Sonning Eye
Earley
Lower Earley
Winnersh
Sindlesham
Hurst
Whistley Green
Ruscombe
Waltham St Lawrence
White Waltham
Littlewick Green
Knowl Hill
Warren Row
Crazies Hill
Cockpole Green
Burchett's Green
Hurley Bottom
Pinkneys Green
Furze Platt
Cookham Dean
Cookham Rise
Bray
Bray Wick
Holyport
Dorney
Boveney
Eton
Eton Wick
Clewer Village
Oakley Green
Fifield
Touchen-End
Hawthorn Hill
Shurlock Row
Paley Street
Woodlands Park
Newell Green
North Ascot
Winkfield Row
South Ascot
Windlesham
Lightwater
Popeswood
Easthampstead
Eastheath
Barkham
Arborfield Cross
Arborfield Garrison
Farley Hill
Swallowfield
Riseley
Beech Hill
Spencers Wood
Three Mile Cross
Grazeley
Wokefield Park
Whitley
Burghfield Common
Burghfield Hill
Sheffield Bottom
Ufton Nervet
Mortimer West End
Aldermaston Soke
Aldermaston Wharf
Beenham
Chapel Row
Midgham
Woolhampton
Wasing
Southend
Frilsham
Tidmarsh
Basildon Park (NT)
Beale Park
Mapledurham House & Mill
Museum of Reading
River & Rowing Mus
Dinton Pastures
Greys Court (NT)
Fawley Court
Stonor Park
Bisham Abbey N.S.C.
Cliveden (NT)
Burnham Beeches
Legoland
Windsor Forest
Look Out Discovery Park
Swallowfield Park
California
Wellington
Thames or Isis
Blackwater
Loddon
Pang
Chosley & Wallingford Rly
M4
M3
A404(M)
A329(M)
A404
A4
A4074
A4130
A4155
A321
A329
A330
A332
A3095
A3290
A322
A30
A33
A340
A417
A308
A327
A4094
B3024
B3018
B3034
B3030
B3349
B3430
B3348
B3031
B3270
B4009
B4526
B471
B481
B480
B4447
B3020
B3022
B386

READING

Area Code 0118

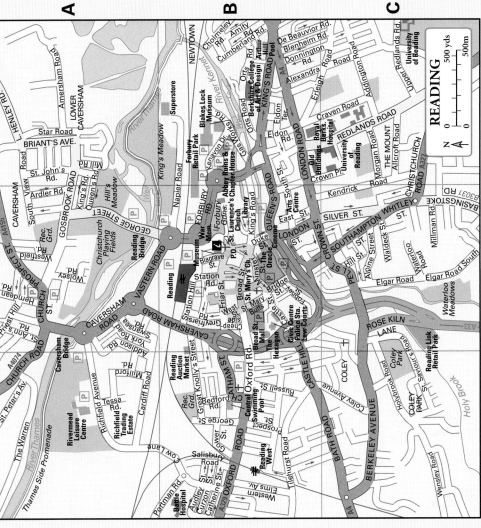

INDEX TO STREET NAMES

Addington Road	C3	Duke Street	B2	Priest Hill	A2
Addison Road	A1	East Street	A1	Prospect Street	A2
Alexandra Road	B3	Eldon Road	B3	Caversham	B3
Allcroft Road	C3	Eldon Terrace	B3	Prospect Street *Reading*	B1
Alpine Street	C2	Elgar Road	C2	Queen's Road	A2
Amersham Road	A3	Elgar Road South	C2	Caversham	
Amity Road	B1	Erleigh Road	B3	Queen's Road *Reading*	B2
Ardler Road	A2	Fobney Street	B2	Redlands Road	C3
Audley Street	B1	Forbury Road	B2	Richfield Avenue	A1
Basingstoke Road	C2	Friar Street	B2	Rose Kiln Lane	C2
Bath Road	C1	Gas Works Road	B2	Russell Street	B1
Bedford Road	B1	George Street	B3	St. Ann's Road	A2
Berkeley Avenue	C1	Caversham		St. John's Road	A3
Blagrave Street	B2	George Street *Reading*	B1	St. Mary's Butts	B2
Blenheim Road	B3	Gosbrook Road	A2	St. Peters Avenue	A1
Briant's Avenue	A3	Gower Street	B1	St. Saviour's Road	C1
Bridge Street	B2	Great Knollys Street	B2	Silver Street	C2
Broad Street	B2	Greyfriars Road	B2	South Street	B2
Cardiff Road	A1	Hemdean Road	A2	Southampton Street	C2
Castle Hill	C2	Hill Street	B2	South View Road	A2
Castle Street	B2	Holybrook Road	C1	Star Road	A3
Catherine Street	B1	Kenavon Drive	B2	Station Hill	B2
Caversham Road	B1	Kendrick Road	B3	Station Road	B2
Chatham Street	B1	King's Road *Caversham*	A2	Swansea Road	C2
Cheapside	B2	King's Road *Reading*	B2	Tessa Road	A1
Cholmeley Road	B3	London Road	B3	The Warren	A1
Christchurch Road	C2	London Street	B2	Tilehurst Road	B1
Church Road	A1	Lower Henley Road	A3	Upper Redlands Road	C3
Church Street	A2	Mill Road	A3	Vastern Road	A2
Coley Avenue	C1	Millford Road	A1	Waldeck Street	C2
Cow Lane	B1	Millman Road	C2	Waterloo Road	C2
Craven Road	C3	Minster Street	B2	Wensley Road	C1
Crown Place	B3	Morgan Road	B3	Western Elms Avenue	B1
Crown Street	C2	Napier Road	A2	Westfield Road	A2
Cumberland Road	B3	Orts Road	B2	West Street	B2
Curzon Street	B1	Oxford Road	B1	Whitley Street	C2
De Beauvoir Road	C2	Pell Street	C2	Wolsey Road	A2
Donnington Road	B3	Portman Road	A1	York Road	A1

TOURIST INFORMATION ☎ 0118 956 6226
TOWN HALL, BLAGRAVE STREET,
READING, RG1 1QH

HOSPITAL A & E ☎ 0118 987 5111
ROYAL BERKSHIRE HOSPITAL, LONDON ROAD,
READING, RG1 5AN

COUNCIL OFFICE ☎ 0118 939 0900
CIVIC CENTRE, CIVIC OFFICES, (OFF CASTLE ST.)
READING, RG1 7TD

Reading *Read.* Population: 213,474. Town, county and industrial town and railway centre on River Thames, 36m/58km W of London. During Victorian times Reading was an important manufacturing town, particularly for biscuit-making and brewing. University. Remains of Norman abbey, founded by Henry I who lies buried there.

WEB-SITE www.reading.gov.uk

LOCAL RADIO BBC RADIO BERKSHIRE 104.4 FM
CLASSIC GOLD 1431 AM, 2-TEN FM 97 FM

Area Code 01722

Wiltshire

SALISBURY

SALISBURY

N
0   200 yds
0   200m

TOURIST INFORMATION ☎ 01722 334956
FISH ROW,
SALISBURY, SP1 1EJ

HOSPITAL A & E ☎ 01722 336262
SALISBURY DISTRICT HOSPITAL, ODSTOCK ROAD,
SALISBURY, SP2 8BJ

COUNCIL OFFICE ☎ 01722 336272
THE COUNCIL HOUSE, BOURNE HILL,
SALISBURY, SP1 3UZ

Salisbury *(Former and official name New Sarum) Wilts.* Population: 39,268. Cathedral city at confluence of Rivers Avon and Nadder, 21m/34km NW of Southampton. Shopping centre and market town, with buildings ranging from medieval to Victorian; several medieval churches. Cathedral, in Early English style, built between 1220 and 1260, has the tallest spire in England at 123m/404ft.

WEB-SITE   www.salisbury.gov.uk

LOCAL RADIO   BBC WILTSHIRE SOUND 103.5 FM, 1368 AM
SPIRE FM 102 FM

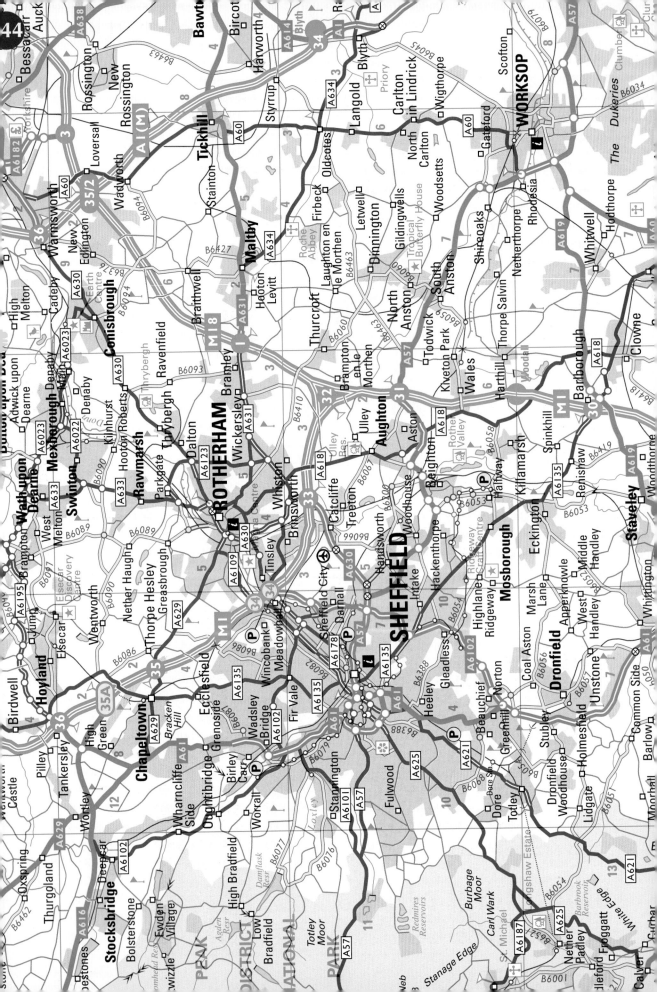

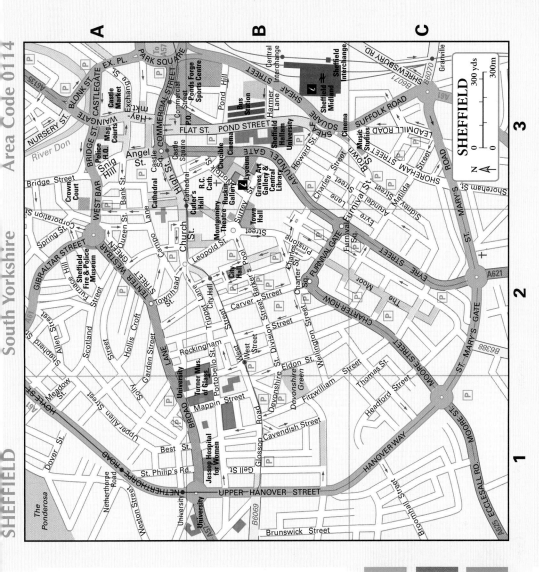

SHEFFIELD

0   300 yds
0   300m

N

INDEX TO STREET NAMES

Allen Street	A2	Eyre Street	A2	Portobello Street	B1
Angel Street	A3	Fitzwilliam Street	A3	Queen Street	A2
Arundel Gate	B3	Flat Street	B3	Rockingham Street	B2
Arundel Street	C2	Furnace Hill	A2	St. Mary's Gate	C2
Bank Street	A3	Furnival Gate	B2	St. Mary's Road	C2
Barker's Pool	B2	Furnival Square	B2	St. Philip's Road	A1
Best Street	A1	Furnival Street	B2	Scotland Street	A2
Blonk Street	A3	Garden Street	A2	Sheaf Square	B3
Bridge Street	A3	Gell Street	A1	Sheaf Street	B3
Broad Lane	B1	Gibraltar Street	A2	Shepherd Street	A2
Broomhall Street	C1	Glossop Road	B1	Shoreham Street	C3
Brown Street	C3	Hanover Way	C1	Shrewsbury Road	C3
Brunswick Street	B1	Harmer Lane	B3	Sidney Street	C2
Campo Lane	A2	Haymarket	A3	Snig Hill	A3
Carver Lane	B2	Headford Street	C1	Solly Street	A1
Castle Square	A3	High Street	A3	Spring Street	A2
Castlegate	A3	Hollis Croft	A2	Suffolk Road	C3
Cavendish Street	B1	Howard Street	B3	Surrey Street	B2
Charles Street	B2/B3	Hoyle Street	A1	Tenter Street	A2
Charter Row	C2	Leadmill Road	C3	The Moor	C2
Charter Square	B2	Leopold Street	B2	Thomas Street	C1
Church Street	A2	Mappin Street	B1	Townhead Street	A2
Commercial Street	A3	Matilda Street	C3	Trippet Lane	B2
Corporation Street	A2	Meadow Street	A1	Upper Allen Street	A1
Devonshire Street	B1	Moore Street	C1	Upper Hanover Street	B1
Division Street	B2	Netherthorpe Road	A1	Waingate	A3
Dover Street	A1	Norfolk Street	B3	Wellington Street	B2
Ecclesall Road	C1	Nursery Street	A3	West Bar	A2
Eldon Street	B2	Pinstone Street	B2	West Street	B2
Exchange Street	A3	Pond Hill	A3	Westbar Green	B1
Eyre Lane	C2	Pond Street	B3	Weston Street	A1

TOURIST INFORMATION ☎ 0114 221 1900
1 TUDOR SQUARE,
SHEFFIELD, S1 2LA

HOSPITAL A & E ☎ 0114 243 4343
NORTHERN GENERAL HOSPITAL, HERRIES ROAD,
SHEFFIELD, S5 7AU

COUNCIL OFFICE ☎ 0114 272 6444
FIRST POINT, 1 UNION STREET,
SHEFFIELD, S1 2LA

WEB-SITE   www.sheffield.gov.uk

LOCAL RADIO   BBC RADIO SHEFFIELD 88.6 FM
MAGIC AM, SOUTH YORKSHIRE 1548 AM, HALLAM FM 97.4 FM

Sheffield *S.Yorks.* Population: 431,607. City, on River Don, 144m/232km NW of London. Former centre of heavy steel industry, now largely precision steel and cutlery industries. University of Sheffield and Sheffield Hallam University. Various museums dedicated to Sheffield's industrial past. National Centre for Popular Music in city centre. Meadowhall shopping centre and Sheffield City Airport, 3m/5km NE of city centre.

Area Code 023

SOUTHAMPTON

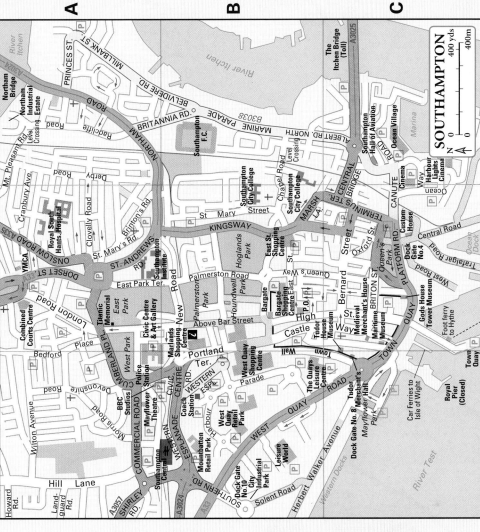

TOURIST INFORMATION ☎ 023 8022 1106
9 CIVIC CENTRE ROAD,
SOUTHAMPTON, SO14 7LP

HOSPITAL A & E ☎ 023 8077 7222
SOUTHAMPTON GENERAL HOSPITAL, TREMONA RD,
SHIRLEY, SOUTHAMPTON, SO16 6YD

COUNCIL OFFICE ☎ 023 8083 3333
CIVIC CENTRE, CIVIC CENTRE ROAD,
SOUTHAMPTON, SO14 7LY

Southampton *S'ham*. Population: 210,138. City, at confluence of Rivers Itchen and Test at head of Southampton Water, 70m/113km SW of London. Southern centre for business, culture and recreation. Container and transatlantic passenger port, dealing with 7 percent of UK's seaborne trade. Site of many famous departures: Henry V's army bound for Agincourt; the Pilgrim Fathers sailed to America on the Mayflower in 1620; maiden voyage of Queen Mary and only voyage of Titanic. Remains of medieval town walls. Medieval Merchant's House (English Heritage) has authentically recreated furnishings. Boat and helicopter ferries to Isle of Wight. Host to many international boating events including Southampton International Boat Show, Whitbread Round the World, and BT Global Challenge. University. Southampton International Airport 1m/2km S of Eastleigh.

WEB-SITE www.southampton.gov.uk

LOCAL RADIO
BBC RADIO SOLENT 96.1 FM
CAPITAL GOLD 1557 AM, POWER FM 103.2 FM, SOUTH CITY 107.8 FM, WAVE 105.2 FM

A533 Bradwall Green A50 A534 CONGLETON Key Green Timbersbrook Heaton Rushton Spencer

Elworth Arclid Hightown Bridestones Meerbro
Sandbach Sta. Brookhouse Green Astbury Newtown Rudyard Resr
Sandbach Spen Green Brownlow Heath Gillow Heath Biddulph Grange Garden Rudyard Lake A523 8

Hassall Green Fourlanes End Little Moreton Hall Biddulph Moor
Wheelock Scholar Green Brown Lees Knypersley Biddulph Horton Rudyard
Winterley Hassall Rode Heath A34 Mow Cop Greenway Bank Blackwood Hill Longsdon Leek
CREWE M6 Alsager Church Lawton Harriseahead Brown Edge A53 Horse Bri
Haslington A50 Kidsgrove Newchapel Brindley Ford Endon Stanley A5
Hardings Wood Norton in the Moors Baddeley Green Deep Hayes
A5020 Radway Green A533 Butt Lane Goldenhill Bagnall Wetley Rocks
Barthomley Coalpit Hill Talke Tunstall Smallthorne Milton Bas Gr
Weston Engleseabrook A500 Butters Green Ceramica Burslem A5009 Cons A520
Chorlton Balterley Audley Red Street A527 A5272 Abbey Hulton Werrington A522 Cellarhead
Halmer End Chesterton W.Moore Hanley Bucknall
Betley Alsagers Bank NEWCASTLE-UNDER-LYME STOKE-ON-TRENT A52 A520
A51 Wrinehill A531 Leycett Silverdale A5271 Parkhall
Blakenhall B5044 A5272 Weston Coyney Dilho
Checkley Madeley Heath Keele A525 Keele A519 Fenton Cookshill Caverswall
Madeley A53 Clayton A50 Longton Foxfield Lt. Rly A521
Woore A525 Onneley Whitmore Hall Hanford Meir Blythe Bridge Forsb
Pipe Gate Aston Whitmore A5182 A500 Hanford Lightwood Blythe Ma
Knighton Dorothy Clive Garden Hanchurch A5035 Trentham A5005 B5029
A51 Baldwin's Gate Knowl Wall Rough Close Meirheath Cresswell
Blackbrook Hill Chorlton Barlaston Fulford
Mucklestone Stableford The Rowe Tittensor Moddershall Middleton
A53 Maer Chapel Chorlton Beech Wedgwood Visitor Cen B5066 Hilderstone Garsh
Ashley Cranberry A519 A51 Oulton Cotwalton
Loggerheads Podmore Swynnerton Aston-by-Stone Milwich
Blore Heath 1459 Hookgate Cotes M6 Stone Burston B5066 Fradsw
Chatcull Standon Walton B5027 A34 Sandon A51
Almington Croxtonbank Millmeece Stafford A51 Gayton
Hales Wetwood Slindon Yarnfield B5066 Hopton Heath 1643
Fairoak Croxton B5026 Sturbridge Norton Bridge Yarlet Salt
Chipnall Sugnall Pershall Chebsey Whitgreave Marston
Cheswardine Outlands Bishop's Offley Cop Mere Eccleshall A5013 Little Bridgeford Great Bridgeford Ancient High House Hopton A513
Soudley Knighton Adbaston Wootton Shire Hall Gallery Tixall
eywood Knighton Reservoir High Offley Ellenhall B5405 A518 Ingestre
Ellerton Shebdon Woodseaves Seighford STAFFORD
Sambrook Weston Jones Norbury Lawnhead Ranton Coton Clanford A518
A41 Pickstock A519 Derrington

Area Code 01782

STOKE-ON-TRENT

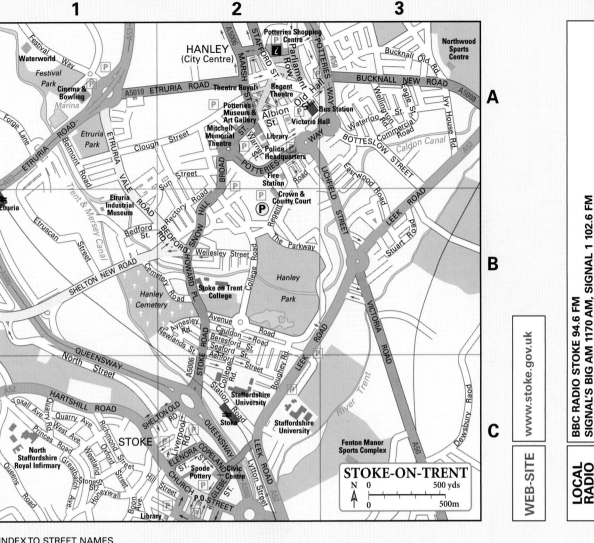

STOKE-ON-TRENT

N 0 .... 500 yds

0 .... 500m

WEB-SITE www.stoke.gov.uk

LOCAL RADIO

BBC RADIO STOKE 94.6 FM
SIGNAL'S BIG AM 1170 AM, SIGNAL 1 102.6 FM

INDEX TO STREET NAMES

**TOURIST INFORMATION ☎ 01782 236000
POTTERIES SHOPPING CENTRE, QUADRANT RD,
STOKE-ON-TRENT, ST1 1RZ**

**HOSPITAL A & E ☎ 01782 715444
NORTH STAFFORDSHIRE ROYAL INFIRMARY,
PRINCE'S ROAD, STOKE-ON-TRENT, ST4 7LN**

**COUNCIL OFFICE ☎ 01782 234567
TOWN HALL, CIVIC CENTRE, GLEBE STREET,
STOKE-ON-TRENT, ST4 1RN**

Stoke-on-Trent *Stoke* Population: 266,543. City, on River Trent, 135m/217km NW of London. Centre for employment, shopping and leisure. Created by an amalgamation of former Stoke-upon-Trent and the towns of Burslem, Fenton, Hanley, Longton and Tunstall in 1910. Capital of The Potteries (largest claywear producer in the world), now largely a finishing centre for imported pottery. Many pottery factories open to public including Wedgewood, Royal Doulton and Spode. Potteries Museum in Hanley charts history of the potteries. Gladstone Pottery Museum in Longton is centred around large bottle-kiln and demonstrates traditional skills of pottery production. Staffordshire University.

ROYAL LEAMINGTON SPA
Warwick
Stratford-upon-Avon
REDDITCH
Alcester
Evesham
VALE OF EVESHAM

Eathorpe
Cubbington
Hunningham
Offchurch
Radford Semele
Ufton
Knightcote
Burton Dassett Hills
Sor Brook
Horley
Hornton
Horley
Wroxton
Balscote

Whitnash
Bishop's Tachbrook
Chesterton Green
Bishop's Itchington
Harbury
Warwick
Gaydon
Northend
Edgehill
Ratley
Middle Tysoe
Shenington
Alkerton

Old Milverton
Leek Wootton
Lord Leycester Hospital
Warwickshire County Mus
Longbridge
Barford
Ashorne
Moreton Morrell
Wellesbourne
Lighthorne
Heritage Motor Centre
Chadshunt
Kineton
Little Kineton
Butlers Marston
Pillerton Hersey
Pillerton Priors
Oxhill
Lower Tysoe
Upper Tysoe
Whatcote
Idlicote
Honington
Tredington

Hatton
Haseley
Shrewley
Budbrooke
Hampton on the Hill
Norton Lindsey
Sherbourne
Wasperton
Hampton Lucy
Charlecote
Charlecote Park (NT)
Alveston
Tiddington
Loxley
Walton
Ettington
Fulready
Halford
Alderminster
Fosse Way
Stour

Rowington
Pinley Green
Preston Bagot
Claverdon
Langley
Edstone
Bearley
Snitterfield
Ingon
Shottery
Anne Hathaway's Cottage
Shakespeare's Birthplace
Clifford Chambers
Atherstone on Stour
Preston on Stour
Newbold on Stour
Armscote
Blackwell
Darlingscott

Henley-in-Arden
Wootton Wawen
Little Alne
Aston Cantlow
Mary Arden's House
Wilmcote
Walcote
Billesley
Red Hill
Temple Grafton
Ardens Grafton
Luddington
Dorsington
Long Marston
Wimpstone
Lower Quinton
Upper Quinton
Mickleton
Ilmington
Meon Hill
Kiftsgate Court
Hidcote Manor (NT)
Broad Marston
Honeybourne
Weston

Tanworth in Arden
Danzey Sta.
Gorcott Hill
Ullenhall
Oldberrow
Beaudesert
Morton Bagot
Great Alne
Haselor
Dovecote (NT)
Coughton Court (NT)
King's Coughton
Ragley Hall
Arrow
Oversley Green
Exhall
Wixford
Broom
Bidford-on-Avon
Barton
Cleeve Prior
North Littleton
Middle Littleton
South Littleton
Bretforton
Badsey

Beoley End
Mappleborough Green
Studley
Studley Common
New End
Sambourne
Cookhill
Weethley
Dunnington
Iron Cross
Salford Priors
Abbots Salford
Harvington
Norton
Aldington
Offenham
Evesham Country Park Shopping & Garden Centre

Gorcott Hill
Hunt End
Wood Bank
Abbots Morton
Rous Lench
Atch Lench
Church Lench

A423 A425 A452 A425 A445 A453 A46 A4177 A429
M40 A46 A439 A3400 A46 A422 A429 A435 A441 A4189
A4023 A448 B4497 B4090 B4088 A46 A4184 A435 A4090
B4085 B4510 B4088 B4081 B4100 B4086 B4455 B4451 B4100 A4100

STRATFORD-UPON-AVON Warwickshire Area Code 01789

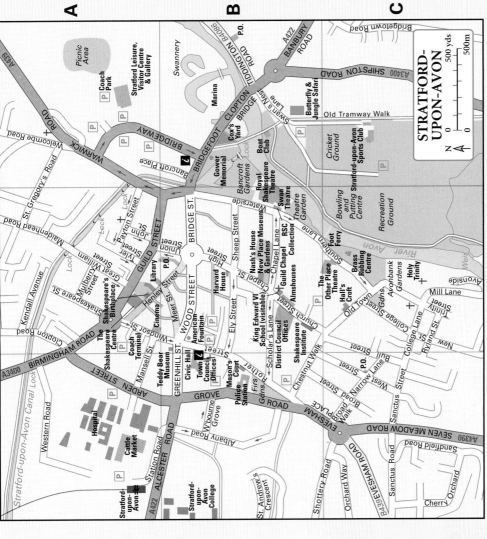

STRATFORD-
UPON-AVON

N

0 500 yds
0 500m

TOURIST INFORMATION ☎ 01789 293127
BRIDGEFOOT,
STRATFORD-UPON-AVON, CV37 6GW

HOSPITAL A & E ☎ 01926 495321
WARWICK HOSPITAL, WAKIN ROAD,
WARWICK, CV34 5BW

COUNCIL OFFICE ☎ 01789 267575
COUNCIL OFFICES, ELIZABETH HOUSE,
CHURCH ST, STRATFORD-UPON-AVON, CV37 6HX

WEB-SITE www.stratford.gov.uk

LOCAL RADIO BBC RADIO COVENTRY & WARWICKSHIRE 94.8 & 103.7 FM
102 FM - THE BEAR 102 FM

Stratford-upon-Avon (Also called Stratford-on-Avon.) *Warks.* Population: 22,231. Town, on River Avon, 8m/13km SW of Warwick. Tourist centre. Many attractive 16c buildings. Reconstructed Shakespeare's Birthplace. Elizabethan garden at New Place. Hall's Croft Eizabethan town house and doctor's dispensary. Royal Shakespeare Theatre. Shakespeare's grave at Holy Trinity Church. Anne Hathaway's Cottage to W, at Shottery.

SOUTH SHIELDS
SUNDERLAND
SEAHAM
Peterlee
Horden
Easington Colliery
Easington
Little Thorpe
Turning the Tide
Nose's Point
Dene Mouth
Cold Hesledon
Dalton-le-Dale
Seaton
Hawthorn
Murton
South Hetton
HOUGHTON LE SPRING
Hetton-le-Hole
Haswell
Ludworth
Shotton
Easington Lane
Littletown
Pittington
Shadforth
Sherburn
Carrville
Shincliffe
DURHAM
Cathedral
Neville's Cross 1346
Framwellgate Moor
Pity Me
Finchale
Sacriston
Witton Gilbert
Bearpark
Ushaw Moor
Esh Winning
Waterhouses
Quebec
Esh
Langley Park
Cornsay Colliery
Cornsay
Satley
Butsfield
Lanchester
Lanchester Valley Walk
Greencroft
Iveston
Leadgate
CONSETT
Delves
Medomsley
Dipton
Ebchester
Derwent Walk
STANLEY
Annfield Plain
South Moor
Tantobie
Tanfield
Burnopfield
Hobson
Rowlands Gill
Highfield
Lintzford
Chopwell
High Spen
Hamsterley
Marley Hill
Sunniside
Gibside Chapel (NT)
Beamish
Beamish Open Air Museum
Grange Villa
CHESTER-LE-STREET
Pelton
Ouston
Newfield
Waldridge
Waldridge Fell
Edmondsley
Kimblesworth
Plawsworth
Craghead
Holmside
Burnhope
Maiden Law
Great Lumley
Lumley
Fence Houses
Bournmoor
Colliery Row
West Rainton
East Rainton
Herrington
Penshaw
Fatfield
Shiney Row
WASHINGTON
Birtley
Angel of the North
Springwell
Wrekenton
Lamesley
Kibblesworth
Team Valley
GATESHEAD
FELLING
Pelaw
Dunston
Metrocentre
Swalwell
WHICKHAM
Winlaton
Winlaton Mill
Blaydon
Ryton
Stella
Greenside
Barlow
Crawcrook
Prudhoe
NEWCASTLE UPON TYNE
Gosforth
Kenton
Blakelaw
Jesmond
Heaton
Byker
Walker
Wallsend
Longbenton
Willington
Newburn
Wallbottle
Lemington
Throckley
Heddon-on-the-Wall
Stephenson's Birthplace
Hebburn
Jarrow
Monkton
Bede's World
BOLDON
East Boldon
West Boldon
Cleadon
Harton
Marsden
Marsden Bay
Whitburn
Whitburn Bay
Roker
Fulwell
Monkwearmouth
National Glass Centre
Southwick
Castletown
South Hylton
Hendon
New Silksworth
Silksworth
Ryhope
A1(M)
A19
A194(M)
A690
A182
A183
A1231
A167
A692
A693
A691
A1018
A184
A186
A187
A188
A189
A191
A694
A695
A696
A69
A6076
B6532
B6313
B6301
B6296
B6168
B1283
B1285
B1284
B1286
B1280
B1432
B1404
B1405
B1296
B1426
B6528
B6315
B6310

Tyne & Wear

Area Code 0191

SUNDERLAND

SUNDERLAND

N

0   400 yds
0   400m

INDEX TO STREET NAMES

TOURIST INFORMATION ☎ 0191 553 2000
50 FAWCETT STREET, SUNDERLAND, SR1 1RF

HOSPITAL A & E ☎ 0191 565 6256
SUNDERLAND DISTRICT GENERAL HOSPITAL,
KAYLL ROAD, SUNDERLAND, SR4 7TP

COUNCIL OFFICE ☎ 0191 553 1000
SUNDERLAND CITY COUNCIL, CIVIC CENTRE, BURDON ROAD
SUNDERLAND, SR2 7DN

Sunderland *T. & W.* Population 183,310. Industrial city and seaport at mouth of River Wear, 11m/17km SE of Newcastle upon Tyne. Previously largest ship-building town in the world; coal mining was also important. Several museums celebrate city's industrial past. Service sector and manufacturing account for largest contribution to local economy. National Glass Centre commemorates importance of stained glass to area. University. Airport 4m/6km W.

WEB-SITE www.sunderland.gov.uk

LOCAL RADIO
BBC RADIO NEWCASTLE 95.4 FM, 1458 AM
SUN FM 103.4 FM

Area Code 01792

SWANSEA

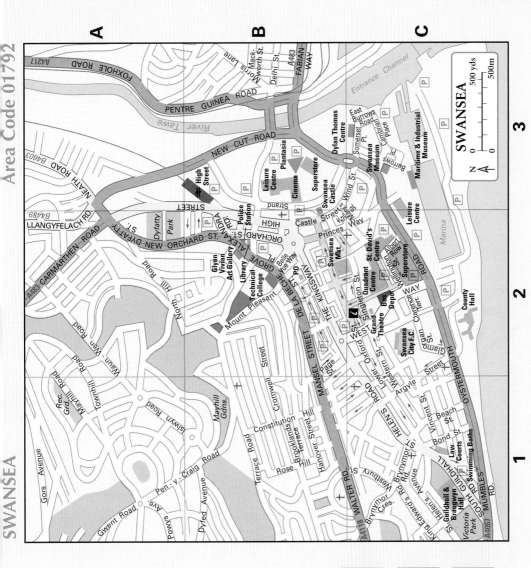

INDEX TO STREET NAMES

Albert Row	C2	Gors Avenue	A1
Alexandra Road	B2	Grove Place	B2
Argyle Street	C1	Gwent Road	A1
Beach Street	C1	Hanover Street	B1
Belle Vue Way	B2	High Street	B2
Bond Street	C1	Islwyn Road	A1
Brooklands Terrace	B1	King Edward's Road	C1
Brynymor Crescent	C1	Llangyfelach Road	A2
Brynymor Road	C1	Lower Oxford Street	C1
Burrows Place	C3	Mackworth Street	B3
Cambrian Place	C3	Mansel Street	B1
Carmarthen Road	A2	Mayhill Road	A1
Castle Street	B2	Morris Lane	B3
Clarence Terrace	C2	Mount Pleasant	B2
Constitution Hill	B1	Mumbles Road	C1
Cromwell Street	B1	Neath Road	A3
De La Beche Street	B2	New Cut Road	B3
Delhi Street	B3	New Orchard Street	C1
Dyfatty Street	A2	North Hill Road	A2
Dyfed Avenue	B1	Orchard Street	B2
East Burrows Road	C3	Oystermouth Road	C1
Fabian Way	B3		
Foxhole Road	A3		
Glamorgan Street	C2		

Page Street	B2	Strand	B3
Pentre Guinea Road	A3	Terrace Road	B1
Pen-y-Craig Road	A1	The Kingsway	B2
Powys Avenue	A1	Townhill Road	A1
Princess Way	B2	Vincent Street	C1
Rose Hill	B1	Walter Road	C1
St. Helen's Avenue	C1	Waun-Wen Road	A2
St. Helen's Road	C1	Wellington Street	C2
St. Mary Street	B2	Westbury Street	C1
Singleton Street	C2	Western Street	C1
Somerset Place	C3	West Way	C2
South Guildhall Road	C1		

TOURIST INFORMATION ☎ 01792 468321
WESTWAY,
SWANSEA, SA1 3QG

HOSPITAL A & E ☎ 01792 702222
MORRISTON HOSPITAL, MORRISTON,
SWANSEA, SA6 6NL

COUNCIL OFFICE ☎ 01792 636000
COUNTY HALL, OYSTERMOUTH ROAD,
SWANSEA, SA1 3SN

Swansea (Abertawe). Population: 171,038. City, port on Swansea Bay at mouth of River Tawe, and Wales' second city, 35m/57km W of Cardiff. Settlement developed next to Norman castle built in 1099, but claims made that a Viking settlement existed before this date. Previously a port for local metal smelting industries. Bombed in World War II, and city centre rebuilt. Birthplace of Dylan Thomas, who described it as 'an ugly, lovely town'. Remains of 14c castle (Cadw) or fortified manor house. University of Wales. Tropical plant and wildlife leisure centre, Plantasia. Airport 5m/9km W at Fairwood Common.

WEB-SITE www.swansea.gov.uk

LOCAL RADIO
BBC RADIO WALES 93.9 FM
SWANSEA SOUND 1170 AM

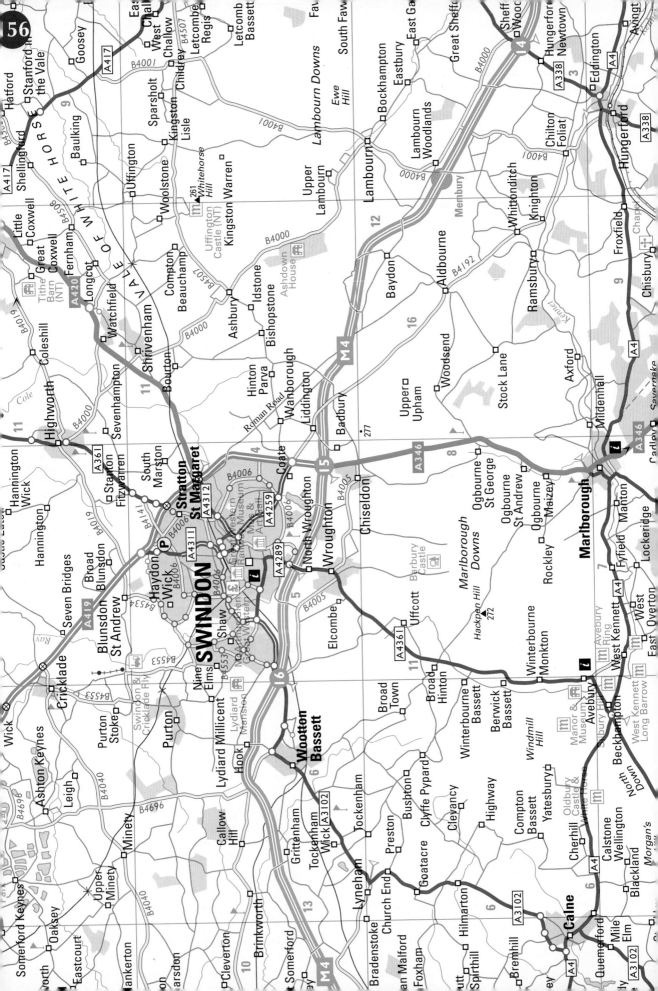

Area Code 01793

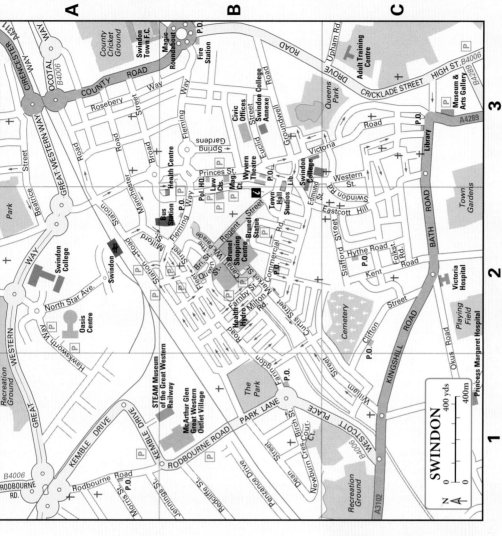

TOURIST INFORMATION ☎ 01793 530328
37 REGENT STREET,
SWINDON, SN1 1JL

HOSPITAL A & E ☎ 01793 604105
THE GREAT WESTERN HOSPITAL, MARLBOROUGH ROAD,
SWINDON, SN3 6BB

COUNCIL OFFICE ☎ 01793 463000
CIVIC OFFICES, EUCLID STREET,
SWINDON, SN1 2JH

Swindon *Swin.* Population: 145,236. Town, industrial and commercial centre, 70m/113km W of London. Large, modern shopping centre. Town expanded considerably in 19c with arrival of the railway. The Museum of the Great Western Railway exhibits Swindon built locomotives and documents the history of the railway works.

WEB-SITE www.swindon.gov.uk

LOCAL RADIO BBC WILTSHIRE SOUND 103.6 FM
CLASSIC GOLD 1161 AM, GWR FM 97.2 FM

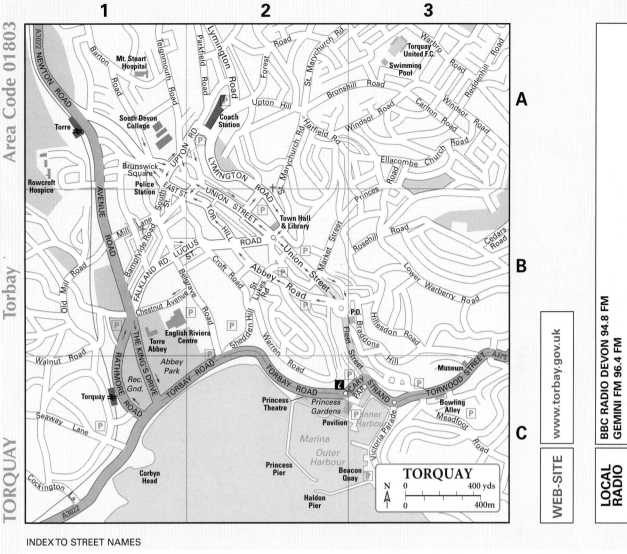

TORQUAY

N

| 0 | | 400 yds |
| 0 | | 400m |

Area Code 01803

Torbay

TORQUAY

www.torbay.gov.uk

WEB-SITE

BBC RADIO DEVON 94.8 FM
GEMINI FM 96.4 FM

LOCAL RADIO

INDEX TO STREET NAMES

TOURIST INFORMATION ☎ 01803 297428
VAUGHAN PARADE,
TORQUAY, TQ2 5JG

HOSPITAL A & E ☎ 01803 614567
TORBAY HOSPITAL, NEWTON ROAD,
TORQUAY, TQ2 7AA

COUNCIL OFFICE ☎ 01803 201201
TOWN HALL, CASTLE CIRCUS,
TORQUAY, TQ1 3DR

Torquay *Torbay* Population: 59,587. Town, 18m/30km S of Exeter. Chief town and resort of Torbay English Riviera district, with harbour and several beaches. Noted for mild climate. Torre Abbey with 15c gatehouse, is a converted monastery housing a collecion of furniture and glassware. Torquay Museum has display on crimewriter Agatha Christie born in Torquay. Kent's Cavern showcaves are an important prehistoric site. Babbacombe Model village 2m/3km N.

WATFORD
Hertfordshire
Area Code 01923

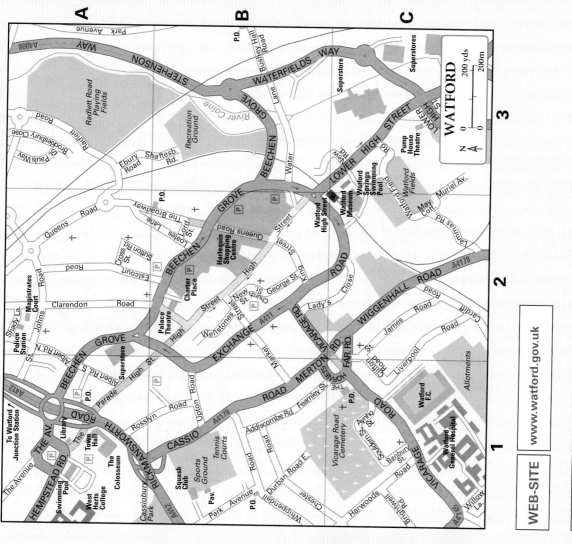

INDEX TO STREET NAMES

Street	Grid
Addiscombe Road	B1
Albert Road North	A1
Albert Road South	A1
Aynho Street	C1
Banbury Street	C1
Beechen Grove	A1/B3
Brightwell Road	C1
Brocklesbury Close	A3
Bushey Hall Road	B3
Cardiff Road	C2
Cassio Road	B1
Chester Road	B1
Church Street	B2
Clarendon Road	A2
Clifton Road	C1
Cross Street	A2
Durban Road East	B1
Ebury Road	A3
Estcourt Road	A2
Exchange Road	B1

Street	Grid
Farraline Road	C1
Fearnley Street	B1
George Street	B2
Harwoods Road	C1
Hempsted Road	A1
High Street	A1/B2
King Street	B2
Lady's Close	B2
Lammas Road	C2
Liverpool Road	C1
Loates Lane	B2
Lord Street	B2
Lower High Street	C3
Market Street	C2
May Cottages	B1
Merton Road	B1
Muriel Avenue	B2
New Road	C3
New Street	B2
Park Avenue	A3
Park Avenue	B1
Queens Road	A2/B2
Radlett Road	A3
Rickmansworth Road	B1

Street	Grid
Rosslyn Road	A1
Shaftesbury Road	A3
Souldern Street	C1
St. James Road	C2
St. Johns Road	A1
St. Pauls Way	A3
Stephenson Way	B3
Sutton Road	A2
The Avenue	A1
The Broadway	B2
The Hornets	C1
The Parade	B2
Upton Road	A1
Vicarage Road	C1/B2
Water Lane	B3
Waterfields Way	B3
Watford	C2
Field Road	
Wellstones	B2
Whippendell Road	B1
Wiggenhall Road	C2
Willow Lane	C1

TOURIST INFORMATION ☎ 01727 864511
TOWN HALL, MARKET PLACE,
ST ALBANS, AL3 5DJ

HOSPITAL A & E ☎ 01923 244366
WATFORD GENERAL HOSPITAL, VICARAGE ROAD,
WATFORD, WD1 8HB

COUNCIL OFFICE ☎ 01923 226400
WATFORD COUNCIL, TOWN HALL,
WATFORD, WD17 3EX

Watford *Herts.* Population: 113,080. Old market town on River Colne, 16m/26km NW of London. Printing and brewing developed as the main industries; now the industrial base is more diverse. Shopping and leisure centre with modern sculptures in redeveloped central area. Parish church of Saint Mary's has 16c chapel. Local history museum housed in Georgian house. Edwardian Palace Theatre originally opened as a music hall in 1908.

WEB-SITE www.watford.gov.uk

LOCAL RADIO
BBC THREE COUNTIES RADIO 103.8 FM, 1161 AM
MERCURY 96.6 FM

WATFORD
0 200 yds
0 200m

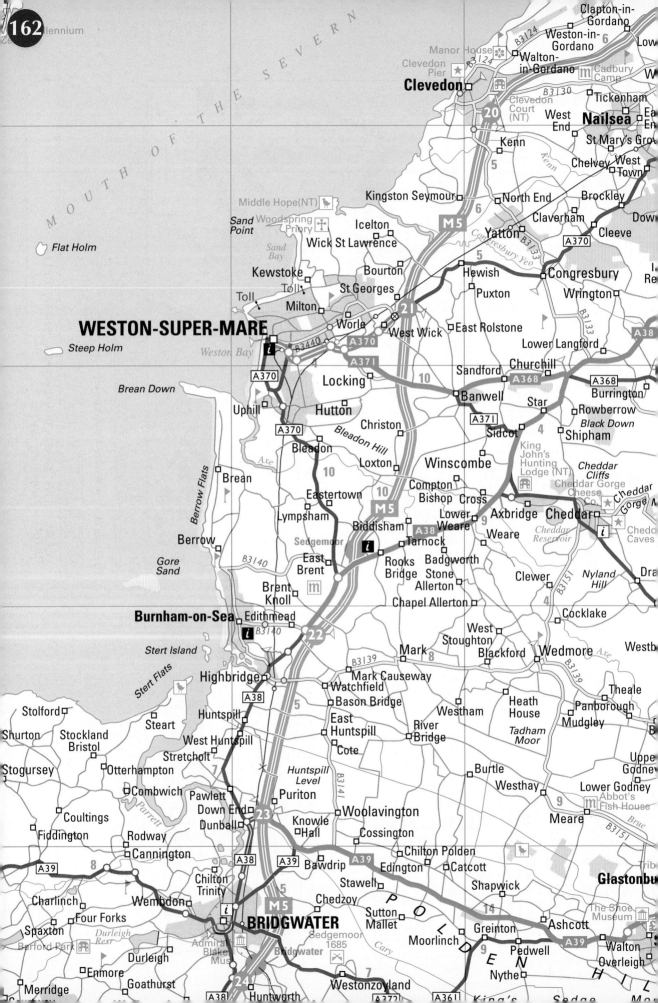

MOUTH OF THE SEVERN

Flat Holm

Steep Holm

Millennium

Clevedon
Manor House
Clevedon Pier
Clevedon Court (NT)

Clapton-in-Gordano
Weston-in-Gordano
Walton-in-Gordano
Cadbury Camp

B3124

20

West End
Kenn

Tickenham
Nailsea
St Mary's Gro
Chelvey West Town
Brockley
Dow

Kingston Seymour
North End
Claverham
Cleeve

Middle Hope(NT)
Sand Point
Woodspring Priory

Icelton
Hewish
Puxton

Yatton
Congresbury
Wrington

A370

B3133

Sand Bay
Wick St Lawrence
Bourton

M5

Congresbury Yeo

A38

Kewstoke
Toll
St Georges
Milton

Worle
West Wick
East Rolstone
Lower Langford

21

B3124

WESTON-SUPER-MARE
Weston Bay
B3440
A370

A371

Sandford
Churchill
Burrington

A368

A368

Locking
Banwell
Star
Rowberrow

A371

Brean Down

Uphill
Hutton
Christon
Sidcot
Shipham

Black Down

A370

Bleadon
Bleadon Hill
Loxton

Winscombe
King John's Hunting Lodge (NT)
Cheddar Cliffs
Cheddar Gorge Cheese Co.

Cheddar
Gorge

Axe

Brean
Eastertown

Compton Bishop
Axbridge

Cheddar Reservoir

Chedd
Caves

Berrow Flats

Lympsham

M5

Biddisham
A38

Lower Weare
Weare
Clewer
Nyland Hill
Dra

Berrow

East Brent

Tarnock
Rooks Bridge
Badgworth
Stone
Allerton

Gore Sand

B3140

Brent Knoll

Chapel Allerton
Cocklake

22

Burnham-on-Sea
Edithmead
B3140

West Stoughton
Blackford
Wedmore

Axe

Stert Island

Mark
B3139

Westb

Stert Flats

Highbridge

A38

Mark Causeway
Watchfield
Bason Bridge

Westham
Heath House
Theale
Panborough
Mudgley

Stolford
Shurton
Stockland Bristol
Stogursey

Huntspill
West Huntspill
Stretcholt

East Huntspill
Cote

River Bridge

Tadham Moor

Uppe
Godne

Combwich
Otterhampton
Pawlett
Down End
Dunball

Puriton
B3141

Burtle
Westhay
Lower Godney

Abbot's Fish House

Meare
B3151

Brue

Coultings
Rodway
Cannington

Fiddington

A39

23

Knowle Hall
Cossington

Woolavington

Chilton Polden
Edington
Catcott
Shapwick

Ashcott

Glastonbu

The Shoe Museum

Charlinch
Wembdon
Chilton Trinity

Bawdrip
Stawell

A39

A38
A39
A39

Greinton
Pedwell
Walton
Overleigh

P O L D E N

Four Forks
Spaxton
Barford Park

M5

BRIDGWATER
Admiral Blake Mus
Bridgwater

Chedzoy
Sutton Mallet
Moorlinch

A39

Durleigh Rest
Durleigh
Sedgemoor 1685

Cary

Nythe

Merridge
Enmore
Goathurst

24

Westonzoyland

King's

Merridge
Courtenay
Huntworth

A38
A361
A372

Sedge Mo

WESTON-SUPER-MARE   North Somerset   Area Code 01934

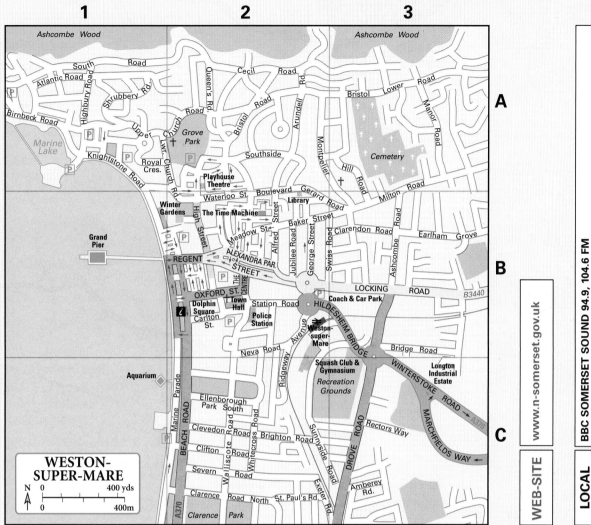

INDEX TO STREET NAMES

TOURIST INFORMATION ☎ 01934 888800
BEACH LAWNS,
WESTON-SUPER-MARE, BS23 1AT

HOSPITAL A & E ☎ 01934 636363
WESTON GENERAL HOSPITAL, GRANGE ROAD,
UPHILL, WESTON-SUPER-MARE, BS23 3NT

COUNCIL OFFICE ☎ 01934 888888
NORTH SOMERSET COUNCIL, TOWN HALL,
WESTON-SUPER-MARE, BS23 1UJ

Weston-super-Mare *N.Som.* Population: 69,372. Town and popular resort on the Bristol Channel, 18m/28km SW of Bristol, situated on Weston Bay and first developed in the 19c. Over 1m/2km of sands with traditional beach donkeys; promenade, marine lake, miniature steam railway and Winter Gardens. Amusement park located on the central Grand Pier, built in 1904. The Aquarium houses ocean and coastal waters display tanks. Local history and heritage museums give an insight into the town as a Victorian seaside resort. Annual motorbike beach race, Enduro, is held in October. International Helicopter Museum at Locking 2m/3km E.

Area Code 01962 · **Hampshire** · **WINCHESTER**

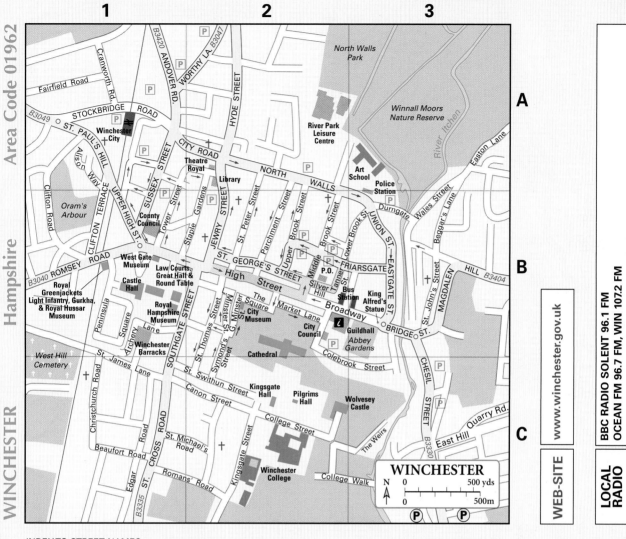

WINCHESTER
N   0   500 yds
     0   500m

WEB-SITE www.winchester.gov.uk

LOCAL RADIO: BBC RADIO SOLENT 96.1 FM · OCEAN FM 96.7 FM, WIN 107.2 FM

INDEX TO STREET NAMES

TOURIST INFORMATION ☎ 01962 840500
GUILDHALL, THE BROADWAY, WINCHESTER
HAMPSHIRE, SO23 9LJ

HOSPITAL A & E ☎ 01962 863535
ROYAL HAMPSHIRE COUNTY HOSPITAL,
ROMSEY ROAD, WINCHESTER, SO22 5DG

COUNCIL OFFICE ☎ 01962 840222
CITY OFFICES, COLEBROOK STREET,
WINCHESTER, SO23 9LJ

Winchester *Hants.* Population: 36,121. City, county town on River Itchen on site of Roman town of Venta Belgarum, 12m/19km N of Southampton. Ancient capital of Wessex and of Anglo-Saxon England. 11c cathedral, longest in Europe with carved Norman font and England's oldest complete choir-stalls. Winchester College, boys' public school founded 1382. 13c Great Hall is only remaining part of Winchester Castle. Westgate Museum is in 12c gatehouse in medieval city wall, once a debtors' prison. 12c hospital of St. Cross. City Mill (National Trust), built over river in 18c. To S across river, St. Catherine's Hill, Iron Age fort. Extensive ruins of medieval Wolvesey Castle, also known as Old Bishop's Palace (English Heritage), 1m/2km SE.

WINDSOR   Windsor & Maidenhead   Area Code 01753

TOURIST INFORMATION ☎ 01753 743900
24 HIGH STREET,
WINDSOR, SL4 1LH

HOSPITAL A & E ☎ 01753 633000
WEXHAM PARK HOSPITAL, WEXHAM STREET,
SLOUGH, SL2 4HL

COUNCIL OFFICE ☎ 01753 810525
COUNCIL OFFICES, YORK HOUSE, SHEET STREET,
WINDSOR, SL4 1DD

WEB-SITE   www.rbwm.gov.uk

LOCAL RADIO   BBC RADIO BERKSHIRE 95.4 FM
STAR FM 106.6 FM

Windsor *W. & M.* Population: 26,369. Town, attractive market town on S bank of River Thames, 2m/3km S of Slough and 21m/34km W of London. Castle is royal residence. Great Park to S of town is open to public; Home Park bordering river is private. St. George's Chapel is impressive. Many Georgian houses, and guildhall designed by Sir Christopher Wren.

Arley
Wolverley
Trimpley
Franche
Low Habberley
Blakebrook
Buttonoak
Wyre
B4194
B4190
A451
Broome
Blakedown
Holy Cross
Clent Hills
Waseley Hills (NT)
B4551
M5
A456
Bell End
Belbroughton
Drayton
KIDDERMINSTER
A491
4
Far Forest
Forest
Wribbenhall
Bewdley
Fairfield
Upper Catshill
Bournheath
Catshill
A4117
Lem Hill
Fingerpost
West Midland
Stone House Cottage
Harvington
Harvington Hall
Chaddesley Corbett
Dodford
Sidemoor
Licke End
M4
Pound Bank
Callow Hill
Ribbesford
A456
A451
Shenstone
Stone
Mustow Green
B4091
4A
17
Bliss Gate
A4202
Top
Rock
Upper Mitton
Wilden
A450
A449
Hereford and Worcester
A448
BROMSGROVE
Aston Fields
Finstall
Tarde
Pensax
Dunley
Astley Cross
Lincomb
Crossway Green
Norchard
Hartlebury
Rushock
Cutnall Green
Elmbridge
A38
Abberley
A451
9
10
A4025
Elmley Lovett
A442
Upton Warren
Stoke Prior
A443
Abberley Hill
Astley
Noutard's Green
The Burf
Acton
Dunhampton
Doverdale
Hampton Lovett
Wychbold
5
Woodg
Abberley Hall
Teme
Great Witley
Eastgrove Cottage Garden
Frog Pool
Shrawley
Sytchampton
Oldfield
Ombersley
Droitwich
Hanbury Hall (NT)
B4203
Stanford Bridge
Woodbury Hill
275
Witley Court
Little Witley
Holt Fleet
A4133
Uphampton
A4133
Spa
The Jinney Ring Craft Centre
Hanbury
Woolmer
Shelsley Walsh
Holt Heath
A449
Salwarpe
Hadzor
B4090
Bradley Green
Shelsley Beauchamp
Holt
Hawford
Hawford Dovecote (NT)
A38
Earl's Common
Clifton upon Teme
Wichenford
Sinton Green
Grimley
Fernhill Heath
Martin Hussingtree
Oddingley
Himbleton
Martley
Moseley
Shoulton
Hallow Heath
Claines
A4538
Sale Green
Tibberton
Huddington
Grafton Flyford
Wafre
Wichenford Dovecote (NT)
Hallow
Hindlip
M5
6
Crowle Green
Flyford Flavell
Horsham
Berrow Green
Peachley
A449
6
Warndon
Crowle
Broughton Hackett
A422
Broad Green
Lower Broadheath
B4204
A443
The Greenfriars
Bredicot
Upton Snodsbury
North Pid
14
Lulsley
Broadwas
WORCESTER
Worc Wds
Spetchley
Churchill
Naunton Beaucham
Knightwick
Cotheridge
Henwick
Cathedral
Commandery
Spetchley Park
Sneachill
White Ladies Aston
Alfrick
Leigh
Rushwick
St John's
A44
Worcester 1651
Whittington
Suckley Hills
Bransford
Bransford Bridge
A4440
7
Peopleton
Bisha
Suckley
Smith End Green
Collett's Green
Leigh Sinton
Powick
A449
Norton
A4538
Stoulton
B4082
Longley Green
A4103
17
A4440
Callow End
Kempsey
Littleworth
Hawbridge
Drakes Broughton
Pinvin
Throckm
Stifford's Bridge
Storridge
Newland
11
Draycott
9
Pirton
Wadborough
Pershore Sta.
Acton Green
Ridgeway Cross
Cradley
West Malvern
Malvern Link
Madresfield
Clevelode
Clifton
Kerswell Green
High Green
Besford
Defford
Pershore
Wyre Piddle
Low Mo
Pow Green
Mathon
Barnard's Green
GREAT MALVERN
Guarlford
Rhydd
Severn Stoke
Abbey
Wick
A4104
Colwall Stone
Lower Wyche
425
Hanley Swan
B4211
Kinnersley
M5
Pensham
Birlingham
Little Comber
Coddington
Upper Wyche
Malvern Hills
B4208
Earl's Croome
B4080
Great Comberton
Colwall Green
Malvern Wells
Three Counties Showground
Hanley Castle
Holly Green
Baughton
Eckington
Strensham
Bredon Hill
293
Elmley Castle
Little Malvern
Welland
Upton upon Severn
A38
Wellington Heath
A449
5
340
Little Welland
Uckinghall
A4104
7
Strensham
Naunton
Stratford
3
8
Bredon's Norton
As
und

Area Code 01905

Worcestershire

WORCESTER

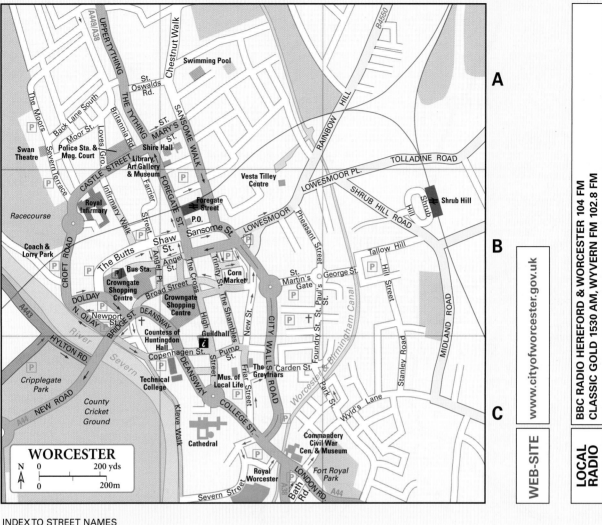

INDEX TO STREET NAMES

Worcester *Worcs.* Population: 82,661. City, on River Severn, 24m/38km SW of Birmingham. Shopping, cultural, sports and industrial centre; industries include porcelain and sauces and condiments. 18c Guildhall. Cathedral mainly Early English includes England's largest Norman crypt, 13c choir and Lady Chapel and tomb of King John. Three Choirs Festival held here every third year. Civil War Centre at the Commandery, headquarters for Charles II during Battle of Worcester. Factory tours and museum at Royal Worcester Porcelain. Elgar's Birthplace, home of composer Sir Edward Elgar, in Broadheath, 3m/5km W.

Thoithorpe
Alne
dwark
Youlton
Tollerton
Linton-
on-
Ouse
rn
rpe
erwood
Nun
Monkton
wth
Newton-on-Ouse
erton
Moor
Monkton
Beningbrough
Beningbrough Hall (NT)
A59
Roman Road
15
arston Moor
Marston Moor 1644
kwith
Hessay
Long Marston
B1224
Bilton
Hutton Wandesley
Angram
Askham Bryan
Askham Richard
Healaugh
Wighill
Bilbrough
Catterton
wton Kyme
A64
A659
A659
Tadcaster
A162
Kirkby Wharfe
tton
Saxton
Barkston
Church Fenton
Bolton Percy
Ulleskelf
Ryther
owton
9
Cawood
Kelfield
Riccall
n in Elmet
Newthorpe
Steeton Hall Gatehouse
South Milford
Lumby
Monk Fryston
B1222
Biggin
8
A63
Hambleton
A162
Hillam
3
A1
A162
Gateforth
Burn
West

Cross Lanes
Huby
Sutton-on-the-Forest
Sutton Park
Shipton
B1363
Skelton
A1237
Overton
Nether Poppleton
Upper Poppleton
P
A19
Rawcliffe
A59
YORK
Nat Rly Museum
Jorvik
A1036
Knapton
Acomb
A1237
A1036
Rufforth
York
P
Bishopthorpe
10
Copmanthorpe
Acaster Malbis
Colton
Acaster Selby
Appleton Roebuck
Stillingfleet
Wharfe
B1223
Ouse
B1222
Wistow
Thorpe Willoughby
Brayton

Stillington
Farlington
West Lilling
Sheriff Hutton
Wiggington
Haxby
Earswick
Towthorpe
Strensall
Strensall Common
18
New Earswick
Huntington
A64
Clifford's Tower
Heslington
Fulford
A64
B1228
McArthurGlen
£
P
Crockey Hill
14
Naburn
Deighton
Escrick
A19
Kelfield
Skipwith
Selby
i
Lund
Cliffe
A163
Barlby
Osgodby
A63
Hemingbrough
7
Barlow
A19
A1041

Welburn
Bulmer
Whitwell-on-the-Hill
Kirkham
Prio
Foston
Crambe
Thornton-le-Clay
Barton-le-Willow
Flaxton
Harton
Howsha
Leppi
Claxton
Bossall
Scrayingham
Sand Hutton
Buttercrambe
B
Sk
Upper Helmsley
Stockton on the Forest
Warthill
Stamford Bridge
Brockfield
Gate Helmsley
A166
Full Sutton
Holtby
Stamford Bridge 1066
Low Catton
High Catton
Murton
Dunnington
Osbaldwick
A1079
Kexby
Wilberfo
11
Newton upon Derwent
Sutton upon Derwent
Elvington
Storwood
East Cottingwith
Ross Moor
Thorn
M
Wheldrake
Thicket Priory
Thorganby
Ellerton
B1228
Aughton
Foggathorp
North Duffield
Harlt
Highfield
Bubwith
Gunby
Wi
South Duffield
Breighton
B1228
Wressle
Brind
12
Howden Sta.
Newsholme
Long Drax
Barmby on the Marsh
Knedlington
Asselby
5

Area Code 01904

YORK

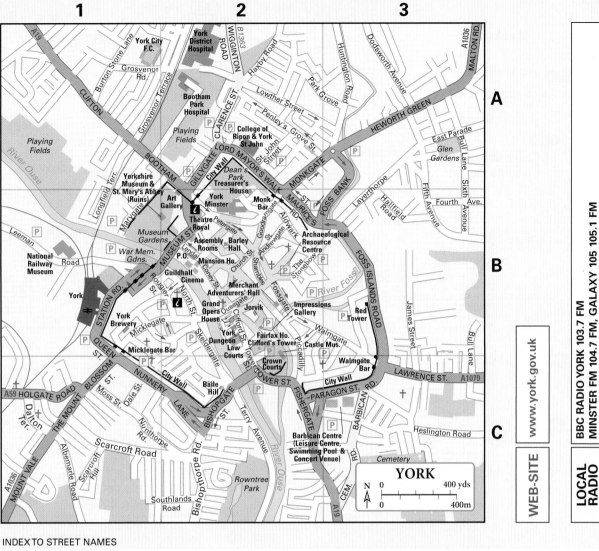

WEB-SITE www.york.gov.uk

LOCAL RADIO BBC RADIO YORK 103.7 FM MINSTER FM 104.7 FM, GALAXY 105 105.1 FM

INDEX TO STREET NAMES

TOURIST INFORMATION ☎ 01904 554488
TIC TRAVEL OFFICE, 20 GEORGE HUDSON ST.,
YORK, YO1 6WR

HOSPITAL A & E ☎ 01904 631313
YORK DISTRICT HOSPITAL, WIGGINTON ROAD,
YORK, YO31 8HE

COUNCIL OFFICE ☎ 01904 613161
THE GUILDHALL,
YORK, YO1 9QN

York Population: 124,609. City, ancient city and archiepiscopal see on River Ouse, 22m/36km NE of Leeds. On site of Roman Eboracum. Constantine the Great proclaimed Roman Emperor in York in AD 306; only emperor to be enthroned in Britain. City fell to Danes in AD 867 and became known as Jorvik. Medieval wall largely intact, other fortifications including Clifford's Tower (English Heritage). York Minster has largest Medieval stained glass window in country. Previously a wool trading, craft and railway centre. Home to National Railway Museum. Jorvik Viking Centre in Coppergate. Merchant Adventurers' Hall in Fossgate is finest remaining guildhall in Europe. University of York at Heslington. Racecourse at Knavesmire.

Ware & Hertford
Harlow, Stansted Airport & Cambridge
Cuffley
Cheshunt
B156
M25
25
Waltham Cross
ENFIELD
thgate
A10
A10
A503
ttenham
Tottenham
nsey
Stoke Newington
Hackney
Bethnal Green
City
est-ster
ea
Camberwell
A202
A2
Brixton
23
Lewisham
A205
Streatham
A212
A21
tcham
Beckenham
BROMLEY
A222
CROYDON
A232
West Wickham
A2022
rley
oulsdon
Warlingham
A22
Caterham
3
7/8
M23
Crawley, Gatwick Airport & Brighton

Waltham Abbey
26
Epping Forest
A121
Theydon Bois
A1168
Loughton
Chingford
WALTHAM FOREST
MII
Woodford
4
REDBRIDGE
Walthamstow
A406
Leyton
A1400
Wanstead
A11
Ilford
A406
East Ham
Stratford
A13
Poplar
A102
Docklands
A2
Greenwich
A205
Woolwich

Epping
MII
4
North Weald Bassett
6
27
Roding
5
Abridge
CHIGWELL
A1112
HAVERING
Romford
Becontree
BARKING
Dagenham
A123
Thames
A2016
London City
Thamesmead
A207
A2
BEXLEY
Sidcup
Chislehurst
A20
A222
A21
New Addington
A233
Biggin Hill
D   O   W
A232
Orpington
Farnborough
A21
A232
4
3/1
4
A224
Hextable
Swanley
Eynsford
West Kingsdown
N
4
S
A225
Otford
M26
A25
5
CLACKET LANE SERVICES
10
M25
A25
Westerham
B2026
Godstone
Oxted
East Grinstead & Eastbourne

A414
A414
A113
Doddinghurst
A128
Ingatestone
A12
Chelmsford, Ipswich & Harwich
BILLERICAY
A1023
BRENTWOOD
8
M25
28
A12
A127
3
Basildon & Southend
A127
Laindon
A128
29
B186
Hornchurch
Upminster
5
Rainham
A1306
A13
South Ockendon
A13
Southend
30
THURROCK SERVICES
GRAYS
Chadwell St. Mary
Purfleet
31
West Thurrock
A126
3
A282
A1089
Tilbury
A206
Dartford
1B
2
1A
A226
Northfleet
GRAVESEND
Swanscombe
1
Wilmington
A2018
A223
3
A2
Rochester, Dover & Margate
A2
M25
2
Darenth
South Darenth
Hartley
Istead Rise
A227
New Ash Green
Meopham
M20
West Kingsdown
A20
Kemsing
Sevenoaks
A21
A225
Borough Green
2
Maidstone & Folkestone
3
M20
2A
A20
A227
Tonbridge & Hastings

2 Full junction

2 Restricted junction

0   2   4 miles
0 2 4 6 kms

Abbreviations

All	Alley	Co	County	Ex	Exchange	Hts	Heights	Pas	Passage	Sta	Station
Allot	Allotments	Coll	College	Exhib	Exhibition	Ind	Industrial	Pav	Pavilion	Sts	Streets
Amb	Ambulance	Comm	Community	FB	Footbridge	Int	International	Pk	Park	Sub	Subway
App	Approach	Conv	Convent	FC	Football Club	Junct	Junction	Pl	Place	Swim	Swimming
Arc	Arcade	Cor	Corner	Fld	Field	La	Lane	Pol	Police	TA	Territorial Army
Av	Avenue	Coron	Coroners	Flds	Fields	Las	Lanes	Prec	Precinct	TH	Town Hall
Bdy	Broadway	Cors	Corners	Fm	Farm	Lib	Library	Prim	Primary	Tenn	Tennis
Bk	Bank	Cotts	Cottages	Gall	Gallery	Lo	Lodge	Prom	Promenade	Ter	Terrace
Bldgs	Buildings	Cov	Covered	Gar	Garage	Lwr	Lower	Pt	Point	Thea	Theatre
Boul	Boulevard	Crem	Crematorium	Gdn	Garden	Mag	Magistrates	Quad	Quadrant	Trd	Trading
Bowl	Bowling	Cres	Crescent	Gdns	Gardens	Mans	Mansions	RC	Roman Catholic	Twr	Tower
Br	Bridge	Ct	Court	Govt	Government	Mem	Memorial	Rd	Road	Twrs	Towers
C of E	Church of England	Cts	Courts	Gra	Grange	Mkt	Market	Rds	Roads	Uni	University
Cath	Cathedral	Ctyd	Courtyard	Grd	Ground	Mkts	Markets	Rec	Recreation	Vil	Villas
Cem	Cemetery	Dep	Depot	Grds	Grounds	Ms	Mews	Res	Reservoir	Vil	Villa
Cen	Central, Centre	Dev	Development	Grn	Green	Mt	Mount	Ri	Rise	Vw	View
Cft	Croft	Dr	Drive	Grns	Greens	Mus	Museum	S	South	W	West
Cfts	Crofts	Dws	Dwellings	Gro	Grove	N	North	Sch	School	Wd	Wood
Ch	Church	E	East	Gros	Groves	NT	National Trust	Sec	Secondary	Wds	Woods
Chyd	Churchyard	Ed	Education	Gt	Great	Nat	National	Shop	Shopping	Wf	Wharf
Cin	Cinema	Elec	Electricity	Ho	House	PH	Public House	Sq	Square	Wk	Walk
Circ	Circus	Embk	Embankment	Hos	Houses	PO	Post Office	St.	Saint	Wks	Works
Cl	Close	Est	Estate	Hosp	Hospital	Par	Parade	St	Street	Yd	Yard

Abbreviations

Aber.	Aberdeenshire	Flints.	Flintshire	Norf.	Norfolk	Som.	Somerset
Arg. & B.	Argyll & Bute	Glos.	Gloucestershire	Northants.	Northamptonshire	Staffs.	Staffordshire
B'burn.	Blackburn with Darwen	Gt.Man.	Greater Manchester	Northumb.	Northumberland	Stir.	Stirling
Beds.	Bedfordshire	Hants.	Hampshire	Notts.	Nottinghamshire	Suff.	Suffolk
Bucks.	Buckinghamshire	Here.	Herefordshire	Ork.	Orkney	Surr.	Surrey
Cambs.	Cambridgeshire	Herts.	Hertfordshire	Oxon.	Oxfordshire	T. & W.	Tyne & Wear
Cere.	Ceredigion	High.	Highland	P. & K.	Perth & Kinross	Tel. & W.	Telford & Wrekin
Ches.	Cheshire	I.o.M.	Isle of Man	Pembs.	Pembrokeshire	V. of Glam.	Vale of Glamorgan
Cornw.	Cornwall	I.o.W.	Isle of Wight	Peter.	Peterborough	W'ham	Wokingham
Cumb.	Cumbria	Lancs.	Lancashire	R.C.T.	Rhondda Cynon Taff	W.Isles	Western Isles (Na h-Eileanan an Iar)
D. & G.	Dumfries & Galloway	Leics.	Leicestershire	S.Ayr.	South Ayrshire		
Derbys.	Derbyshire	Lincs.	Lincolnshire	S.Glos.	South Gloucestershire	W.Loth.	West Lothian
Dur.	Durham	Med.	Medway			W.Suss.	West Sussex
E.Ayr.	East Ayrshire	Mersey.	Merseyside	S.Lan.	South Lanarkshire	W.Yorks.	West Yorkshire
E.Loth.	East Lothian	Mon.	Monmouthshire	S.Yorks.	South Yorkshire	Wilts.	Wiltshire
E.Riding	East Riding of Yorkshire	N.Lan.	North Lanarkshire	Sc.Bord.	Scottish Borders	Worcs.	Worcestershire
		N.Lincs.	North Lincolnshire	Shet.	Shetland	Wrex.	Wrexham
		N.Yorks.	North Yorkshire	Shrop.	Shropshire		

Abbeytown	29 E2	Adlington	25 D3	Alvie	42 A4	Ardvasar	40 C4	Aucholzie	39 D1
Abbots Bromley	20 C3	Adwick le Street	26 B3	Alyth	39 D2	Arinagour	36 B2	Auchterarder	38 B4
Abbotsbury	8 A4	Ainsdale	24 C3	Ambergate	21 D2	Arisaig	36 C1	Auchtermuchty	39 D4
Aberaeron	12 B3	Aintree	24 C4	Amble	35 F4	Armadale	34 A1	Auchtertool	34 B1
Aberaman	7 D1	Aird Asaig	47 D3	Amblecote	20 B4	Armitage	20 C3	Audlem	20 A2
Aberavon	6 C1	Aird of Sleat	40 B4	Ambleside	29 F4	Armthorpe	26 B4	Audley	20 A2
Abercanaid	7 E1	Airdrie	33 G2	Ambrosden	15 E3	Arncliffe	25 E1	Aughton Lancs.	24 C4
Aberchirder	43 D2	Airidh a'Bhruaich	47 E2	Amersham	15 F3	Arnisdale	40 C4	Aughton S.Yorks.	26 A4
Abercynon	7 E1	Airth	34 A1	Amesbury	8 C2	Arnol	47 E1	Auldearn	42 B2
Aberdare	7 D1	Airton	25 E1	Amlwch	18 B1	Arnold	21 E2	Aultbea	41 D1
Aberdaron	18 A3	Aith Ork.	48 C2	Ammanford	6 C1	Arnprior	38 A4	Aultguish Inn	41 E2
Aberdeen	43 F4	Aith Shet.	49 E3	Ampthill	15 F2	Arrochar	37 F4	Aveley	10 C1
Aberdeen Airport	43 E4	Akeld	35 E3	Amulree	38 B3	Arundel	10 A4	Aviemore	42 B4
Aberdour	34 B1	Albrighton	20 A3	Ancaster	21 F2	Ascot	9 F1	Avoch	42 A2
Aberdyfi	12 C1	Alcester	14 C1	Ancroft	35 E2	Asfordby	21 E3	Avonbridge	34 A1
Aberfeldy	38 B2	Aldbourne	14 C4	Ancrum	35 D3	Ash Kent	11 F2	Avonmouth	7 F2
Aberffraw	18 A2	Aldbrough	27 D2	Andover	9 D1	Ash Surr.	9 F1	Awre	14 A3
Aberfoyle	38 A4	Aldeburgh	17 F2	Andreas	24 B2	Ashbourne	20 C2	Awsworth	21 D2
Abergavenny	7 E1	Aldenham	16 A4	Angle	12 A2	Ashburton	5 D2	Axminster	5 F1
Abergele	19 D1	Alderbury	8 C2	Angmering	10 A4	Ashbury	14 C4	Aycliffe	31 D3
Abergynolwyn	12 C1	Alderholt	8 C3	Anlaby	27 D3	Ashby de la Zouch	21 D3	Aylesbury	15 E3
Aberkenfig	7 D2	Alderley Edge	20 B1	Annan	29 E1	Ashchurch	14 B2	Aylesford	11 D2
Aberlady	34 C1	Aldershot	9 F1	Annbank	33 E3	Ashcott	7 F3	Aylesham	11 F2
Aberlemno	39 E2	Aldingham	24 C1	Annfield Plain	30 C2	Ashford Kent	11 E2	Aylsham	23 E3
Aberlour	42 C3	Aldington	11 E3	Anstey	21 D3	Ashford Surr.	10 A1	Ayr	33 E3
Abernethy	38 C4	Aldridge	20 B4	Anstruther	39 E4	Ashington	31 D1	Aysgarth	30 C4
Aberporth	12 A3	Alexandria	33 E1	An Tairbeart	47 E3	Ashkirk	34 C3	
Abersoch	18 A3	Alford Aber.	43 D4	An t-Ob	47 D4	Ashley	16 C1	**B**
Abersychan	7 E1	Alford Lincs.	22 B1	Aoradh	32 A3	Ashton	19 F2	Babworth	26 B4
Abertillery	7 E1	Alfreton	21 D1	Appleby-in-Westmorland	30 A3	Ashton-in-Makerfield	25 D4	Backaland	48 B2
Aberuthven	38 C4	Allanton	34 A2	Appleby Magna	20 C3			Backwell	7 F2
Aberystwyth	12 C2	Allendale Town	30 B2	Applecross	40 C3	Ashton-under-Lyne	25 E4	Bacup	25 E3
Abhainnsuidhe	47 D3	Allenheads	30 B2	Appledore Devon	6 B4	Ashurst Hants.	9 D3	Badcaul	44 A4
Abingdon	15 D4	Allhallows	11 D1	Appledore Kent	11 E3	Ashurst Kent	10 C3	Badenscoth	43 E3
Abington	34 A3	Allnabad	44 C2	Appleton Thorn	19 F1	Ashwick	8 A1	Badlipster	45 F2
Aboyne	43 D4	Alloa	38 B4	Appley Bridge	25 D3	Askern	26 B3	Badsey	14 B2
Abram	25 D4	Allonby	29 E2	Arbirlot	39 E3	Aspatria	29 E2	Bagh a' Chaisteil (Castlebay)	46 A4
Accrington	25 E3	Alloway	33 E3	Arbroath	39 E3	Astbury	20 A1	
Achadh Mòr	47 E2	Almondsbury	14 A4	Ardchiavaig	36 B4	Aston Clinton	15 F3	Bagillt	19 E1
Achahoish	32 C1	Alness	42 A2	Arden	33 E1	Aston on Trent	21 D2	Baglan	6 C1
Acharacle	36 C2	Alnmouth	35 F4	Ardentinny	33 E1	Astwood Bank	14 B1	Bagshot	9 F1
Achavanich	45 E2	Alnwick	35 F4	Ardeonaig	38 A3	Atherington	6 C4	Baildon	25 F2
Achfary	44 B2	Alresford	17 D3	Ardersier	42 A2	Atherstone	20 C4	Baile Ailein	47 E2
Achiltibuie	44 A3	Alrewas	20 C3	Ardfern	37 D4	Atherton	25 D4	Baile a'Mhanaich	46 A2
Achintee	41 D3	Alsager	20 A1	Ardgay	44 C4	Attadale	41 D3	Baile Mhartainn	46 A1
Achnacroish	37 D3	Alston	30 A2	Ardleigh	17 D3	Attleborough	23 D4	Baile Mòr	36 B3
Achnasheen	41 E2	Altnafeadh	37 F2	Ardlui	37 F4	Attlebridge	23 E3	Bainbridge	30 B4
Achosnich	36 C2	Altnaharra	44 C2	Ardlussa	32 B1	Auchallater	38 C1	Bainton	26 C2
Achriesgill	44 B2	Alton Hants.	9 F2	Ardmair	44 A4	Auchenblae	39 E1	Bala	19 D3
Ackworth Moor Top	26 A3	Alton Staffs.	20 C2	Ardminish	32 B2	Auchenbreck	32 D1	Balbeggie	38 C3
Acle	23 F3	Altrincham	25 E4	Ardmolich	37 D1	Auchencairn	29 D2	Balblair	42 A2
Acomb	30 B1	Alva	38 B4	Ardrishaig	32 C1	Auchencrow	35 E2	Balcombe	10 B3
Adderbury	15 D2	Alvechurch	14 B1	Ardrossan	33 E3	Auchindrain	37 E4	Balderton	21 E2
Addingham	25 F2	Alveley	20 A4	Ardtalnaig	38 A3	Auchinleck	33 F3	Baldock	16 A2
Addlestone	10 A2	Alveston	14 A4	Ardtoe	36 C2	Auchmull	39 E1	Baldslow	11 D4
		Alves	42 B2			Auchnagatt	43 F3	Balemartine	36 A3

Houbie 49 F1
Houghton le Spring 31 D2
Houghton Regis 15 F2
Houndslow 35 D2
Houston 33 E2
Houton 48 B3
Hove 10 B4
Hoveton 23 E3
Hovingham 26 B1
Howden 26 B3
Howwood 33 F2
Hoylake 19 E1
Hoyland 26 A4
Hucknall 21 D2
Huddersfield 25 F3
Huggate 26 C2
Huish Episcopi 7 F4
Huisinis 47 D3
Hull 27 D3
Hullavington 14 B4
Hullbridge 11 D1
Humberside International Airport 27 D3
Humberston 27 E4
Humbie 34 C2
Hundleby 22 B1
Hundleton 12 A2
Hungerford 9 D1
Hunmanby 27 D1
Hunstanton 22 C2
Hunter's Quay 33 E1
Huntingdon 16 A1
Huntly 43 D3
Hurlford 33 F3
Hursley 9 D2
Hurstbourne Tarrant 9 D1
Hurst Green 11 D3
Hurstpierpoint 10 B3
Hurworth-on-Tees 31 D3
Husbands Bosworth 21 E4
Huttoft 22 B1
Hutton Cranswick 27 D2
Hutton Rudby 31 D4
Huyton 19 F1
Hyde 25 E4
Hythe *Hants.* 9 D3
Hythe *Kent* 11 E3

I

Ibstock 21 D3
Icklesham 11 D4
Icklingham 16 C1
Idrigil 40 B2
Ilchester 7 F4
Ilford 10 C1
Ilfracombe 6 B3
Ilkeston 21 D2
Ilkley 25 F2
Ilminster 7 F4
Immingham 27 D3
Inchbare 39 E2
Inchnadamph 44 B3
Inchture 39 D3
Ingatestone 16 C4
Ingleton *Dur.* 30 C3
Ingleton *N.Yorks.* 25 D1
Inglewhite 25 D2
Ingoldmells 22 B1
Inkberrow 14 B1
Innellan 33 D2
Innerleithen 34 C3
Insch 43 D3
Inveralligan 40 C2
Inverallochy 43 F2
Inveraray 37 E4
Inverarity 39 D3
Inverarnan 37 F4
Inverbervie 39 F1

Invercassley 44 C4
Invercharnan 37 E2
Inverey 38 C1
Invergarry 41 E4
Invergordon 42 A2
Inverinan 37 E4
Inverkeilor 39 E2
Inverkeithing 34 B1
Inverkirkaig 44 A3
Inverlael 41 E1
Invermoriston 41 F4
Inverneil 32 C1
Inverness 42 A3
Inverness Airport 42 A2
Invernoaden 37 E4
Inverurie 43 E4
Ipplepen 5 D2
Ipstones 20 B2
Ipswich 17 E2
Irchester 15 F1
Irlam 25 D4
Ironbridge 20 A3
Irthlingborough 15 F1
Irvine 33 E3
Isbister (Mainland) *Shet.* 49 E1
Isbister (Whalsay) *Shet.* 49 F2
Isleham 16 C1
Isle of Man Airport 24 A3
Isle of Whithorn 28 C2
Iver 10 A1
Ivinghoe 15 F3
Ivybridge 4 C3
Iwade 11 D2
Ixworth 17 D1

J

Jarrow 31 D1
Jaywick 17 E3
Jedburgh 35 D3
Jemimaville 42 A2
John o' Groats 45 F1
Johnston 12 A2
Johnstone 33 F2
Johnstonebridge 34 B4

K

Kames 32 D1
Kearsley 25 D4
Kedington 16 C2
Keelby 27 D3
Keele 20 A2
Kegworth 21 D3
Keighley 25 F2
Keillmore 32 C1
Keiss 45 F1
Keith 43 D2
Kellas *Angus* 39 D3
Kellas *Moray* 42 C2
Kelso 35 D3
Kelty 38 C4
Kelvedon 17 D3
Kelvedon Hatch 16 B4
Kemnay 43 E4
Kempsey 14 B2
Kempston 15 F2
Kendal 30 A4
Kenilworth 14 C1
Kenmore 38 B2
Kennacraig 32 C2
Kennethmont 43 D3
Kennington 15 D3
Kennoway 39 D4
Kensaleyre 40 B2
Kensworth 15 F3
Kentallen 37 E2
Kenton 5 D2
Kesgrave 17 E2
Kessingland 23 F4
Keswick 29 F3

Kettering 21 F4
Kettletoft 48 C2
Kettlewell 25 E1
Ketton 21 F3
Kewstoke 7 F2
Keyingham 27 D3
Keymer 10 B4
Keynsham 8 A1
Keyworth 21 E2
Kibworth Harcourt 21 E4
Kidderminster 20 B4
Kidlington 15 D3
Kidsgrove 20 B2
Kidwelly (Cydweli) 6 B1
Kielder 35 D4
Kilberry 32 C2
Kilbirnie 33 E2
Kilburn 21 D2
Kilcadzow 34 A2
Kilchattan 36 B4
Kilchenzie 32 C3
Kilchiaran 32 A3
Kilchoan 36 C2
Kilchoman 32 A3
Kilchrenan 37 E3
Kilconquhar 39 E4
Kilcreggan 33 E1
Kildonan Lodge 45 D3
Kildrummy 43 D4
Kilfinan 32 D1
Kilgetty 6 A1
Kilham *E.Riding* 27 D1
Kilham *Northumb.* 35 E3
Kilkhampton 6 A4
Killamarsh 26 A4
Killay 6 C1
Killean 32 C2
Killearn 33 F1
Killichonan 38 A2
Killiecrankie 38 B2
Killin 38 A3
Killinghall 26 A1
Killingworth 31 D1
Killundine 36 C2
Kilmacolm 33 E1
Kilmalieu 37 D2
Kilmaluag 40 B2
Kilmarnock 33 F3
Kilmartin 37 D4
Kilmaurs 33 E3
Kilmelford 37 D4
Kilmington 5 F1
Kilmory *Arg. & B.* 32 C1
Kilmory (Rum) *High.* 40 A4
Kilninian 36 B2
Kilninver 37 D3
Kiloran 36 B4
Kilrenny 39 E4
Kilsyth 33 G1
Kilwinning 33 E2
Kimberley *Norf.* 23 D4
Kimberley *Notts.* 21 D2
Kimbolton 16 A1
Kimpton 16 A3
Kinbrace 45 D3
Kincardine 34 A1
Kincardine O'Neil 43 D4
Kincraig 42 A4
Kingarth 33 D2
Kinghorn 34 B1
Kinglassie 39 D4
Kingsbarns 39 E4
Kingsbridge 4 C3
Kingsbury 20 C4
Kingsbury Episcopi 7 F4
Kingsclere 9 E1
Kingsdown 11 F2

Kingshouse 38 A3
Kingskerswell 5 D2
Kings Langley 15 F3
Kingsley *Ches.* 19 F1
Kingsley *Staffs.* 20 B2
King's Lynn 22 C3
Kingsnorth 11 E3
King's Sutton 15 D2
Kingsteignton 5 D2
Kingsthorne 13 F4
Kingston 42 C2
Kingston Bagpuize 15 D3
Kingstone 13 F4
Kingston Seymour 7 F2
Kingston upon Hull 27 D3
Kingswear 5 D3
Kingswood *S.Glos.* 14 A4
Kingswood *Surr.* 10 B2
Kings Worthy 9 E2
Kington 13 E3
Kingussie 42 A4
Kinloch 40 B4
Kinlochard 38 A4
Kinlochbervie 44 B2
Kinlocheil 37 E1
Kinlochewe 41 D2
Kinloch Hourn 41 D4
Kinlochleven 37 E2
Kinloch Rannoch 38 A2
Kinloss 42 B2
Kinmel Bay 19 D1
Kinross 38 C4
Kintbury 9 D1
Kintore 43 E4
Kintour 32 B2
Kintra 32 A2
Kinver 20 B4
Kippax 26 A3
Kippen 38 A4
Kirby Muxloe 21 D3
Kirkbean 29 D2
Kirkbride 29 E2
Kirkburton 25 F3
Kirkby 24 C4
Kirkby in Ashfield 21 D1
Kirkby Lonsdale 25 D1
Kirkby Malzeard 25 F1
Kirkbymoorside 31 E4
Kirkby Stephen 30 B4
Kirkcaldy 34 B1
Kirkcolm 28 A1
Kirkconnel 33 G4
Kirkcowan 28 B2
Kirkcudbright 28 C2
Kirkham 24 C2
Kirkinner 28 B2
Kirkintilloch 33 F1
Kirkliston 34 B1
Kirk Michael *I.o.M.* 24 A2
Kirkmichael *P. & K.* 38 C2
Kirkmichael *S.Ayr.* 33 E4
Kirkmuirhill 34 A2
Kirknewton *Northumb.* 35 E3
Kirknewton *W.Loth.* 34 B2
Kirkoswald *Cumb.* 30 A2
Kirkoswald *S.Ayr.* 33 E4
Kirkpatrick Durham 29 D1
Kirkpatrick -Fleming 29 F1
Kirk Sandall 26 B3
Kirkton 37 D4
Kirkton of Culsalmond 43 D3
Kirkton of Durris 39 F1

Kirkton of Glenisla 39 D2
Kirkton of Kingoldrum 39 D2
Kirkton of Menmuir 39 E2
Kirkton of Skene 43 E4
Kirktown of Auchterless 43 E3
Kirktown of Deskford 43 D2
Kirkwall 48 B3
Kirk Yetholm 35 E3
Kirriemuir 39 D2
Kirtlington 15 D3
Kirton *Lincs.* 22 A2
Kirton *Suff.* 17 E2
Kirton in Lindsey 26 C4
Knaresborough 26 A2
Knayton 31 D4
Knebworth 16 A3
Knighton 13 E2
Knock 36 C3
Knockandhu 42 C3
Knottingley 26 A3
Knowle 20 C4
Knucklas 13 E2
Knutsford 20 A1
Kyleakin 40 C3
Kyle of Lochalsh 40 C3
Kylerhea 40 C4
Kylestrome 44 B2

L

Laceby 27 D4
Lacock 8 B1
Ladybank 39 D4
Ladykirk 35 E2
Ladysford 43 E2
Lagg 32 D3
Laggan (Invergarry) *High.* 37 F1
Laggan (Newtonmore) *High.* 38 A1
Lagganulva 36 C3
Laide 41 D1
Lairg 44 C4
Lakenheath 16 C1
Laleston 7 D2
Lamberhurst 11 D3
Lambourn 15 D4
Lamlash 32 D3
Lampeter 12 C3
Lamport 15 E1
Lanark 34 A2
Lancaster 24 C1
Lanchester 30 C2
Landore 6 C1
Lane End 15 E4
Langford 16 A2
Langham 21 F3
Langholm 29 F1
Langold 26 B4
Langport 7 F4
Langtoft 26 C1
Langwathby 30 A3
Lanivet 4 A2
Lapworth 14 C1
Larbert 34 A1
Largoward 39 D4
Largs 33 E2
Larkhall 33 G2
Larkhill 8 C1
Larling 23 D4
Latchingdon 17 D4
Latheron 45 E2
Latheronwheel 45 E3
Lauder 34 C2
Laugharne 6 B1
Launceston 4 B1
Laurencekirk 39 E2
Laurieston 28 C1

Place	Map	Grid
Marston Magna	8	A2
Marston Moretaine	15	F2
Martham	23	F3
Martlesham	17	E2
Martley	14	A1
Martock	7	F4
Marybank	41	F2
Marykirk	39	E2
Marypark	42	C3
Maryport	29	E2
Marywell (Deeside)	39	E1
Masham	25	F1
Matlock	20	C1
Matlock Bath	20	C1
Mauchline	33	F3
Maud	43	F3
Maughold	24	B2
Maybole	33	E4
Mayfield	20	C2
Mealsgate	29	E2
Meare	7	F3
Measham	21	D3
Medstead	9	E2
Meidrim	12	A4
Meigle	39	D3
Meikle Kilmory	33	D2
Meikleour	38	C3
Melbourn	16	B2
Melbourne	21	D3
Melksham	8	B1
Melmerby	30	A2
Melrose	34	C3
Melsonby	30	C4
Meltham	25	F3
Melton	17	E2
Melton Mowbray	21	E3
Melvaig	40	C1
Melvich	45	D1
Memsie	43	F2
Menai Bridge	18	B1
Menston	25	F2
Menstrie	38	B4
Mere	8	B2
Meriden	20	C4
Merthyr Tydfil	7	D1
Messingham	26	C4
Metfield	17	E1
Metheringham	21	F1
Methlick	43	E3
Methven	38	C3
Methwold	22	C4
Mevagissey	4	A3
Mexborough	26	A4
Mey	45	F1
Miabhig	47	D2
Mickleton *Dur.*	30	B3
Mickleton *Glos.*	14	C2
Mid Ardlaw	43	F2
Midbea	48	B2
Middle Barton	15	D2
Middleham	30	C4
Middlemarsh	8	A3
Middle Rasen	27	D4
Middlesbrough	31	D3
Middlesmoor	25	F1
Middleton *Gt.Man.*	25	E4
Middleton *Norf.*	22	C3
Middleton Cheney	15	D2
Middleton-in-Teesdale	30	B3
Middleton-on-Sea	10	A4
Middleton-on-the-Wolds	26	C2
Middleton Stoney	15	D3
Middlewich	20	A1
Midhurst	9	F2
Midlem	34	C3
Midsomer Norton	8	A1
Mid Yell	49	F1
Milborne Port	8	A2
Milborne St. Andrew	8	B3
Mildenhall	16	C1
Mile End	17	D3
Milfield	35	E3
Milford	9	F2
Milford Haven	12	A2
Milford on Sea	9	D4
Millbrook	4	B3
Millhouse	32	D1
Millom	24	B1
Millport	33	D2
Milltown of Rothiemay	43	D3
Milnathort	38	C4
Milngavie	33	F1
Milnrow	25	E3
Milnthorpe	25	D1
Milovaig	40	A2
Milton *High.*	41	F3
Milton *P. & K.*	38	B3
Milton Keynes	15	F2
Milton of Campsie	33	F1
Milverton	7	E4
Minard	37	E4
Minchinhampton	14	B3
Minehead	7	D3
Minera	19	E2
Minnigaff	28	B1
Minster (Sheppey) *Kent*	11	E1
Minster (Thanet) *Kent*	11	F2
Minsterley	13	F1
Mintlaw	43	F3
Mirfield	25	F3
Misterton	26	B4
Mitcheldean	14	A3
Mobberley	20	A1
Modbury	4	C3
Moelfre	18	B1
Moffat	34	B4
Mold	19	E2
Molescroft	27	D2
Moniaive	33	G4
Monifieth	39	E3
Monimail	39	D4
Monkokehampton	4	C1
Monks Eleigh	17	D2
Monmouth (Trefynwy)	7	F1
Monreith	28	B2
Montgomery (Trefaldwyn)	13	E1
Montrose	39	E2
Moorends	26	B3
Morar	36	C1
Morebattle	35	D3
Morecambe	24	C1
Morenish	38	A3
Moresby	29	E3
Moreton	19	E1
Moretonhampstead	5	D1
Moreton-in-Marsh	14	C2
Morfa Nefyn	18	A3
Morley	26	A3
Morpeth	30	C1
Morriston	6	C1
Mortehoe	6	B3
Mortimer's Cross	13	F3
Morton (Bourne) *Lincs.*	22	A3
Morton *Lincs.* (Gainsborough)	26	C4
Morville	20	A4
Mosborough	26	A4
Moscow	33	F3
Mossat	43	D4
Mossblown	33	E3
Mossley	25	E4
Mosstodloch	42	C2
Motherwell	33	G2
Moulsecoomb	10	B4
Moulton *Lincs.*	22	A3
Moulton *Suff.*	16	C1
Mountain Ash	7	E1
Mountbenger	34	C3
Mountsorrel	21	E3
Moy	42	A3
Muchalls	39	F1
Much Wenlock	20	A4
Muirdrum	39	E3
Muirhead	39	D3
Muirkirk	33	G3
Muir of Fowlis	43	D4
Muir of Ord	41	F2
Mulbarton	23	E4
Mulben	42	C2
Mullion	3	E4
Mundesley	23	E2
Mundford	22	C4
Munlochy	42	A2
Murton	31	D2
Musbury	5	F1
Musselburgh	34	C1
Muthill	38	B4
Mybster	45	E2
Mytholmroyd	25	E3

N

Place	Map	Grid
Nailsea	7	F2
Nailsworth	14	B3
Nairn	42	A2
Nantwich	20	A2
Nantyglo	7	E1
Narberth	6	A1
Narborough *Leics.*	21	D4
Narborough *Norf.*	22	C3
Nateby	30	B4
Nazeing	16	B4
Near Sawrey	29	F4
Neath	6	C1
Necton	23	D4
Needham Market	17	D2
Needingworth	16	B1
Nefyn	18	A3
Neilston	33	F2
Nelson	25	E2
Nenthead	30	B2
Neston	19	E1
Nether Langwith	21	D1
Netherley	39	F1
Nether Stowey	7	E3
Netherton	35	E4
Nethy Bridge	42	B4
Nettlebed	15	E4
Nettleham	21	F1
New Abbey	29	D1
New Aberdour	43	E2
New Addington	10	B2
New Alresford	9	E2
Newark-on-Trent	21	E1
New Ash Green	10	C2
Newbiggin-by-the-Sea	31	D1
Newbigging	34	A2
Newbold Verdon	21	D3
Newborough	22	A4
Newbridge	7	E1
Newburgh *Aber.*	43	F3
Newburgh *Fife*	39	D4
Newburn	30	C1
Newbury	9	E1
Newby Bridge	29	F4
New Byth	43	E2
Newcastle	13	E2
Newcastle Emlyn	12	B4
Newcastle International Airport	30	C1
Newcastleton	29	F1
Newcastle-under-Lyme	20	B2
Newcastle upon Tyne	30	C1
New Cumnock	33	F4
New Deer	43	E3
Newent	14	A2
New Galloway	28	C1
Newhaven	10	C4
Newick	10	B3
Newington	11	D2
New Leeds	43	F2
New Luce	28	A1
Newlyn	3	D3
Newmachar	43	E4
Newmains	34	A2
Newmarket *Suff.*	16	C1
Newmarket *W.Isles*	47	F2
Newmill	43	D2
New Mills	25	E4
Newmilns	33	F3
New Milton	9	D3
New Mistley	17	E3
Newnham	14	A3
New Pitsligo	43	E2
Newport *Essex*	16	B2
Newport *High.*	45	E3
Newport *I.o.W.*	9	E4
Newport *Newport*	7	F2
Newport *Pembs.*	12	A4
Newport *Tel. & W.*	20	A3
Newport-on-Tay	39	D3
Newport Pagnell	15	F2
New Quay *Cere.*	12	B3
Newquay *Cornw.*	3	F2
New Radnor	13	E3
New Romney	11	E3
New Rossington	26	B4
New Scone	38	C3
Newton *Arg. & B.*	37	E4
Newton *Lancs.*	25	D2
Newton Abbot	5	D2
Newton Aycliffe	31	D3
Newton Ferrers	4	C3
Newtonhill	39	F1
Newton-le-Willows	19	F1
Newton Mearns	33	F2
Newtonmore	42	A4
Newton Poppleford	5	E1
Newton St. Cyres	5	D1
Newton Stewart	28	B1
Newtown *Here.*	14	A2
Newtown (Y Drenewydd) *Powys*	13	E2
Newtown St. Boswells	35	D3
New Tredegar	7	E1
Newtyle	39	D3
Neyland	12	B2
Ninemile Bar or Crocketford	29	D1
Ninfield	11	D4
Nisbet	35	D3
Norham	35	E2
Normanton	26	A3
Northallerton	31	D4
Northam	6	B4
Northampton	15	E1
North Baddesley	9	D2
North Ballachulish	37	E2
North Berwick	34	C1
North Cave	26	C2
North Cheriton	8	A2
North Cowton	31	D4
North Duffield	26	B2
North Elmham	23	D3
North Ferriby	26	C3
Northfleet	10	C1
North Grimston	26	C1
North Hykeham	21	F1
Northill	16	A2
North Kessock	42	A3
Northleach	14	C3
North Leigh	15	D3
North Middleton	34	C2
North Molton	6	C4
North Queensferry	34	B1
North Shields	31	D1
North Somercotes	27	E4
North Sunderland	35	F3
North Thoresby	27	E4
North Walsham	23	E3
North Weald Bassett	16	B4
Northwich	20	A1
North Wingfield	21	D1
Northwood	9	E3
Norton *N.Yorks.*	26	C1
Norton *Suff.*	17	D1
Norton Canes	20	B3
Norton Fitzwarren	7	E4
Norwich	23	E4
Norwich Airport	23	E3
Norwick	49	F1
Nottingham	21	D2
Nuneaton	21	D4

O

Place	Map	Grid
Oadby	21	E4
Oakdale	7	E1
Oakengates	20	A3
Oakham	21	F3
Oakley *Bucks.*	15	E3
Oakley *Fife*	34	A1
Oakley *Hants.*	9	E1
Oban	37	D3
Ochiltree	33	F3
Ockbrook	21	D2
Ockle	36	C2
Oddsta	49	F1
Odiham	9	F1
Ogmore	7	D2
Ogmore Vale	7	D1
Okehampton	4	C1
Oldbury	20	B4
Old Clipstone	21	E1
Old Colwyn	18	C1
Old Dailly	33	E4
Old Felixstowe	17	E2
Oldham	25	E4
Oldland	8	A1
Old Leake	22	B2
Oldmeldrum	43	E3
Old Town	25	D1
Olgrinmore	45	E2
Ollaberry	49	E2
Ollerton	21	E1
Olney	15	F1
Olveston	14	A4
Ombersley	14	B1
Onchan	24	B3
Onich	37	E2
Orford	17	E2
Ormesby St. Margaret	23	F3
Ormiston	34	C1
Ormskirk	24	C3
Orpington	10	C2
Orrell	25	D3
Orton	30	A4
Orton Longueville	22	A4
Oskaig	40	B3
Ossett	26	A3
Oswaldkirk	26	B1
Oswaldtwistle	25	D3
Oswestry	19	E3
Otford	10	C2
Otley *Suff.*	17	E2
Otley *W.Yorks.*	25	F2

DISTANCE IN KILOMETRES

Cities (diagonal, top-left to bottom-right):
ABERDEEN, ABERYSTWYTH, AYR, BIRMINGHAM, BRADFORD, BRISTOL, CAMBRIDGE, CARDIFF, CARLISLE, COVENTRY, DERBY, DONCASTER, DOVER, EDINBURGH, EXETER, FISHGUARD, FORT WILLIAM, GLASGOW, GLOUCESTER, HARWICH, HOLYHEAD, HULL, INVERNESS, KENDAL, LEEDS, LEICESTER, LINCOLN, LIVERPOOL, MANCHESTER, NEWCASTLE UPON TYNE, NORWICH, NOTTINGHAM, OXFORD, PENZANCE, PERTH, PLYMOUTH, PORTSMOUTH, SALISBURY, SHEFFIELD, SHREWSBURY, SOUTHAMPTON, SOUTHEND-ON-SEA, STOKE-ON-TRENT, STRANRAER, THURSO, WORCESTER, YORK, LONDON

Upper triangle — kilometres (read by rows):

689 288 652 525 779 772 787 348 678 631 554 208 896 776 253 235 723 869 679 566 169 420 531 660 624 531 533 377 789 628 779 1069 135 977 904 866 584 628 872 858 592 370 365 689 509 816
492 179 285 217 319 187 341 211 224 278 476 489 335 87 681 494 164 444 175 366 761 269 293 235 306 158 228 447 417 248 238 507 554 407 340 274 251 121 307 396 174 507 958 153 335 340
455 328 583 571 591 151 481 435 385 734 127 700 579 227 53 526 682 483 402 333 224 335 470 449 335 336 238 613 436 554 872 153 772 681 634 388 423 668 666 388 82 529 484 340 621
182 138 161 161 304 32 66 153 286 452 256 267 64 457 82 265 232 209 787 232 175 68 142 142 125 331 249 84 98 428 517 328 225 179 122 69 201 232 68 470 903 45 206 171
309 249 333 177 190 117 55 426 323 439 372 517 330 253 354 254 106 578 100 15 162 119 100 56 156 283 122 270 599 389 499 397 352 61 164 377 351 114 343 774 217 51 312
235 72 431 148 204 288 388 579 117 248 771 584 56 311 368 348 832 359 314 185 264 261 253 470 328 222 108 290 644 190 146 82 261 167 117 259 195 597 1028 100 346 196
286 425 129 146 179 185 549 340 404 752 565 193 105 383 201 826 348 228 101 134 270 240 381 93 127 127 497 637 425 200 225 179 232 211 101 191 591 1022 166 256 85
439 185 227 314 351 587 190 175 779 592 93 364 343 370 840 367 336 222 301 261 275 491 380 245 161 362 652 262 217 150 286 167 185 299 220 605 1036 116 367 237
330 283 233 582 148 549 428 340 153 375 531 331 251 401 72 183 319 298 183 185 90 460 285 402 721 212 621 529 483 237 272 517 515 237 166 597 333 187 470
72 151 253 497 265 304 669 483 92 233 262 183 731 257 187 37 116 174 151 330 219 77 76 438 542 338 203 162 134 100 179 200 93 496 927 66 204 138
87 309 431 322 311 623 436 150 251 248 146 684 211 109 45 82 129 90 264 217 24 148 494 496 394 272 235 56 103 251 240 56 449 880 116 140 187
364 346 417 365 573 286 237 303 267 74 607 161 50 106 64 130 80 179 228 17 217 578 418 478 344 314 27 158 320 280 105 399 803 203 53 262
718 396 581 932 745 312 188 533 386 996 517 420 264 319 426 404 566 262 306 209 554 808 460 201 256 365 352 220 116 346 748 1192 296 441 114
697 576 225 69 523 661 480 357 261 220 330 476 415 331 333 167 579 418 570 869 72 769 697 658 383 420 665 650 385 200 457 481 301 608
365 888 702 174 399 486 449 949 416 431 303 381 378 370 587 430 340 212 158 761 69 203 140 378 285 171 344 312 715 1146 217 463 282
768 581 269 537 262 423 829 356 383 322 393 254 315 534 504 335 335 537 640 438 394 330 338 208 365 475 261 594 1025 238 422 430
187 715 871 591 108 412 523 658 637 523 525 415 801 624 742 1061 171 961 869 822 576 612 856 855 576 309 285 673 526 810
528 684 484 404 280 225 336 471 451 336 338 228 615 438 555 874 100 774 882 636 389 425 669 668 389 135 476 486 340 623
277 282 275 776 303 257 129 208 212 196 414 286 171 74 346 587 246 171 106 211 119 143 232 138 541 972 43 290 175
497 306 922 462 352 206 238 368 341 486 129 232 203 557 734 468 253 259 293 333 264 97 288 697 1118 290 361 117
346 732 259 262 274 299 148 198 397 465 272 325 658 544 528 457 389 191 162 425 463 191 497 929 238 306 402
620 200 88 146 68 198 148 190 232 132 257 637 431 537 385 346 105 216 360 303 162 417 816 277 64 278
473 584 713 677 584 586 430 842 681 832 1122 188 1030 958 919 637 681 925 911 645 415 196 742 562 869
111 246 225 111 121 138 383 220 330 649 285 549 457 410 161 200 444 451 164 238 669 261 142 406
154 114 114 64 154 278 114 265 603 396 504 393 354 53 172 360 343 116 349 780 212 37 304
79 162 135 291 182 40 111 475 525 375 238 200 101 114 214 195 82 484 909 103 159 150
195 151 248 164 58 190 554 489 454 317 278 74 185 303 235 134 463 874 174 122 211
50 249 346 148 249 550 396 451 383 320 110 93 341 357 80 349 780 171 150 325
219 307 100 227 542 397 443 351 311 61 108 331 330 58 351 782 161 108 303
412 251 402 760 241 660 529 491 208 307 505 483 270 256 626 380 125 441
193 220 587 653 515 296 319 235 296 304 164 274 626 1038 259 286 171
157 512 492 417 278 240 61 127 254 228 80 451 877 122 125 192
397 644 298 127 97 209 162 103 156 169 568 1028 87 277 95
933 125 360 298 576 443 328 502 484 887 1318 375 636 439
842 769 731 449 492 737 723 457 235 385 554 373 681
272 209 451 354 240 414 385 787 1226 286 536 351
64 336 290 32 191 293 695 1154 214 397 124
306 225 35 204 246 649 1115 150 373 142
130 307 290 77 402 834 171 84 253
262 301 53 438 877 76 214 240
200 280 682 1122 171 380 130
274 681 1107 220 357 63
402 842 97 161 245
612 499 352 636
938 758 1072
256 171
315

Lower triangle — miles (left-hand side, read by rows):

428
179 306
405 111 283
326 177 204 113
484 135 362 86 192
480 198 355 100 155 146
489 116 367 100 207 45 178
216 212 94 189 110 268 264 273
421 131 299 20 118 92 80 115 205
392 139 270 41 73 127 91 141 176 45
344 173 239 95 34 179 111 195 145 94 54
586 296 456 177 265 210 115 218 362 157 192 226
129 304 79 281 201 360 341 365 92 309 268 215 446
557 208 435 159 273 73 211 118 341 165 200 259 246 433
482 54 360 166 231 154 251 109 266 189 193 227 361 358 227
157 423 141 400 321 479 467 484 211 416 387 356 579 140 552 477
146 307 33 284 205 363 351 368 95 300 271 240 463 43 436 361 116
449 102 327 51 157 35 120 58 233 57 93 147 194 325 108 167 444 328
540 276 424 165 220 193 65 226 330 145 156 188 117 411 248 334 541 425 172
422 109 300 144 158 229 238 213 206 163 154 166 331 298 302 163 417 301 175 309
352 209 250 130 66 216 125 230 156 114 91 46 240 222 279 263 367 251 171 190 215
105 473 207 439 359 517 513 522 249 454 425 377 619 162 590 515 67 174 482 573 455 385
261 167 139 144 62 223 216 228 45 160 131 100 321 137 296 221 256 140 188 287 161 124 294
330 182 208 109 9 195 142 209 114 116 68 31 261 205 268 238 325 209 160 219 163 55 363 69
410 146 292 42 101 115 63 138 198 23 28 66 164 296 180 200 409 293 80 128 170 91 443 153 96
388 190 279 88 74 164 83 187 185 72 51 40 198 258 237 244 396 280 129 148 186 42 421 140 71 49
330 98 208 88 62 162 168 162 114 108 80 81 265 206 235 158 325 209 122 212 123 92 364 75 40 84 31
331 142 209 78 35 157 149 171 115 94 56 50 251 207 230 196 326 210 122 212 212 123 92 364 75 40 84 31
234 278 148 206 97 292 237 305 56 205 164 111 352 104 365 332 258 142 257 302 247 118 267 86 96 181 154 155 136
490 259 381 155 176 204 58 236 286 136 135 142 163 360 267 313 498 382 178 80 289 144 523 238 173 113 102 215 191 256
390 154 271 52 78 138 79 162 177 48 15 45 190 260 211 208 388 272 106 144 169 82 423 157 71 25 36 92 62 156 120
484 148 344 61 168 67 79 100 250 47 92 135 130 354 132 208 461 345 46 126 202 160 517 205 165 69 118 155 141 250 137 94
664 315 542 266 372 180 309 225 448 272 307 359 344 540 98 334 659 543 215 346 409 396 697 403 375 295 344 342 337 472 365 318 247
84 344 95 321 242 400 396 405 132 337 308 260 502 45 473 398 106 62 365 456 338 268 117 177 246 326 304 246 247 150 406 306 400 580
607 253 480 204 310 118 264 163 386 210 245 297 286 478 43 272 597 481 153 291 328 334 640 341 313 233 282 280 275 410 320 259 185 78 523
562 211 423 140 247 91 124 135 329 126 169 214 125 433 126 245 540 424 106 157 284 239 595 284 244 148 197 238 218 329 184 173 79 224 478 169
538 170 394 111 219 51 140 93 300 101 146 195 159 409 87 205 511 395 66 161 242 215 571 255 220 173 199 193 305 198 149 60 185 454 130 40
363 156 241 76 38 112 111 178 147 83 35 17 227 238 235 210 358 242 131 182 146 65 396 100 33 63 46 39 38 129 146 38 130 358 279 280 209 190
390 75 263 43 102 104 104 169 62 64 98 219 261 177 129 380 264 61 203 104 131 134 423 124 107 71 115 58 67 203 184 79 101 275 306 220 180 140 81
542 191 415 234 73 131 115 321 111 156 199 137 413 106 227 532 416 89 264 224 575 276 224 133 188 212 206 314 189 158 64 204 458 149 20 22 191 163
533 246 414 144 218 161 63 186 320 124 149 174 72 404 214 295 531 415 240 88 288 566 280 213 121 146 222 205 300 102 142 97 312 449 257 119 127 180 187 124
368 108 241 42 71 121 119 137 147 58 35 65 215 239 194 162 358 242 86 179 119 101 401 102 72 51 83 50 36 168 170 50 105 301 284 239 182 43 33 174 170
230 315 51 292 213 367 376 103 308 279 248 465 124 444 369 192 34 336 433 309 259 258 148 217 301 288 217 218 189 280 353 551 146 489 432 403 250 272 424 423 250
227 595 329 561 481 639 635 644 371 576 547 499 741 284 712 637 177 296 604 695 577 507 122 416 485 565 543 485 486 389 645 545 639 819 239 762 717 693 518 545 697 688 523 380
428 95 301 28 135 62 103 72 207 41 72 126 136 299 135 148 418 302 27 180 148 172 461 162 132 64 108 106 100 236 161 76 54 233 344 178 133 93 106 47 106 137 60 310 583
316 208 211 128 32 215 159 228 116 127 87 33 274 187 288 262 327 211 180 224 190 40 349 88 23 99 76 30 67 178 78 172 395 232 333 247 232 52 133 236 222 100 219 471 159
507 211 386 106 194 122 53 147 292 86 116 163 71 378 175 267 503 387 109 73 250 173 540 252 189 93 131 202 188 274 106 119 59 273 423 218 77 88 157 149 81 39 152 395 662 106 196